FORD
TOUGH

FORD TOUGH

BILL FORD AND THE BATTLE TO
REBUILD AMERICA'S AUTOMAKER

DAVID MAGEE

WILEY

John Wiley & Sons, Inc.

Published by John Wiley & Sons, Inc., Hoboken, New Jersey.
Published simultaneously in Canada.
Photos appear courtesy of Ford Motor Company.

For general information on our other products and services please contact our Customer Care Department within the United States at (800) 762-2974, outside the United States at (317) 572-3993 or fax (317) 572-4002.

Wiley also publishes its books in a variety of electronic formats. Some content that appears in print may not be available in electronic books. For more information about Wiley products, visit our web site at www.Wiley.com.

Library of Congress Cataloging-in-Publication Data:
Magee, David, 1965–
    Ford tough : Bill Ford and the battle to rebuild America's automaker / David Magee.
            p.   cm.
    Includes bibliographical references and index.
    ISBN 0-471-47966-7 (cloth)
    1. Ford Motor Company—History.   2. Ford, Bill, 1957–   I. Title.
    HD9710.U54F644   2004
    338.7'6292'0973—dc22   629.22
2004008609

Printed in the United States of America.

10 9 8 7 6 5 4 3 2 1

For William, Hudson, and Mary Halley

Failure is only the opportunity
to begin again more intelligently.
—Henry Ford

There are no crown princes at the Ford Motor Company.
—Henry Ford II

I'm energized by the pressure
and bound and determined to succeed.
—William Clay (Bill) Ford Jr.

CONTENTS

PROLOGUE

This is the story of an American struggle. It revolves around a 100-year-old company and a leader who bears its name, but is not a tale of the ages. Instead, it is about a modern-day battle for the things we value most in life, including family, tradition, and a promising future.

Founded in Dearborn, Michigan, by Henry Ford in 1903, no company has been written about in our lifetime as much as Ford Motor Company, which put the world on wheels, revolutionized manufacturing, and helped engineer social change. And certainly no family with industrial roots has been written about more than Henry Ford and his three generations of descendants, whose mix of vibrant leadership, quiet philanthropy, and occasional dustups has colored the family as the aristocracy of American business. The names alone bring up images of power and influence: Henry Ford, Edsel B. Ford, Henry Ford II, William Clay Ford, Edsel Ford II, and William Clay "Bill" Ford Jr.

The many valuable and interesting works about the company, the family, or both, typically only add insight to a remarkable story that we already generally know. Our lives, over generations, have been so deeply intertwined with Ford Motor Company and its milestones that if we have not read it, we have, at least in part, lived it, from the introduction of the Model T (1908) to the first moving assembly line at Highland Park, Michigan (1918); military production and support in World War II; the launch of the Thunderbird (1954); the end of the Edsel (1959); the birth of the

Mustang (1964); the hapless Pinto (1970); the import-whipping Taurus (1985); the segment-birthing Explorer (1990); and the best-selling truck in the United States, the F-Series pickup.

But while Ford Motor Company celebrates its rich past with zeal, anyone who has ever spent any time in Dearborn knows that Henry Ford was all about the future. His great-grandson, William Clay "Bill" Ford Jr., today the leader of one of the world's largest automakers, has the same focus, saying he prefers to learn from past victories and mistakes rather than bask in them or dwell on them. So a contemporary story about the company fighting to position itself in a new era of business as it approached the end of its first century of operation, with the founder's great-grandson leading the way, only makes sense.

An American celebrity figure of sorts by virtue of his rich bloodline and the company television ads he starred in, Bill Ford is a golden-boy heir grown into a family-man executive, the first Ford family member to run the company since Henry Ford II retired in 1979. He is also a self-professed environmentalist, the father of four soccer-playing children, and widely considered a nice guy. His ascension first to chairman of the board and then to chairman and chief executive officer reminds us that Ford Motor Company is not just another overgrown, faceless conglomeration of American corporations. The simple fact that a member of the Ford family is still involved after 100 years of business is remarkable in its own right and worthy of study.

Henry Ford II took Ford Motor Company public in 1956, but the family maintained control of over 40 percent of the voting rights through special Class B shares. The family's ownership and involvement persevere because they pledge unity on business issues and do not allow Class B shares to be sold outside the family. Today, the company has worldwide sales in excess of $140 billion; more than 340,000 employees;

ownership of such valued global brands as Ford, Volvo, Jaguar, Land Rover, and Aston Martin; and controlling interest in Japanese automaker Mazda—and the Ford family still maintains a controlling interest in the company.

If only it were so easy. When Bill Ford took over as chairman of the board in 1999 at the same time Jacques Nasser was elevated to CEO, Ford Motor Company was on top of the world, flush with cash and annual profits. An assortment of problems developed, however, ranging from lack of focus to poor capital investments. As the U.S. stock market's bubble burst, so did Ford's plans of diversifying its business. The company lost $5.45 billion in 2001 and $980 million in 2002, and faced a scary $7.3 billion U.S. pension shortfall at the end of 2002. The company had to give deep incentives to car buyers over both years to keep domestic market share from taking a complete, devastating dive. By early 2003, rumors of severe financial stress swirled.

Automakers are accustomed to hard times. The cyclical nature of the business caused drastic industry downturn/upturn swings several times during the 20th century, and Ford Motor Company was not immune to the predictable scenario. The economy goes up, profits soar, and shareholders and executives gloat. But as quickly as the Michigan seasons change, costs escalate, focus is lost, and the economy weakens before books celebrating the previous successes even hit shelves. This happened as recently as 1991, when U.S. automakers were being dominated by the Japanese and hemorrhaging so badly that the Big Three lost a combined $7.5 billion, unheard-of at the time. Predicting the end of Detroit would have been easy, and many took that route, assuming America's last industrial stronghold had faced its day of reckoning: failure due to poor quality, design, and management. But by 1994, after a great awakening, the American automakers were back with striking products and record earnings, intriguing domestic customers romanced by the auto once again.

Ford Motor Company in particular has experienced severe turns in its fortunes several times since its founding and each time has come back from the brink with either timely leadership or a great product. As early as July 1903, one month after incorporation, Henry Ford's company was almost broke. Five years later, the Ford Motor Company was selling thousands of Model Ts and reaping millions in profits. Henry Ford was well on his way to becoming an American business icon.

The best example of a recovery at Ford Motor Company might be the job Henry Ford II did in 1945 when taking over for his grandfather, Henry Ford, at the young age of 28. The automaker was in disarray as the elder Ford's health deteriorated. The company's founder had been turning increasingly to a family outsider but trusted adviser, Harry Bennett, who was running the company more like a communist country than a big business. Henry Ford II used his familial influence to gain control at just the right moment and turned the company around by surrounding himself with fresh, new, outside talent—the famed "Whiz Kids"—who instituted badly needed financial controls and reinvigorated the product cycle plan. Ford Motor Company prospered during postwar growth years and paced the auto industry with cars like the Thunderbird and Mustang that had almost mythic appeal.

The boom cycle ran its course, though, and Ford Motor Company was struggling once again as the 1970s wound down. The U.S. auto industry was facing quality issues and a product identity crisis amid an onslaught of better-designed and better-built Japanese products. In addition, two energy crises had dampened customers' appetites for large cars. Henry Ford II stepped down as chairman in 1980. Ford lost $1.4 billion that year, which only slightly trailed Chrysler's

$1.7 billion loss, and bill-paying cash was scarce. Americans were turning away in droves from cars designed and built in the United States that looked and drove like cardboard boxes.

New Ford management, led by CEO Philip Caldwell and President Donald Petersen, empowered a product team to design and build a car with only the customer in mind. The end result was the revolutionary Taurus, launched in 1985 and derided by short-sighted critics as "the jellybean." But the Taurus quickly became a best-seller and ushered in an era of functional aerodynamic design. The Taurus helped send the company to more than a decade of strong performance, reviving the domestic auto market, and ultimately igniting the American economy. This rise-fall-rise saga has become the U.S. auto industry as we know it, Detroit's hubris burgeoning from success before giving way to humility derived from failure.

However, the predicament of Ford Motor Company as it approached its 100th anniversary made it clear this was not just another story about an industrial giant with a colorful leader working to emerge from yet another typical cyclical downturn. Ford Motor Company was teetering, leaning perilously close to losing its footing as world leader and ending up as another proud company living blushingly off its glorious past. Automotive operations were still losing money, raising doubts about creditworthiness as the economy remained in painfully slow recovery and a revived product pipeline could not deliver fast enough. Incentive wars raged. The first Japanese full-size pickup truck was on its way to America, along with dozens of other formidable competitive products. And that was only part of Ford's centennial adventure. When Henry Ford founded Ford Motor Company in 1903 there were 88 companies building cars in the United States, including 15 in Detroit alone.

After the $36 billion takeover of Chrysler by German Daimler-Benz in 1998, only Ford and General Motors could truly be called American. The Big Three were now the Big Two, and one of them was quite troubled.

Approaching its 100th anniversary, Ford Motor Company was down and fighting not only to survive, but to build a new foundation strong enough to launch and sustain an entire second century of business as a U.S. company with global reach, power, and influence. But the path to success was not clear. Ford Motor Company had set the standards for world transportation at the beginning of the 20th century by building affordable, reliable cars for the masses. But the early days of the 21st century revealed that America was approaching an automotive crossroads. Consumers were still seeking and enjoying the luxuries of large, lavish SUVs on one hand, but asking for environmental and sensible alternatives on the other. Faith in the American corporation was weakened, yet reliance on corporate responsibility increased. No industry in America had the opportunity to deliver and respond to the calls for change like the automotive industry, which accounts for roughly 15 percent of the U.S. economy when considering suppliers, dealers, and finance.

Bill Ford, the leader, was fighting not only for his family but also for the thousands of families who have relied on the company for generations, and for ideals bred from a century of leadership. But he was under repeated attack for being cold-hearted toward the environment, too nice a guy, and not really needing or wanting the CEO responsibility in the first place. Needs in Dearborn were many, from can't-miss products to strong, timely leadership to unique, long-term vision—and all in a hurry if this industrial giant was to emerge from this crisis as a company worthy of leading the nation and the world in a new century of business.

The Rouge

On the first day of February 1999, times at Ford Motor Company could seemingly have not been better. America was at the peak of the go-go 1990s, and its love affair with bigger, faster, better had translated for the automaker into sports utility vehicle (SUV) sales by the millions, accompanied by extraordinary profits.

The company had introduced the Explorer in 1990 and created a sensation. That first year and every year since, Explorer has been the world's best-selling SUV. The larger Expedition and even larger Excursion followed in subsequent years, scoring with customers as well as stockholders, who admired their profitability. For six consecutive years beginning in 1993, Ford averaged more than $5 billion in annual profits. By 1998, Ford Motor had one-year gross sales in excess of $140 billion. More important, the company sat on a whopping $22 billion in excess cash in 1999. The only question in Dearborn and on Wall Street seemed to be, how could it be used best to make a giant company bigger and stronger?

William Clay "Bill" Ford Jr., the great-grandson of Ford Motor Company founder and industrial revolutionary Henry Ford, was in just the first day of his second month on the job as chairman of the board of the world's second-largest automaker. He was the first member of the Ford family since Henry Ford II retired as chairman in 1979 to hold a senior leadership position at Ford, but he was not widely known inside the company other than by his family name. Bill Ford had risen through company ranks with 15 jobs and had served on its board of directors since 1988, but at 41 years old, with boyish looks and an athletic frame, he was still seen and known by many as the son of longtime influential director William Clay Ford.

Bill Ford Jr. joined the automaker as an entry-level product planner after graduating from Princeton in 1979. He advanced through an array of jobs, moving to another department every 10 to 12 months, in Ford Motor Company tradition, where any manager who stays in the same job for too long may not stay on an executive track. Long a part of Ford's develop-leaders-within culture, the idea was that executives in the making must learn about all areas of the business, from finance to sales and marketing to product development. Bill Ford was doing just that, following a mobility path to executive leadership similar to one once followed by his father.

———

A short but trim amateur tennis champion and scratch golfer with a personality becoming of a Southern gentleman, Bill Ford Sr. married the former Martha Firestone (granddaughter of tire magnate Harvey Firestone) in 1947. He was well-known at Ford Motor Company in the 1940s and 1950s as a product design and development guru. So talented was the elder Ford that he was given his own company division to run, Continental. The Continental Mark II luxury car was to be more prestigious than the Cadillac, an exclusive, limited-edition product destined to be a corporate loss leader, but an enhancement beyond the company's grassroots image. An updated version of the graceful, hand-built Lincoln Continental manufactured in 1939 under the leadership of Bill Ford Sr.'s father, Edsel B. Ford, the Continental Mark II was launched in 1955 to rave reviews.

"My dad," says Bill Ford, "is a very talented artist. He clearly inherited his father's eye for design."

The only problem was that Bill Ford Sr.'s brother, Ford Motor chairman Henry Ford II, was preparing to take the company public in 1956 and believed the money-losing Continental division would trouble potential shareholders. A great car by all accounts, the Continental was killed before it ever got started, its remnants folded into the profitable Lincoln division. Bill Ford Sr. soon left the employment of Ford Motor Company, remaining only as a member of the board of directors.

Bill Ford Sr. and Martha Ford lived in Grosse Pointe Shores and had four children—three girls and one boy. William Clay Ford Jr. was born in 1957. They called him Billy, a nickname still used by his mother but dropped by most others in the mid-1990s. Despite his lineage and plush, wealthy home in Detroit's suburbs, Bill Ford was not raised as a crown prince of Ford Motor Company. No longer working for the automaker, his father purchased the Detroit Lions, a storied National Football League franchise, in 1963 and instilled in his son and daughters a passion to compete in whatever they did.

"Everything we did in our house was hypercompetitive," Ford says, "whether it was playing cards, a trivia game . . . even our conversations were competitive, like who knew the stats better of some athlete.

"My sisters were a part of it," Ford says, smiling. "The most innocent after-dinner game became cutthroat. There were no gracious winners and no good losers."

A student and athlete first, Bill Ford made straight As in school, spending much of his spare time playing and following sports. He was a youth leagues soccer and hockey hound who on fall Sunday afternoons could be found in the stands at Lions games. Under the spell of football, he watched the championship-starved Lions play amid occasional heckles from nearby fans, directed at the team's owner—his father. "Get us a winner, Ford." "Can't you afford a decent quarterback, Ford?"

Bill Ford's mother did not want him spoiled. She signed him up for youth league play in nearby St. Clair Shores, a blue-collar town, and drove him across town on weekends to play hockey with boys who did not know or care about his wealthy background. He never had bodyguards or chauffeurs, and his mother picked him up from grade school by waiting in line with all the other mothers.

"I think they wanted me to have as normal a childhood as possible," Ford said. "That was important to them. They ultimately wanted me to sink or swim on my own merits."

He learned to fish, hike, and understand and appreciate the outdoors at Fontinalis, a private fishing club the family belonged to in northern Michigan. The family membership dated back to Ford's grandfather, Edsel Ford. Neither of his parents fished, but his mother believed it was important that her son be exposed to the outdoors. She took him there for the first time when he was five or six and it was love at first sight. Ford begged his mother to take him there at any opportunity. He says she "sat on the porch for four days" while he'd "hang out" with camp caretaker Walter Babcock, learning to fly-fish for trout along the Sturgeon River. Ford so loved Fontinalis, and Babcock in particular, that a trip there was all he asked his parents for as a birthday present. He and the caretaker would spend 16 to 17 hours outdoors in a single day.

"[Babcock] had a profound influence on my life," Ford says. "He spent hours with me in the woods. Not only did he teach me how to fish, but . . . he would grab edible plants or say, 'See that tree? That's a beech tree,' or 'See those marks? Those are slash marks from a bear.'

"I was so fascinated," Ford says, "that he could read things where I would just walk past them. He was so patient with me, he'd spend hours and I would ask him a million questions about everything. Sometimes he could not answer, but he would go home and research or check with a friend and get back with me. He always answered eventually."

To earn money, Ford worked one summer at Henry Ford's

Greenfield Village. He was a gardener, punching in and out on a clock for minimum wage along with other workers. One day he was told to fertilize a plant bed, using fertilizer mixed in water colored with blue dye. It was a windy day. A lady in a white dress walked by, getting sprayed with the blue solution by Henry Ford's great-grandson.

"It probably took all the money I earned to pay for that dress," Ford says.

In school and on the playing field, Ford's tenacity helped him gain an edge. He became a fierce competitor, routinely engaging in battle on the ice in hockey as a teen or excelling in the classroom. Following family tradition, he left home as a teenager to attend Hotchkiss School, a prestigious prep boarding high school in Lakeville, Connecticut—the same school from which his father and grandfather had graduated. When Ford did research at Hotchkiss, it was in the Edsel B. Ford Library. If he played tennis, it was on courts that bore the name William Clay Ford Tennis Courts, in honor of his father. But these were only minor distractions for Bill Ford. He captained the football team, starred on the hockey team, and continued to make good grades. And when he called home, Ford was far more likely to check on the progress of his beloved Lions football team than to inquire about the automobile business.

"I was never terribly aware of [Ford Motor Company] when I was young," Ford says. "I was concerned with how my friends were doing, how the team I was on at the moment was doing. . . . That's just the nature of a kid, and I was not any different."

At Princeton University, Ford majored in history and studied great leaders like Abraham Lincoln, fueling a passion for Civil War history that continues today. Around campus, he traveled in his high school graduation present, a metallic green Ford Mustang. It was the first car that was officially his, as his parents only let him use an extra family car—often a Ford station wagon—the first three years he had a driver's license. The Mustang had a special, one-of-a-kind paint job picked out from the studio by his father.

"It was so metallic," Ford says, "it swam in the sun, which was great, except that it was a show color never meant for extreme use. I took it one day up to northern Michigan in the middle of winter and the temperature dropped below zero. I woke up the next morning and the paint was literally standing up in strips. It had torn off the car."

Ford played rugby and sported a bumper sticker on his green Mustang: "In rugby there are no winners, only survivors." He was exposed to and intrigued by Eastern mysticism, studying philosophy and beginning to ask himself questions about social responsibility. In his senior year at Princeton, Ford was elected president of Ivy, the oldest and most prestigious club on campus. When a female classmate tried to diversify the all-male club amid threats and complaints, it was Ford who extended friendship and the invitation of an interview to join. Her entry was denied by the club membership as a whole, but the student never forgot the classmate willing to give her a chance.

During his senior year, Ford met his future wife, freshman Lisa Vanderzee, who was also from Grosse Pointe, though they had not previously known each other. A friend introduced them.

"She had three great-looking roommates," Ford says. "Because I knew Lisa, I had an in. My friends were jealous."

Ford's senior thesis at Princeton, "Henry Ford and Labor: A Reappraisal," was a work he produced in six days. While he blushingly passes it off as something less than his best effort, the fact that he turned to family and Ford Motor Company history as his college career came to a close showed the young Ford was becoming more aware of and interested in his roots. Upon graduation, he announced that he wanted to work at Ford Motor Company, in the family tradition. His father was pleased, though he had never pushed his son into the automotive business.

"The only advice my dad ever gave me," Ford says, "was

when it came time for me to graduate [from college]. He said, whatever you decide to do, give it one hundred percent. If it is Ford, fine, but make sure you do what you really want to do and then give it all you've got."

<hr>

When Bill Ford joined Ford Motor Company in 1979, he took extra steps to try to blend in as just another employee. During his first days on the job, he tried to work incognito under the name William Clay, not wanting to draw attention and advantage with his name and heritage. Once fellow workers figured out his identity, Ford worked hard to overcome any notions that he was a privileged employee, but it was not easy.

"Many superiors," he says, "were either afraid to give me meaningful direction and feedback or bitter and harsh. I was self-conscious for a lot of years, frankly, because I never wanted anyone to say I was not pulling my weight. I thought it was important to change coffee filters and stand over the copy machine making copies."

Ford's father worked diligently from all angles to make sure Ford learned the business properly. Bill Ford Sr. got his 25-year-old son on the company's labor negotiations team in 1982 during a year of crucial UAW talks. When Ford took a job in commercial truck engineering years later, he thought it wise to learn the intricacies of driving an 18-wheeler. He took classes to obtain a commercial truck license, driving an 18-wheeler with a full load on a round-trip from Detroit to Toledo as a final exam. The hardest part, he says, was maneuvering the truck backwards through a busy McDonald's parking lot.

Ford's first opportunity to lead an operating unit came when he was named managing director of Ford of Switzerland in 1987. The division was small but troubled. The assignment was clearly a test of the young Ford by then-chairman and CEO Donald Petersen. The automaker had been entrenched in Europe for decades, and assignments there were typical for company rising stars. If you earned results in Europe, you found promotion in North America. Ford was married with one child (Eleanor Clay, born in 1985) at the time and was understandably homesick on occasion, calling to his parents in the United States on fall Sunday afternoons for Lions game updates, even asking his mother to put the telephone receiver close to the television set so he could hear game action. Still, he turned Ford of Europe's Swiss operations around in a short time, restoring profitability and earning the respect of dealers in that country, who still talk today about his hands-on leadership.

When Henry Ford II died in September 1987, Bill Ford Sr. believed it was time to directly involve the family's fourth generation in the leadership of Ford Motor Company. He wanted his son and his nephew, Edsel B. Ford II (Henry Ford II's son), to have seats on the company's board of directors so they could learn while he was still an active member. At the time, Bill Ford Sr. was the only Ford family member serving on the board. Bill Ford Jr. and his cousin Edsel Ford were just young employees of the company, but they were representative of future Ford family involvement. Donald Petersen was chairman and CEO of the company, and the automaker was in the midst of record performance, due in large part to the success of the Taurus, launched in 1985. This success, combined with the death of Henry Ford II, gave Petersen the feeling that he could and should distance Ford Motor Company from the Ford family, even though members still controlled 40 percent of the voting rights. Petersen outwardly resisted having "the Ford boys" join the board, on the premise that the company was outgrowing its founding family and needed more experienced, qualified directors from the outside.

"There was a feeling among some at that time," remembers Carl Reichardt, a Ford Motor Company board member since 1986 and the former chairman and CEO of Wells Fargo (he retired in 1994), "that the [Ford] family was great, but having independent management would serve all shareholders better.

They thought the family should be on one side and management on another."

With the support of Reichardt and other outside directors, Bill Ford Sr. persuaded Petersen to go along with the addition of Bill Ford and his cousin Edsel Ford to the company's board.

"My dad did the heavy lifting on this," says Ford.

Born in 1948, Edsel is older than his first cousin Bill and had been working at Ford Motor Company since graduating from Babson College, near Boston, in 1973. Edsel Ford rose through the company on a fast track himself (he retired as president of Ford Credit in 1998). The ascension of the fourth-generation duo to the board represented a youth movement that would signal family involvement in Ford Motor Company for years to come.

Reichardt had delivered memorable results at Wells Fargo (the company's stock price rose 1,668 percent during his 11-year tenure) and earned a reputation among management and investment leaders for his ability to deliver growth through extraordinary focus on primary principles of business. He had known members of the Ford family since meeting Henry II years before when the then-Ford chairman was securing financing through Wells Fargo Bank for the massive Renaissance Center project he orchestrated in downtown Detroit. As one of the board members to thoroughly question the board-hopeful Fords, Reichardt remembers seeing glimpses of Henry Ford II, the legendary industrial leader who led Ford Motor Company for 35 years, on the faces of Bill and Edsel Ford.

"I thought, they are young," says Reichardt, still an influential member of Ford's board, "but on the other hand, they had essentially been with the company since they were babies. These guys understood the car business. When they would wake up in the morning, that's what they talked about at the breakfast table."

The Fords were appointed to the board in 1988, but in an attempt to restrict their influence, Petersen refused to assign Bill and Edsel Ford to any decision-making committees. Barely 30 at the time, Bill Ford says he was "probably not completely prepared" for a seat on the board, but was eager to learn. In all, there were 19 Ford Motor Company directors in 1988, but only Bill and Edsel Ford had no committee assignment. The duo sat speechless at board meetings for most of the first year until they could not take it anymore, and then they fought back publicly.

"I've made it clear on one or two occasions to Mr. Petersen," Edsel Ford said in a *Fortune* magazine interview in 1988, "that it does seem a bit odd to me that there are three classes of directors: inside, outside, and Billy and me."

One public swing was all it took. In May of 1989, the fourth generation Ford family members received meaningful assignments and became active participants in the board management of Ford Motor Company. Bill Ford was appointed to the company's powerful finance committee and Edsel Ford was appointed to the executive committee. They never sat silent again, despite the fact that Ford Motor Company's board, including the likes of Reichardt and former Hallmark Chairman and CEO Irv Hockaday, contained some of the biggest names in American business. Bill Ford saw the lineup of heavy hitters as a gift and took advantage by constantly searching for opportunities to amass business wisdom.

"I was like a sponge," he says. "I would quiz all of them about this business and also about their own companies."

With Ford Motor Company's top leadership, however, Bill Ford's position on the board was a delicate situation, considering he was still just a middle-level company employee who was questioning the CEO—his boss—during board meetings. Ford says he tried to "always be respectful," but found occasions when he considered it important to get his point across on matters of consequence.

In the midst of a major downturn in the U.S. economy in

1990, Petersen retired a year earlier than expected, due largely to his inability to deliver the payoff from the diversification efforts he had pushed for in the late 1980s, and what could be best termed a lack of long-term corporate vision. Harold "Red" Poling took over upon Petersen's retirement and led the company for the next three years.

Serving on the company's finance committee during the trying times of 1990 and 1991, when Detroit's Big Three automakers posted record losses and appeared to be crumbling under pressure from the Japanese, Bill Ford began to assert himself in a more vocal and substantial manner. By late 1990, when Ford Motor Company was flush with investment cash—holding almost $10 billion—voices of reason from the family members, who maintained long-term corporate views as opposed to the quick, profit-purging approaches that often satisfy short-term investors, were becoming more valuable to the company. At a time when the U.S. auto industry was in the midst of a cyclical decline, Ford Motor Company reinvested much of its cash in key, existing plants like the Louisville truck plant and Taurus facilities in Chicago and Atlanta and began to look toward global diversification, hoping to alleviate some of the cyclical nature of the American car business. For his part, Bill Ford emerged during this period as a vital player on the company's powerful finance committee. His leadership resulted in his being named head of the finance committee in 1995, a move that required him to cease being employed by the company.

"He earned it," Reichardt says of the appointment. "We would not have put a lightweight on as chairman of finance."

———————

Out of a day-to-day job at Ford Motor Company due to his new role, Bill Ford assumed duties as vice chairman of the Detroit Lions, the National Football League team owned by his father. He ran the team, dismissing one coach and hiring another, restructuring operations, and instituting a comprehensive marketing plan that included putting the Lions on the Internet before the cyber world was fully developed. He also met egocentric NFL owners head-on over issues he felt were important to Detroit and the Lions. At his first NFL team owners meeting in 1995, the opening topic of business was moving the traditional Thanksgiving game away from Detroit and the Lions, rotating it among a number of hosting cities. Ford fought back and won.

"This game does not belong to you or us," he told owners. "It belongs to the fans who've been watching it since 1934—which predates most of the franchises trying to take it away."

Ford spent the rest of his work time in his role as chairman of the finance committee, focusing on the financial well-being and long-term success of Ford Motor Company as the automaker amassed billions in surplus cash while profits soared during the SUV boom. It was during this stretch that fellow board members and Ford executives respected his desires and stopped calling him by his childhood name.

"He earned the right," Reichardt says, "to be called Bill."

When Alex Trotman announced near the end of 1998 that he was stepping down as chairman and CEO one year earlier than expected, Henry Ford's great-grandson was convinced by supportive family members that the time was right for the first Ford to step into a top leadership role at the company since his uncle Henry Ford II retired in 1979. Ford board members agreed. The much-anticipated move, a Ford returning to Ford's future, was made public in fall of 1998. Few were surprised, including Trotman, who used to taunt his successor behind his back by calling him "Prince William." Ford did not deny the obvious—his heritage—but pointed to his constant aspiration to be more than just an extension of a rich bloodline.

"I grew up in a wealthy neighborhood," Ford said, "where there were plenty of second- and third-generation kids who were crushed by their family's expectations. I always thought I was good enough to go beyond that, but I was never sure whether I'd have the opportunity."

Some questioned why he would take the responsibility at all, considering that with a net worth estimated at more than $100 million (including 2.7 million shares of Ford stock), Bill Ford could do anything in the world he wanted, avoiding the responsibilities of a job altogether. But not working was never an option for Ford.

"My dad said, 'A vacation is not a vacation if it is not earned,'" Ford says.

He found opportunity at Ford Motor Company as chairman, but the vision and directive from the board of directors was clear. Still young and with a wife and four children ranging in ages from 3 to 13 at his Grosse Point, Michigan, home, Bill Ford was not viewed as having the hard-core automotive experience or the time to run the company day to day. He had paid his dues, advancing through more than a dozen jobs and earning a master's degree from MIT (1984) since joining the company in 1979. During that time, he had amassed significant operating experience, running Ford divisions large enough to stand on their own among most publicly traded companies in the world. But Ford was believed by some to lack the killer instinct and hard-nosed car savvy gained from years of experience in the cutthroat, global automotive industry. His job was to run the board, just as he had run the finance committee of the board. The power of running the $160 billion Ford Motor Company would go to a seasoned executive.

Jacques Nasser, who earned the nickname "Jac the Knife" for his cost-cutting prowess as president of Ford Motor Company, was a blunt-talking, high-ego personality who helped the company raise profit margins in a short period by cutting billions in costs and reducing personnel. What Bill Ford was believed to lack in grit and in-the-trenches experience, Nasser more than made up for with a military-like approach, commanding presence, and numbers-driven results from top-level responsibilities.

When Trotman retired, the duties of chairman and CEO were effectively split: Nasser was given the job of CEO of Ford, running the day-to-day operations; Bill Ford ran the board. Analysts praised Nasser as an industry hero of Ford's SUV-driven success of the 1990s and believed his leadership was perfect for taking the company into its second century of business.

"Jac's been the catalyst," said Lehman Brothers auto analyst Joseph S. Phillippi in late 1998. "Jac's the general."

Nasser joined Ford of Australia as a financial analyst in 1968 after earning a business degree from the Royal Melbourne Institute of Technology. He advanced with international assignments in places like Thailand, the Philippines, Venezuela, and Argentina, honing his fluency in four languages (English, Arabic, Spanish, and Portuguese) and his reputation as a diminutive (he's five-foot-six), hard-driving manager with a charismatic personality, a quick trigger finger, and a taste for fine wine and clothes.

Nasser returned to Australia in 1990 to lead the Ford division he had started in, and found an operation losing money and market share. He cut Ford of Australia's workforce of 15,000 in half, improved productivity by 40 percent, and earned a promotion to head of Ford of Europe in 1993, before moving to the United States in 1996 as head of automotive operations at Ford Motor Company. He was named president of automotive operations in 1997.

The mix of Nasser as CEO and Ford as chairman seemed odd only because philosophically and personally they were so different. A prime example: Ford believed internal combustion engines would be obsolete in his lifetime; Nasser did not. Ford preferred a quiet room to think; Nasser liked a room full of listeners. But the two were friendly, having worked together in the 1980s when Bill Ford was a financial analyst in charge of Venezuela and Nasser was head of finance for Latin America and Asia.

"We have a running start on this," Ford told Mary Connelly of *Automotive News.* "We've known each other a long time. We find we are in sync more than we are not."

The fit seemed to be perfect from the perspective of Ford Motor Company's board of directors and Wall Street investors. Fifty-two at the time, Nasser was considered the business guru who appeared to be in complete command of himself and the company, while Ford was considered the quiet chairman with long-term interests and the right last name, an obvious balance to Nasser's edge.

"We had the strong operations guy and the guy who was strategic and visionary," Reichardt says. "It seemed like the ideal situation."

From the start, Nasser moved fast. That was part personality (he was known during his 30-plus years at Ford for nonstop energy and drive) and part reflection of the times. The business he inherited from Trotman was old-economy in a raging new-economy world, and Nasser believed that required expedient action on his part. Ford Motor Company had morphed in the 1990s from a car company that made some trucks into a truck company that made some cars. This transformation produced record automotive operation profits, but hardly excited investors mesmerized by the dot-com craze. Nasser pledged to reposition the company, and it was no secret that along the way he hoped to position himself in the pantheon of management leadership circles with General Electric's Jack Welch and IBM's Lou Gerstner. Nasser, who stood out in a crowd despite his diminutive frame, consulted with University of Michigan business professor Noel Tichy, co-author of the best-selling business management book *The Leadership Engine: How Winning Companies Build Leaders at Every Level* (New York: HarperBusiness, 1997), and had barely been announced as Ford Motor Company's CEO-elect in late 1998 when he was already making headlines for restructuring management and shaking Ford's corporate trees at the highest levels.

Ford Motor Company was blowing past slumping rival General Motors at the time, claiming 25 percent of U.S. market share and on its way to record profits of more than $7 billion. General Motors was still the biggest, but Ford was widely considered the best, delivering higher profit margins and owning a superior product lineup. Yet Nasser trimmed the number of vice presidents from 45 to 40 and rolled out a new performance-based profit-sharing plan before he even officially moved into the CEO office. The tactics made him a hero on Wall Street, where investment bankers overwhelmingly approved his aggressive mind-set. The company's stock price reached all-time high levels in anticipation of the growth ahead as Nasser prepared to take complete charge of operations.

Like Bill Ford, Nasser was in just the first day of his second month on his new job on February 1, 1999, when the pieces for a rich and robust future appeared to all be in place. Nasser was out of the office and the country, traveling in Europe on Ford Motor Company business. Ford was in his car, not far from World Headquarters, returning from lunch, when the news came over the radio:

"There has been an explosion at Ford's Rouge manufacturing facility. The full extent of damage is not known, but there are injuries."

Ford looked out his car window toward the distant massive Rouge complex, which sits along the river from which it took its name and rises above the flat, treed landscape in the Dearborn area. He saw smoke billowing toward the sky.

The Rouge was the brainchild of Ford's great-grandfather, Henry Ford, who dreamed of building a car from start to finish, raw materials and all, in one location. Henry Ford had the Rouge constructed in 1918 to accomplish just that. Raw materials entered, fully completed cars exited, and there was nothing like it anywhere else. The vertical integration process gave Ford Motor Company total self-sufficiency in owning, operating, and coordinating all the resources needed to build complete automobiles. The 1,100-acre complex was for many years the world's largest auto manufacturing facility, employing 100,000 workers at its peak in the 1940s. But by 1999, the entire complex was showing its age. Fewer than 10,000 employees worked at Ford's six plants in operation at the time, and facilities were in need of renovation. Plans were already under way to replace the 78-year-old powerhouse that energized the Rouge. The powerhouse was still capable of producing enough juice to light the entire city of Boston, but the aged facility was a throwback to the heyday of the massive complex.

Boiler control room 6 was the biggest of the seven control rooms on the third floor of the powerhouse, with space to store coffee pots and snacks. Workers often congregated there to snack and chat during break times. Half a dozen men were gathered just before 1 P.M. on February 1. They had no idea that imminent spontaneous combustion would take some of their lives and change the course of a corporation.

Made with one-inch steel and standing 60 feet high, boiler 6 was heated by a furnace that consumed about 400,000 cubic feet of natural gas each hour. The firebox, in turn, heated its water capacity of up to 28,000 gallons to a temperature as high as 550 degrees. The boiler was in shutdown mode for annual inspection just before 1 P.M. Four workers had blanked the flow, physically preventing gas from entering the boiler. After lunch, the men planned to blank the natural gas line. Gas was building up in the firebox inside the boiler while they took a break for lunch, becoming an accident in waiting. Something, maybe a small ember of coal dust, caused ignition, and in an instant the boiler exploded like a gigantic pipe bomb with a force felt blocks away, strong enough to split it open, spewing heat and water in excess of

300°F on nearby workers. Fire from the explosion shot across the room to other boilers, catching them on fire as well.

Like many employees at Ford Motor Company, Jim Vella had not spoken with Bill Ford before February 1, 1999. But as director of manufacturing public affairs, Vella took the company lead in crisis management in the absence of Ford vice president of public affairs Vaughn Koshkarian, who, like Nasser, was out of town on business when the Rouge explosion occurred. Koshkarian had a finance background but had been appointed by Nasser to lead the company's public affairs, despite having no experience in the field. In his absence and in the need for an experienced professional in crisis, Vella stepped forward, speaking with the new company chairman on his mobile phone to brief him on the startling event.

"The accident is serious. There are injuries, maybe deaths. The site is unstable. We are in contact with authorities."

Bill Ford Jr. drove to World Headquarters and was met in his 12th floor office by Vella and by Neil Golightly, who was in his first weeks as director of the chairman's office, with duties that were part public affairs and part executive assistant for Bill Ford. Golightly remembers Ford being visibly concerned and distraught when he walked into the office and sat down for updated information on the accident. Details were still sketchy.

"Do you think I should go?" Ford asked.

Golightly was barely three weeks into his job and still getting to know and understand the man he worked for. The company's CEO was out of the country. Its head of public affairs was out of town. The chairman bore the company name, and the Rouge was an unstable accident scene at a volatile, 78-year-old powerhouse with boilers fed by natural gas. Golightly followed his first gut reaction and advised Ford not to go.

"That's ridiculous," Ford said. "I've got to go."

"Generals don't go to the front lines," another company adviser told the chairman.

"Bust me down to private then," Ford responded, "because I'm out of here."

Ford went straight to the accident scene at the Rouge, taking Golightly along. When they arrived, heavy gray smoke was still escaping from the windows of the powerhouse and a dozen ambulances lined the streets around it. Water from the boilers and from fire extinguishing efforts flooded the street, while coal ash and smoke filled the air. An emergency command center was set up in an adjacent building and Bill Ford went there first, talking to doctors, firemen, paramedics, and employees—searching for answers about how many might have been injured and what their conditions were.

The news was not good. One person was known to be dead. Nineteen others were severely injured, most with burns, and being transported to hospitals throughout the region. Ford worked to stay out of the way in the command center, letting emergency personnel do their job, but wanted to help and offer support because he felt like he needed to do something. Most people did not recognize him. But once they learned he was a Ford, bearing the DNA of the man who had founded the company and built the Rouge, they gravitated toward him and found stability in the difficult moment through his presence.

Ford stayed at the Rouge for almost two hours. When it became obvious there was nothing more to do at the scene, he wanted to go to hospitals where injured employees had been taken. On the way out of the Rouge complex in his car, he passed a throng of media gathered and waiting for updated information on the accident. Realizing his initial thought of keeping the chairman away from the accident scene had been a mistake, Golightly advised Ford that stopping and speaking with reporters would be a good idea since thousands of employees at Ford Motor Company plants throughout the country were watching live news broadcasts, concerned about the fortunes of fellow workers and deserving of first-hand information.

A light rain was falling and smoke was still pouring from the powerhouse in the background when the cameras rolled, but the face of Bill Ford, showing visible emotion, said it all. Cameras zoomed in close as the company chairman spoke with no script, voice quivering. This was not a staged public relations event, but a moment of pure concern and sorrow.

"It's awful," Ford said. "Everyone who works for Ford is an extended member of the family. This is the worst day of my life."

Ford drove to hospitals treating the injured and met with families filling waiting rooms. He gave them the cash from his wallet and offered credit cards to buy food, hotel rooms, anything they might need. He returned the next day and the next as injured employees fought for their lives in intensive care units. Two families asked Ford to visit badly burned employees at bedside, and he obliged, witnessing and sharing the pain firsthand. Other family members of injured employees simply wanted to be near him, finding strength from his heritage and outward compassion.

The days and weeks that followed were long, and there was little good news. Six more Ford employees died, bringing the total deaths from the Rouge accident to seven. There was anger, some directed toward the company for using the aging equipment at the Rouge, but Ford remained personally involved, assuring those around him it was "the right thing to do."

Koshkarian, who had been head of Ford's developing China operations before being handpicked by Nasser to lead the company's 250-person PR staff, was away at public relations firm Burson Marsteller, taking a one-on-one course in public relations when the accident occurred. Koshkarian did not call back to Dearborn to see if anything had happened during the workday until 5 P.M., hours after the explosion. In his absence, the crisis management lead at World Headquarters went to Vella, a native of Detroit who had worked in television news management for 14 years before joining Ford.

Vella led the company's response team, providing employees and news media with up-to-date information on rapidly changing details surrounding the Rouge accident.

In the tragic days that followed, Vella, at Bill Ford's request, helped plan employee funerals. He, Bill Ford, Nasser, and other Ford executives went to each of the services, grieving with the families. After the seventh, they were exhausted, worn out from the unexpected crisis and mental anguish of burying Ford employees. The Rouge explosion and ensuing weeks had been devastating for Ford Motor Company, its employees, and its new chairman. It would be more than a year before the rest of corporate America would face a rude awakening from its blissful times, but Bill Ford and Ford Motor Company got their taste of disaster when the Rouge explosion rocked, rattled, and violently disrupted the destiny of leadership and corporate direction. The pall of death fell heavily over the satisfaction of prosperity in Dearborn. But in the face of tragedy, a new leader emerged.

"Bill earned the respect of a hell of a lot of people that day," says Carl Reichardt.

CHAPTER

2

Lessons
in Leadership

J ac Nasser had a plan when he took over as CEO of Ford
Motor Company. As he saw it, shareholders suffered from
an undervalued stock price because they owned shares in
what was primarily a manufacturing company. By 1999, most
of Wall Street was bored with old-economy companies, even
one like Ford, which has been traded so long on the New
York Stock Exchange that its symbol is just a single letter, F.
Manufacturing companies design and build product, getting it
out of their hands as quickly as possible for someone else to
sell. Manufacturing companies react to economic data, not
whims. They operate on caution, common sense, and time-
tested fundamentals, protecting jobs, security, and dividends.

Never mind that in early 1999, Ford's stock hit an all-time
high of more than $66 per share. The American investment
world was falling under the spell of a technology-driven consumer age in which the mere hint of a newfangled business
model drew raves and investment dollars. Amazon.com,
founded as an Internet bookseller by Jeff Bezos in 1995, had
gone public in 1997 at $18 a share, closing the same day of
its initial public offering (IPO) at $23.50. The company
made nothing in terms of profits and was little more than an

order-fulfilling bookstore with a warehouse and a Web address. It lost $124 million in 1998 on sales of $610 million, yet by the end of the year was trading at a 97.4 multiple over sales, not earnings, at more than $300 per share. The online auctioneer eBay, which went public in September 1998 and originally derived income by facilitating sales of such products as Beanie Babies and helping collectors exchange trading cards, turned a razor-slim profit of $215,000 on revenues of $14.9 million in the first half of 1999, despite owning little besides a functional Internet site. But eBay's stock had a market value of more than $20 billion and was trading at roughly 1,600 times revenues.

These companies, Amazon.com and eBay, were hardly exceptions to the get-big-fast basis of the new-economy promise, which reached a fever pitch at precisely the moment Nasser moved into Ford Motor Company's CEO office with a checkbook linked to accounts containing billions in loose investment cash. For the man with a big plan, it was a dream come true. He wanted to take Ford Motor Company, arguably among the least nimble of the giant U.S. corporations, and remake it into an agile, diversified, global powerhouse, worthy of commanding price-to-earnings ratios three to four times higher than it had historically enjoyed.

The concept, according to Nasser, was relatively simple. Ford Motor Company was an automobile manufacturer linked in parallel to its financing arm, Ford Credit. This business translated into cyclical swings following along the lines of economic times in the United States.

In 1999, Ford Motor Company was at a peak, the top of a cycle. The company had become one of the world's most profitable automakers and its stock price reflected as much, rising 130 percent since the end of 1996, easily outdistancing the 71 percent gain of the Standard & Poor's 500 stock index and gains by rival auto company stocks over the same period. With cyclical stocks and companies, what goes up will always come down. Ford Motor Company, reasonably, was headed toward another downturn sooner or later, most likely when SUV profits dried up. Nasser was looking at consumer-based growth companies like Amazon.com, which in late 1998 passed manufacturers like Alcoa, Caterpillar, and International Paper in market capitalization before ever making a dime in profits, simply because they were Internet based. His idea was to move Ford Motor Company closer to consumers through technology and diversification.

Of course, Nasser was a lifelong company man who had no intention of totally abandoning the automotive business. He simply wanted to take Ford's prowess and capital and expand and diversify the company so that it more closely resembled a consumer company, like, say, General Electric or Coca-Cola—companies that commanded price-to-earnings ratios closer to 36 and 40, instead of 9 to 12—and throw a little Internet presence on top for good measure. In addition to delivering higher returns to shareholders, this diversification and foray into the consumer world would reduce stock price swings from the up-again, down-again cyclical auto industry and help Ford Motor Company keep up with the blue-chip growth stocks that under pre-Nasser circumstances would presumably zoom by on the big board while the automaker searched for the next big thing in cars and trucks.

It was not hard for Nasser to get buy-in for his big plan from Ford's board of directors. As the company's largest shareholders, the Ford family has always maintained a long-term view when it comes to cash and strategy, adamantly favoring reinvestment over divestment. Experienced auto executives and business leaders also remember the hardest days of the industry down cycles, like 1980, when Ford Motor Company was nearly broke due to the hard times, with no apparent place to turn. These memories made many board members more than willing to follow Nasser's vision, which promised to diminish the painful yo-yo effect of manufacturing.

The plan Nasser preached was that Ford Motor Company should become "a leading consumer company for automotive products and services." Nasser's basis for this approach came from breaking the profit life cycle of the automobile down into four stages by percentages, noting that the supplier takes 10 percent of this profit; the manufacturer, 40 percent; dealers, 30 percent; and the aftermarket, including service, body work, and resale, 20 percent. This meant that Ford Motor Company, by not participating at the consumer level of business, was giving up 50 percent of the profit potential available for the cars and trucks it designed and built.

To capture more of this potential profit, Nasser wanted to expand Ford Motor Company's product lineup with more flair and global diversity, branch into other auto-based consumer businesses worldwide, and invest moderately to heavily in the Internet to better reach consumers and raise the overall value of the company. The fast-moving Nasser, who was known to work 18-hour days, often seven days a week, and jet all over the world chasing power meetings or deals, wasted nary a moment in his new job before putting his plan into motion all at once.

Talks had been going on behind the scenes at Ford with Volvo to purchase the Swedish automaker's passenger car business before Nasser filled the CEO office, and the deal was not one he wanted to lose. Ford Motor Company had first purchased an outside automaker in 1921 when it bought Lincoln Motor, an American company. Ford did not buy another until it acquired handmade sports car maker Aston Martin of England in 1987—Ford paid just $33 million for controlling interest in the tiny British car company—and luxury sports car and sedan maker Jaguar, also of England, in 1989, for the pricey sum of $2.52 billion after a bidding war with rival General Motors. (Executives were criticized for grossly overpaying for Jaguar because the luxury company was struggling at the time of Ford's investment, needing a $1.5 billion cash infusion just to survive.) Ford Motor Company also acquired a controlling interest in struggling Japanese automaker Mazda in 1996 and had a true global lineup in place by the time Nasser and Ford pulled off the purchase of Volvo's car division for $6.47 billion in early 1999, gaining a company with a distinctive product typically driven by upper-income customers seeking safety and upscale quality from an unpretentious vehicle.

Later in the same year, Nasser began talks with BMW to purchase its Land Rover division, an English-based company that produced four-wheel-drive SUVs that were widely considered "the toughest civilian vehicles around." Ford Motor Company closed the deal in early 2000 for $3 billion, rounding out a global lineup that gave the company heavy luxury presence and, perhaps as important, more vehicles under the Ford Motor Company umbrella that Nasser, a man of expensive tastes, was willing to drive. Ford's CEO was an engineer at heart with a big passion for design. He loved luxury and cars, and he could be very specific and sometimes quite picky and instructive on certain elements, from hood ornaments to body lines, making it no secret in Dearborn that a Land Rover got more of his attention than a Ford. By picking up Volvo and Land Rover so quickly, he put in place elements of his plan that he hoped would put new shine on Ford's blue oval.

In little more than a blink of an eye, Nasser packaged the company's new luxury brands together in a new company division called the Premier Auto Group (PAG), where the stars in this company, which had made its mark and money for almost an entire century selling millions of cars and trucks to middle-class Americans, now became high-priced luxury vehicles. The PAG, which also included Ford's Lincoln division, was run primarily outside of Dearborn, with marketing functions based in California and daily management operations based largely in Europe. Even though the division was geographically distant, its importance to the parent company was very much present.

"Ford Motor Company," *BusinessWeek* reported on October 11, 1999, "brought an impressive stable of brands to the

Frankfurt Auto Show last month: Jaguars, Volvos, Mazdas, even Aston Martins. Just one thing seemed to be missing: Fords. Cars carrying the trademark oval huddled in a corner of Ford's exhibition space, next to the espresso bar and the free food."

Nasser and Ford Motor Company quickly expanded into other areas of the automotive business outside of manufacturing to help fulfill his mission of finding more opportunity in the profit life cycle of a product. Ford Motor Company had long been recognized within the industry for having the strongest dealer network in the United States. This strength dates back to the company's early days when corporate secretary James Couzens, essentially a chief operating officer, took painstaking efforts to qualify and hand-select the company's first dealers in America's emerging auto market. No other U.S. automakers took the time to weed the weak from the strong applicants. Combined with Henry Ford's promise of quality and that any Ford Motor Company cars needing repair would be fixed at the dealership from which they were bought, the approach eliminated part-time and fly-by-night dealerships from Ford's network, helping the dealer base develop into the world's strongest. Ford's retail network continued to thrive throughout the years, with many dealerships remaining in the family for generations.

But under the business model championed by Nasser, Ford Motor Company was empowering others at the retail level to make money it should and could be earning. Large public companies like AutoNation Inc. were getting involved in dealership consolidation, and some executives in Dearborn believed the automaker should experiment with its own retail model. The company began acquiring what would total almost 50 dealerships in areas like Oklahoma City and Tulsa; Rochester, New York; San Diego; and Salt Lake City. Packaged by Ford Motor Company as the "Auto Collection," the dealerships were essentially a consolidation of area retail outlets into one umbrella superstore where the company set no-haggle pricing. The dealerships used to build Ford's Auto Collection were acquired from willing sellers, but the company's entry into the retail arena was unpopular among many of its 4,000 franchise dealers for obvious reasons. Many felt the company was involved in major encroachment.

Ford Motor Company's relationships with dealers also suffered with the announcement of the new Blue Oval Certified program in April 2000. Blue Oval was designed to make Ford Motor Company dealers aspire to higher business standards by tying cash bonuses to such business basics as the way they sell and service cars, deal with customers, and use technology in daily operations. The Blue Oval program based dealer certification on standards including improved customer service scores, the presence of one staff person dedicated to Internet sales and information requests, and upgraded showroom and service facilities. Qualified dealerships received a payment of 1.25 percent of the invoice price of every vehicle they sold.

From the start, the Blue Oval program was unpopular with many Ford dealers, who accused the company of simply raising wholesale prices of its vehicles without raising the retail prices, thus forcing the dealers to work harder to get their money back on sales. Others argued it created a two-tiered franchise pricing scheme that unfairly rewarded some dealers. A lawsuit was filed in November 2000 by five Ford franchisees to stop implementation of the program. Nasser, however, seemed unfazed by the backlash.

"Anyone," he said, "who is going to hide behind legal fences better have an exit strategy because it won't work long-term. For the best dealers, they can see it as an opportunity. For those dealers who see it as a threat, then maybe there is a threat in it for them."

Ford Motor Company also branched into the service and repair business, paying $1.6 billion for Kwik-Fit, a chain of almost

2,000 service centers in Britain. Kwik-Fit, presumably, moved the company closer to Nasser's goal of finding more profits over the life cycle of a car by moving the company closer to the consumer and keeping it in touch with the car longer. For example, Nasser figured a $20,000 car would generate another $48,000 in revenue over a decade, when considering maintenance, spare parts, gas, and insurance. Kwik-Fit not only gave Ford Motor Company an immediate entry into the consumer automotive business, it was also intended to serve as a learning tool for the automaker as it expanded similar services throughout the world as well as in the United States, allowing the company to parlay its trusted and time-tested brand into endless new dollars through a cradle-to-grave approach to the automobile. And Nasser did not stop there. He also bought Greenleaf, a junkyard business in the United States that held the promise of teaching the company more about recycling; Collision Team of America, a chain of body shops; and an 80 percent stake in Howard Basford Accident Repair, among other acquisitions.

"He wanted to own the value chain under Ford Motor Company," says a former aide.

With a love of fine cigars and a loathing of downtime, Ford's CEO would talk passionately about theories on the subject to anyone who would listen. He often used stories relating to consumer giant Coca-Cola to help others better understand his hyperspeed rush to diversity at Ford Motor Company. The man who always dressed impeccably, wearing three-button Savile Row suits and Patek Philippe Swiss watches, held court about the benefits of becoming a consumer company at the annual Ford/media Christmas party, telling a group of jaw-dropped journalists who could not get a word in edgewise how Coke was going to take over the consumer world because company leaders had the sense and ability to parlay its brand into the sale of something as simple as water. Nasser was waving a bottle of Dasani water as he spoke, his voice rising in intensity with every sentence as he espoused Coke's wonderful new product. He pointed to the bottle, covered in its sleek, blue label and containing the simplest of all product inventions. Looking into the eyes of his onlookers and daring them not to get the point of his simplicity, Nasser said that was exactly what Ford was going to do—use its brand muscle to open completely new doors.

Nasser would leave the bottled water business to Coke and others, but his point was not to be missed. On his watch, Ford Motor Company was expanding beyond car and truck design, manufacturing, and finance, and daring anyone to try to stop it.

———

Married to his wife Jennifer for almost 30 years and having four children, Nasser was hardly in one place for long in the early days and months of his leadership at Ford, flying from meeting to meeting around the globe in company jets and fidgeting during in-house sessions that were not moving his way fast enough. He was known to sleep just a few hours each night and rarely took time off from work, slowing down only at Christmas for an annual family vacation. He worked out at the office in the lavish exercise room he installed for himself at World Headquarters. So he would not have to slow down his frenetic pace on weekends, Nasser was known to take Ford executives and managers with him on a company jet bound for Europe, where, because of time zone differences, he squeezed in more work time on the clock. Nasser, whose only hobbies included collecting Swiss watches (more than 100) and drinking fine wines, often drove himself to work in an Aston Martin DB7 with a 12-cylinder engine. At the office, he worked and simultaneously watched one of several televisions mounted along the wall of his 12th floor suite that were constantly tuned to business news stations. The broadcasts helped him keep track of market news and the excitement as the dot-com craze soared along with share prices of companies such as Cisco, Microsoft, Amazon.com, and eBay.

The daily blitz only fueled his beliefs that there had to be an easier way for Ford Motor Company than relying almost solely on the steel-stamping, labor-intensive auto manufacturing business. The car as it related to the Internet and the consumer was far more interesting and valuable to him and to Wall Street than the car as it related to the Rouge. So rather than concentrate his energy pushing for manufacturing innovation, Nasser looked for Internet technology to energize his stodgy business. He launched several interactive web sites, such as FordDirect.com, so potential car buyers could shop for products in detail online before being referred to dealers for product pickup and purchase. Ford Motor Company also invested in other dot-com entities, including Microsoft's MSN CarPoint, in which Ford made a sizeable investment and took 25 percent ownership. The company joined with Yahoo! to "develop personal services for the vehicle owners online," took a 31 percent ownership position in CarClub.com, and took positions in or partnered for e-business initiatives with such companies as Vehix.com, iVillage.com, Trilogy Software, and Bolt.com.

"We're forming Internet joint ventures left and right," Bill Ford Jr. said in December 1999. "The good news is that every time I meet with John Chambers from Cisco, Scott McNealy from Sun, Steve Ballmer from Microsoft—we meet with them all the time and everybody tells us we are way ahead of anybody else in the [auto] industry as far as the Internet is concerned."

Nasser planned to quickly acquire ownership in enough businesses with either an "e-" prefix or a ".com" suffix to enable him and Ford Motor Company to bundle them and spin the group off as its own entity, capitalizing on rich IPO returns. The sweetest piece of the spin-off pie, he figured, would come from a mangled, Web-based deal he concocted between UUnet, Hewlett-Packard, and a new company named PeoplePC, which would ultimately result in all 350,000 Ford employees worldwide getting a personal computer, printer, and Internet services for the nominal fee of $5 per month. Nasser's grand scheme revolved around a strategy that involved Ford Motor Company buying the computers and equipment that it would give away to employees for nothing from PeoplePC, the Internet computer retailer. Nasser recommended to Ford's board of directors that the company buy a stake in PeoplePC and they obliged, taking 6 percent ownership in the company. He figured that Ford Motor Company, after purchasing such a large quantity of equipment from one source, would spin off its ownership in PeoplePC, easily generating a $250 million profit from the skyrocketing stock—returning to the company the cost of giving each employee a computer.

Often, Nasser acted more in haste than grand design, fueled by his strong desire not to let others beat him to a technology twist. Journalists who regularly cover Ford Motor Company remember attending a press conference at a Specialty Equipment Manufacturers Association meeting in late 1999, where the automaker and Nasser were showing off customized Ford trucks. In the middle of the press conference, Nasser announced he had another, more important press conference that was just about to start. Ford's CEO had apparently heard whispers upon arriving at the conference that rival General Motors was about to announce an e-purchasing program that would allow its suppliers to bid and sell automotive parts online. Not to be outdone, Nasser made a hasty deal with Oracle and called the reporters from the middle of one press conference to another to announce, before GM's press conference, that Ford was in fact forming an e-purchasing venture. Journalists filed into the mostly empty, unprepared pressroom and listened as the president of Oracle announced via speakerphone the Ford partnership, with Nasser standing by. Oracle and Ford would form AutoXchange, an e-business designed to streamline the automaker's supply chain. But before Oracle's president was finished talking, Nasser, either bored or needing to be somewhere else, walked out. The throng of media followed him, like the Pied Piper, leaving a near-empty room with details of the Ford-Oracle venture echoing over the speakerphone as the unaware Oracle president kept on talking.

Not so hasty was one part of Nasser's grand plan, which, ironically, was to divest Ford Motor Company of a part of Nasser's so-called profit chain that the company already owned—its auto parts division, Visteon Automotive Systems. It was rumored around Detroit and Wall Street for a couple years that Ford Motor Company was considering spinning off or selling its primary supplier. Nasser and the majority of Ford's board of directors felt the company was finding new cost-savings opportunities through its Internet business initiatives and would be best served by testing the equities market—a trial run of sorts for the ultimate spin-off of Internet assets—and making Visteon an independent entity. Visteon went public on the New York Stock Exchange in June 2000, taking more than 70,000 employees and $19 billion in revenue from Ford Motor Company, but returning billions in cash from the IPO.

Nasser planned to manage the more diversified, spread-out, technology-based Ford Motor Company he was quickly creating by bringing in people he identified as top industry talent who would be loyal to his sweeping plans and hard-driving style. He first started recruiting outsiders into the company immediately after arriving in 1996, but stepped up the pace as CEO. One of Nasser's first hires at Ford was James C. Schroer, a former RJR Nabisco marketing chief who became Ford's global marketing vice president. One year later, in 1997, he brought in J Mays, a star designer who had won widespread acclaim by sketching Volkswagen's New Beetle and the Audi TT sports coupe. Nasser also brought in engineer Chris Theodore from Chrysler to shore up luxury car development, and former BMW number two man Wolfgang Reitzle to lead Ford's luxury automotive group that included the new Volvo and Land Rover acquisitions as well as Aston Martin and Jaguar.

By so quickly and radically changing the executive faces of Ford and its strategies, Nasser hoped to alter the company's culture, which for decades had thrived on an internal hire-and-promote-within system that rewarded longevity, loyalty, and a more conservative approach to growth and new direction. Ford had traditionally operated under an employee grade level system, which determined hierarchy at the company. A middle manager with a salary grade 10 job had earned eligibility for a subsidized company lease car. A salary grade 13 manager had reached the lowest ranks of senior management and would receive a bonus, stock options, and other perks that usually lasted until retirement. Some top executives kept a running list of managers beneath them with birthdays attached, in order to know exactly who was in line for promotion at any given moment. Under Nasser, this old system was abandoned. Nasser aggressively went after youthful new top talent and devised a strategy to teach the old executives, managers, and employees new ways of thinking and working.

Nasser formed the Business Leadership Initiative (BLI) at Ford, a program he crafted with the help of Noel Tichy, the University of Michigan business professor and consultant. The aim of BLI was to get executives and managers to think and act outside of typical corporate bureaucracy, responding more quickly to consumer needs, recognizing shareholder needs, and focusing on challenges such as company cost and quality in targeted, 100-day blocks. The BLI was a 3-day course, while 100-day projects were an extra-credit assignment of sorts in which high-potential Ford managers, grouped in small teams outside of their regular jobs, were given problems to solve in just over three months' time. One example of the more than 5,000 projects tackled: A team at

Ford of Europe was charged with cutting the cost of sending engineers from headquarters on extended assignments during factory start-ups. They concluded that it was cheaper to rent apartments instead of staying in hotels and cheaper to drive company fleet cars than rentals, and that by using mobile phones instead of hotel phones, the company would save money. Ultimately, they found that a 60-person launch team could save almost $500,000 in a year.

At a cost of between $30 and $40 million to establish in 1999, the BLI program also taught salaried employees such business basics as the meaning of *shareholder value* while driving home Nasser's philosophy of turning Ford Motor Company into a consumer-based business. Included in BLI was a half-day community service project, where executives and managers teamed up for such grassroots jobs as painting a house in a poor neighborhood or landscaping a hospice.

"This leadership effort is about as scaled up as any that I've ever participated in," Tichy said. "As far as leadership goes, Jack Welch was ahead of his time. But he had time. In today's world, he would have to do what he did 10 times faster."

In the classroom, Nasser would teach the classes to executives himself, stalking the room in shirtsleeves, and they, in turn, taught managers, who taught departmental salaried workers. Before and after meetings, Nasser handed out index cards printed on two sides, containing guidelines under the Ford Motor Company "Strategy Pyramid" on one side and Ford Motor Company "Financial Milestones" on the other. At the top of the strategy pyramid was "Superior Shareholder Returns." Second was "World's Leading Consumer Company for Automotive Products and Services," followed by "Transformation and Growth." At the bottom were "Corporate Citizenship" and "Best Total Value to the Customer."

The other side of Nasser's card stated the bottom line, that "Ford Motor Company's Goal Is to Provide Total Shareholder Returns in the *Top Quartile* of the S&P 500 over Time." It also listed strategic priorities for the company, including "customer satisfaction, e-business, superb execution in all we do, and business structure improvements."

Nearly all of Ford's 100,000 salaried workers completed BLI, a Ford 101 course as concocted by Nasser. When he taught the class himself, Nasser was known to raise his voice and get worked up over and over again when diagramming his plan for transforming Ford Motor Company into a company closer to Coca-Cola or General Electric. If anyone questioned aspects of his plan, like the removal of focus from core automotive design and manufacturing, he could easily lose his temper.

"You just don't get it," he might say.

Nasser even suggested to one class of new junior executives that if playing at this level did not make "the hair stand up on the back of your neck when you talk about it, then go somewhere else. Go to our competition. We'd love it."

Getting rid of Ford Motor Company's weaker employees along with the ones who did not excel in BLI classes or enthusiastically jump on board with Nasser's bold, new plan was exactly what he wanted. Every company, Nasser believed, was damaged by the 10 percent of its workforce that accomplished the least. Taking a lead from his favorite executive example, GE's Jack Welch, Nasser and his top human resources aide, confidant David Murphy, instituted a plan at Ford called Performance Management Program (PMP), or "10-80-10." The basic intent of PMP was to weed the weak from Ford's payroll, strengthening the company over time.

In its original form, PMP called for an A-B-C grading scheme of Ford's top 18,000 management-level employees, with 10 percent getting the A grade, 80 percent receiving the B grade, and 10 percent getting a C grade. Two consecutive years of C grades meant the employee was of little or no value to the company and could lead to termination. At the very least, one C grade meant he or she would not be eligible for bonus checks or merit raises, the money going instead to A group employees deemed to be performing best.

The grading system caused deep friction within middle to high ranks at Ford Motor Company from its beginning. Managers and executives who had been bred for decades in a system that was not unlike the military, in that it placed high value on loyalty and service, could not understand how their futures were now directly in the hands of Jac Nasser, the man who could speak loud and clear if he chose through Ford's human resources department.

"Jac," says one Ford manager, "had about 200 employees who would die on the sword for him. The other 350,000 loathed him."

CHAPTER

3

Ground Zero

I t is not often an employee gets to break the nose and ribs of his company's chairman of the board and get away with it, much less earn his respect in doing so. But Dan Murray, who runs the in-house photography department at Ford Motor Company, has "beaten the hell" out of Bill Ford and is still around on payroll to tell about it.

Ford first met Murray in 1995 when flying to Brazil on a company jet for a photo shoot involving an initiative with Conservation International. As a member of the environmental organization's board, Ford was taking a group on a fact-finding mission. Murray, who did not know the company's youngest board member, was sitting near the front of the aircraft reading a martial arts magazine. By day, Murray was a photographer with Ford Motor Company, but at night and on weekends, he became one of the toughest martial arts instructors and fighters in the state of Michigan.

A former student of martial arts, Bill Ford walked by Murray and, noticing his reading material, struck up a conversation with the company photographer. With a third degree black belt in Tae Kwon Do, Murray revealed a passion for fighting and teaching that intrigued Ford. He talked about his motto, "It's always better to give than receive when fighting," and about how he believed martial arts should be taught for dealing with the real world, including self-defense in a hostile or violent situation.

One year after the Brazil trip, Murray went with Bill Ford on another Conservation International excursion, this time to Mexico, where the men talked more about martial arts. The co-owner of a martial arts school, Murray had taught thousands of students through the years and trained regularly with a Lansing, Michigan, group that included bouncers, police officers, and former military personnel. He had fighting experience in dozens of sanctioned tournaments and other "unreputable events" for "money and perverse pleasure," he says. Murray talked to Ford about the differences in learning martial arts as a fighter and learning them for show. His hard-nosed approach got Bill Ford's attention. Not long after the second trip, Murray got a call, asking if he would teach Ford Tae Kwon Do.

"I said, sure," says Murray. "As long as he's not like Elvis and he's willing to work, which basically meant, I'm going to kick his ass. He loved it and I started working with him."

Ford, who admiringly calls Murray "a nut," began taking lessons from him two to four times a week for at least an hour each lesson, training on his own outside of class. Murray taught Ford with an all-out, winner-take-all approach, never letting up in the heat of battle, even when his pupil was elevated to chairman of the board of the company he worked for. Murray says Ford was understandably tentative fighting at first, adjusting to the new, full-contact approach, but their conflicts, as Ford gained experience and more "killer instinct," became nothing-held-back brawls. Murray broke Ford's ribs and nose, but the young chairman with the public persona of the gentle heir kept coming back for more "ass kicking," delivering more attack in return with each passing week.

Ford wanted to achieve black belt status and Murray prodded him along, taking him increasingly to task. Murray brought in other martial arts experts to train with Ford, giving him experience with different body types and ages, but Ford says Murray was the toughest, fighting like he never felt pain.

"I could hit him as hard as I could right in the head and he never flinched," Ford says. "He used to beat the hell out of me. I told him, 'You are doing this for 375,000 people.'"

Both Ford and Murray recall one fight when the instructor's finger became dislocated after a blow to the pupil's head during a sparring match. Murray stopped and held out his hand to show Ford his injured finger. They both "died out laughing" at its mangled nature, Murray remembers.

"Then he grabbed it," Murray says, "and snapped it back into place."

They resumed fighting.

"People mistake his kindness and gentleness as a weakness," Murray says. "But when things get uglier and nastier, he is ruthless. He's rare because he can maintain humanity, but he is tough."

———

Tae Kwon Do is one hobby Bill Ford did not cut back on after accepting the company's chairmanship in 1999, but his life changed in many other ways, including less personal time for his passions, a higher public profile, and a more demanding schedule. He was already used to being in the spotlight as a descendant of Henry Ford and from the sporadic media attention he received in the Detroit area due to his management involvement with the NFL Lions from 1995 to 1999. But leading the board of directors of the world's second-largest automaker and stepping into shoes once famously filled by his great-grandfather, Henry Ford, and uncle, Henry Ford II, was different. He was well aware that accepting the responsibility meant letting go of his ability to slide in and out of public places without causing a stir, being asked for an autograph, or getting an earful of suggestions on how to run the company. But protecting his family time, as well as his family's privacy, just as his mother and father had done for him and his sisters, became a primary goal. Ford was willing to accept a higher profile, but he and his wife were not willing to compromise the lives of their four children. They moved the family from Grosse Pointe, where his grandfather, Edsel B. Ford, had first moved the Ford family in 1929, to the outskirts of Ann Arbor, Michigan's cozy and thriving university town.

In Ann Arbor, the automotive industry is typically only talked about in macrocosmic assessment in the halls and offices of the business school on the University of Michigan campus. A neighborhood job or a visit to a nearby Starbucks by the chairman drew only a few, if any, glances, giving him the distance he sought outside of work. The Fords found an executive home in Ann Arbor, situated on 17 acres with frontage along the Huron River, providing a secluded, outdoor feel near an intimate college setting.

Bill Ford was not the first Ford Motor Company executive to make the 45-minute commute from Ann Arbor, either. Robert McNamara, one of the famed "Whiz Kids" hired by Henry Ford II who helped save the company in the 1940s and 1950s, found comfort in the college town, due to its academic inspiration and distance from the all-auto mentality of metropolitan Detroit. Bill Ford fit right into the college town atmosphere as well, Rollerblading through the streets, wearing jeans around town, and cutting up with his children and their friends on the weekends. The older Ford children enrolled at an independent school, making As and playing multiple sports, while his youngest, a son, enrolled at a public elementary school near the family's home. In Ann Arbor, the Fords were also near Bill's sister, Sheila, and her family (Bill is close to Steve Hamp, his brother-in-law), and their children attended the same two schools. Ford drove himself to work in Dearborn every day, usually in either a Mustang or an F-150, in his position as nonexecutive chairman, having direct involvement in the company's activity as the leader of the board of directors. Ford, however, was completely removed from daily operations of the company, staying out of Nasser's way.

"There were a lot of people," Ford said, "saying, 'Let's hope he doesn't get too close to the real business.'"

At the time, there was little question whether the automaker could make money, and Nasser was fully empowered in operations, making the conventional wisdom among many that Bill Ford's operational leadership was not needed or wanted. The most obvious option remaining for chairman Ford was to help in areas he cared most about— primarily pushing Ford Motor Company to become a better corporate citizen, determining along the way exactly what that meant in the rapidly changing global business environment. No job seemed better suited for him than being the gatekeeper to responsibility and long-term vision at a company needing both. Ford Motor Company was the world leader in manufacturing SUVs and trucks, and consequently lagging behind in environmental issues such as gas mileage and emissions controls, making the company an easy target for drum-beating environmentalists concerned about the greenhouse effect. And while Jac Nasser was effectively managing the corporate growth factor, there was nothing Bill Ford wanted to do more than position Ford Motor Company as a leader in areas he personally believed were critical as the automaker positioned itself for the 21st century. A new-economy manufacturer, of course, needed to be driven by new-economy ideals, and he believed there was room for new age industrialist planning.

Bill Ford had first showed signs in youth as a person who placed high value on outdoor activity and natural resources, but these qualities increasingly took hold during his maturity and ascension at Ford Motor Company. Having developed a passion for fly-fishing, he co-owned, for a time, a popular fly rod company and was known to chase the perfect river or catch all over the world.

"I define a good day of fishing," said brother-in-law Steve Hamp, "as just being there. His definition is being there, but also producing. He's always got a couple of buckets that he's trying to fill."

Ford loves snow skiing with his family in the Colorado Rockies—they own a house in Colorado and often spend holidays there—and hiking outdoors. He dons jeans and boots or tennis shoes and gets outdoors at every possible moment to avoid a cooped-up feeling from sitting in an office too long. He remembers one particular moment working in Ford's product development division in a cramped, stuffy room as a ladder-climbing employee. The window was sealed with insulating rubber cement and would not open.

"So I got an X-Acto knife," he said, "and sliced the rubber cement. And then I got an Allen wrench and opened the window. What I didn't realize was the pressure that was in the building, and everything in my office went flying out of the window—*whoosh!*"

When he was named to the company's board of directors in 1988, Ford talked openly with environmental groups, making it no secret that he was troubled by the company's more than occasional collisions over environmental stances. This frank talk was the opposite of typical auto exec dialogue, angering some board members who thought he was behaving like a dilettante instead of an automotive leader responsible and loyal to the industry creed of production over environmental concern. Some board members asked him to stop. He responded, bluntly, "Absolutely not."

Bill Ford was not the first Ford family member working for the automaker to fight for a cause others considered a distraction to business. Great-grandfather Henry Ford's life, certainly, centered on the development and production of affordable cars, but he was never accused of having limited horizons. He spent time and effort on such noble causes as social engineering with the $5 a day wage and trying to stop World War I with his peace ship concoction. Ford family biographer Robert Lacey wrote in his book *Ford: The Men and the Machine* (Boston: Little, Brown and Co., 1986) that Henry Ford was even an early-day environmentalist of sorts, buying up farmland and forests around Dearborn as soon as he starting making money. Ford used the land, Lacey writes, partly for primitive tractor experiments and party to serve as bird sanctuaries. In 1912, Ford developed a relationship with author, poet, and bird lover John Burroughs, who encouraged him to help support a bill before Congress that would protect migratory birds. The bill had been stagnant in Congress for years, but by mobilizing his company's strong dealer network throughout America, Henry Ford got the Weekes-McLean bill passed and it became a law in 1913, providing unprecedented migratory bird protection in the United States.

Like his great-grandfather, Bill Ford had been striving on a personal level since his time at Princeton for more understanding about himself and the world around him. Since his initial exposure in college to Buddhist texts, Ford has continued to study Zen, Tibetan, and Vipassana Buddhism, saying only that they give him "perspective." He also believes in the benefits of alternative medicine, has seen an acupuncturist, and focuses on healthful eating—he eschews red meat—because of a history of family heart disease. Bill Ford does not often drink alcohol, either. His father was an alcoholic in his days at Ford Motor Company in the 1950s and 1960s, and was not known for punctuality until he abruptly stopped drinking one day, for good, in 1965. A young, pajama-clad Bill Ford unknowingly greeted Alcoholics Anonymous members arriving for meetings in the family's Grosse Pointe home, and though he does not recall such incidents (his mother does), Bill Ford confines his drinking to an occasional glass of red wine. Otherwise, he sticks mostly to water and espresso, saying only that alcohol "does not improve" his personality.

The cornerstone of Bill Ford's idealistic world, though, involves land, soil, and air.

"Nature," he says, "is where my heart is."

Ford Motor Company was earning more than $2,000 for every vehicle it sold in the late 1990s, allowing the company to play off its strength as Bill Ford aggressively pushed a "better world" corporate mantra that he believed would propel the automaker into the 21st century as a manufacturing giant willing and able to lead as a global corporation with a conscience. Ford talked openly about "resolving social and environmental issues" that had long plagued Ford Motor Company, and he began his chairmanship by initiating "a process of stakeholder engagement to bring a fresh perspective to our view of the world."

In a highly publicized move, Ford pulled his company out of the Global Climate Coalition, an organization fighting against environmental organizations like the Sierra Club on behalf of large industrial companies that argued the global-warming threat was nonsense. Ford felt the organization was "an impediment" to company credibility and true environmental responsibility. He also led Ford Motor Company to publish its first corporate citizenship report, documenting and measuring the company's impact on the economy, the environment, and society. The 98-page report acknowledged, in part, that SUVs, with low gas mileage and relatively high emissions, presented the company with challenges in terms of balancing the needs of shareholders, customers, and society.

"A few people," says Ford, "said we were attacking our own vehicles, or confessing a laundry list of failures. We weren't. All we were really trying to do was begin an honest dialogue."

Ford Motor Company got involved with 50 other companies in endorsing the 10-point code of environmental conduct set out by the Coalition for Environmentally Responsible Economics (CERES), which resulted from almost three years of dialogue between the corporations and such organizations as the Sierra Club and the Interfaith Center on Corporate Responsibility. The company also became the first automaker to certify all of its 140 plants around the world under ISO 14001, the international management standard that regulates and independently audits air, water, chemical handling, and recycling. And among Ford Motor Company's operations expansions was TH!NK, a new division launched in early 2000 to build and sell electric zero-emission cars and bicycles worldwide. TH!NK's battery-powered vehicles were intended to help Ford Motor Company meet escalating government emissions requirements and offer transportation alternatives for short, low-speed trips.

"I have been a lifelong environmentalist," Bill Ford said in his keynote address at the Fifth Greenpeace Business Conference in London in 2000. "When I joined Ford Motor Company 20 years ago, I struggled to reconcile my environmental ethic with working for an industrial company. . . . And now, as chairman of one of the world's largest corporations, I am in a unique position to be a catalyst for change."

Ford's environmental vision and activity were evident during the early months of his leadership in the planning and execution of two major building projects, each a blend of new and regenerative construction, and both benefiting the Detroit metropolitan area.

Ford's father had moved his Detroit Lions football franchise from deteriorating downtown Detroit to the suburbs of Pontiac, 30 miles from downtown, to play in the indoor Silverdome in 1976. But sensing the community needed the NFL franchise in its ailing downtown at the same time the Lions needed a new stadium, Bill Ford led the construction effort of a 65,000-seat, $500 million dome, built in the heart of the Motor City around the historic Hudson's Warehouse, constructed in 1920. The warehouse was slated to be demolished, but Bill Ford, working with public sources such as the City of Detroit, Wayne County, and the Detroit Downtown Development Authority, and with private sources including Ford Motor Company, the Lions, and Comerica Bank, pulled off financing for the stadium project. It utilized the existing Hudson's Warehouse in its design—locker rooms, for example, are in the original warehouse basement—making Ford Field one of the most unique stadiums in the country, a state-of-the-art facility, contributing to urban regeneration by recycling an aging, seemingly useless landmark. During construction of the stadium, NFL owners named Ford Field as the host site of the 2006 Super Bowl.

It was also in the early months of 1999 that Bill Ford took the lead in making a long-talked-about redesign and update of the sprawling, aging Rouge manufacturing complex. A debate had raged inside Ford Motor Company for some time as to what to do with the Rouge. The Rouge River was among the dirtiest in America, and leadership in the Detroit area was determined to clean it up. Ford Motor Company, owning and occupying the largest eyesore along Rouge banks, explored for almost a decade what to do with the complex. In 1992, when the Ford Mustang was the only car still built at the Rouge, the company considered closing Dearborn Assembly, replacing the Mustang with a front-wheel-drive car that would have been built at Mazda's Flat Rock, Michigan, plant. This would have meant the end of automobile manufacturing at the Rouge.

However, UAW Local 600 fought with a successful "Save the Mustang" campaign, ultimately resulting in a renewed commitment to the Rouge by Ford Motor Company and a redesign and reintroduction of the Mustang. In 1997, the company and UAW Local 600 membership approved the Rouge viability agreement, which called for an entirely new power plant in 2000. It was not yet in place when the tragic Rouge accident occurred in February 1999.

The tragedy reinforced the thought of some that the outdated plant should be abandoned. The company was patching aging facilities together and facing regulatory fines and issues due to its outdated nature. But a small group of others, most notably Bill Ford, felt differently, considering it a reminder that the company's future hinged upon its past. The Rouge was still the largest industrial complex in the world, containing assembly, engine, glass, tool and die, frame, and stamping operations, in addition to Rouge Steel Company and the Double Eagle Steel Company. It may have been an eyesore, but it was Ford Motor Company's eyesore.

Architect Bill McDonough did not know Bill Ford before 1999, but he had some ideas of his own about what to do with the Rouge. The Charlottesville, Virginia, resident had studied at Dartmouth and Yale and in the 1980s and 1990s led such lauded architectural designs as the Herman Miller Factory in Zeeland, Michigan, and the Gap corporate offices in California. In 1995, the part-time University of Virginia professor founded a firm with German chemist Michael Braungart, specializing in "environmentally safe manufacturing processes and materials," suggesting that "everything from cars to computers to urban centers can be designed so that they never pollute." In February 1999 McDonough saw Bill Ford on the news, talking about his "worst day," and read ensuing stories about the tragedy at the Rouge. On a chance, McDonough, familiar with Bill Ford's environmental stance, used personal contacts to weave his way through roadblocks that typically protect Ford and other corporate leaders. He reached Ford Motor Company's chairman and set up a meeting to discuss the Rouge and possibilities for global impact through industrial leadership.

"I went up to his office and he said, 'Why are you here?' " McDonough remembered. "I said, 'What interests me is that you can change the world. With $80 billion of purchase orders, all you have to do is say you want a different way, and things start to move.' "

The meeting was supposed to last a half hour, but McDonough and Bill Ford talked most of the afternoon about the architect's principles relative to the future of industrial manufacturing, where the biggest corporations have the ability to lead to a world of sustainability and no waste through their large-scale impact. Bill Ford listened intently and thought about his great-grandfather, Henry Ford, whose vertical integration vision for the Rouge had been an industrial epiphany of the 20th century. Bill Ford imagined the overhauled, environmentally engineered Rouge being the same in the 21st century, an entirely new approach to large-scale manufacturing, the demonstration that industry and environment can peacefully coexist.

Not long after their initial meeting, McDonough and Ford attended a luncheon together at The Henry Ford (at the time it was called Henry Ford Museum and Greenfield Village) where Bill Ford, on the museum's board of directors, was the featured speaker. He talked about Ford Motor Company's commitment to being a socially and environmentally responsible company. Then, speaking off the cuff, with no firm plans in place, Ford announced that the Rouge would be rebuilt according to environmental plans laid out by McDonough and the sweeping project would completed in two years. McDonough was sitting by Steve Hamp, Bill Ford's brother-in-law and president of The Henry Ford, when the chairman forced the issue of the Rouge's dubious future by pledging an architectural miracle of sorts. Hamp, who had started work at The Henry Ford in 1978, had seen a little bit of everything in community development circles. But the 1999 Michiganian of the Year (named so by the *Detroit News*) turned in surprise at his brother-in-law's commitment and looked at McDonough.

"When [McDonough] heard Bill say, 'We are going to do this, and we are going to do it in this time frame,' his jaw dropped," Hamp says, "because he had not heard any of it. It was a gut thing for Bill. He just said, 'We are going to do it because I said we are going to do it.' He's at his best when he follows his gut."

Renamed the Ford Rouge Center, the Rouge complex would be redesigned to feature the world's largest living roof atop a new assembly facility, 2.5 million-square-foot Dearborn

Truck Plant. The roof, a sedum-planted surface, would be designed to reduce storm water runoff, insulate the building, and last longer than traditional roof materials—ultimately costing the company less.

"I could feel eyes rolling behind my back," Ford says. "To say [people] were skeptical is an understatement.

"There was a lot of pressure not to do it. Some people thought I was just trying to fuel my wild-eyed enthusiasm. But to me, we had to do it. . . . We desperately needed to change the dialogue from one of paying fines and trying to comply with the law to one of changing the paradigm."

The 600-acre Rouge redevelopment, planned to open in 2004, would also include the interactive Ford Rouge Factory Tour, allowing visitors to the Detroit area to see and experience American automobile manufacturing via a multimedia visitor experience similar to something one might find at Disney's Epcot. The tour also includes a bird's-eye view survey of Ford's new truck plant, manufacturing the popular F-150.

"Bill," says Hamp, "said from the start this is not going to be industrial philanthropy, and at the end of the day, the company is going to save money by doing this."

The planned $2 billion Rouge renovation was not a slam dunk with Ford's board of directors, who had to be sold on the idea that the long-term savings of such a massive product would pay off for the company.

"I remember thinking," said Ford board member and former U.S. Secretary of the Treasury Bob Rubin, "there are a lot of intangibles here. But as hard as they are to measure, there are some compelling benefits. Bill is a kind of unique, maybe special, person with a real feel for maximizing success over a longer-term horizon than most of us look at."

———

Ford's desire for the automaker to contribute to a better world was parlayed into product planning as well. He was outspoken in the industry on the opinion that the gas-powered combustible engine as we know it would go away in our lifetime, stating flatly, "It will happen," despite strong objections from industry leaders. He showed a personal interest in emerging technologies, asking questions of anyone he believed had answers.

Ford Motor Company studied environmentally friendly alternatives through its electric TH!NK car division and experimentation with hydrogen and multiple other engine technologies, but the attention grabber came at the 2001 Los Angeles Auto Show. The automaker announced it would produce a hybrid gas-electric Escape (based on the company's popular compact Escape SUV) in 2003, to be America's first mass-produced and marketed environmentally friendly SUV. The hybrid would be powered by a combination of a conventional combustion engine and an electric motor, drastically improving gas mileage and emissions by electrically powering the vehicle on idle and in low-speed circumstances. This was a significant technology step for Ford away from its U.S. competition, namely General Motors, which was betting on small improvements to conventional power trains until a far-off day when hydrogen-powered cars became practical. While hydrogen may be the ultimate environmental solution for the automotive industry, hybrids are viewed by many as being a practical, near-term improvement that can bridge the gap to a hydrogen future. This realization prompted Bill Ford to say at the time that hybrids could represent "20 percent of the market in 10 years."

Ford Motor Company also made proactive commitments to the federal government, breaking ranks with other U.S. automakers. Ford announced, to the surprise of many inside the industry, that fuel mileage for all Ford SUVs—leading targets among environmentalists—would be increased 25 percent by 2005. This increase of roughly five miles per gallon would be well ahead of government mandates and the timeline other competitive automakers were following.

All was not flowing so easily, however, in the upper levels of leadership at Ford Motor Company. From the earliest days of his CEO reign, Nasser was miffed at the easy attention and following that Bill Ford drew, especially from the inadvertent publicity resulting from the Rouge accident. Nasser liked being an executive star and, in the height of the age that America revered its corporate leaders, he was working overtime to be the poster-perfect American CEO, pitching a contemporary spin to anyone who would listen. Bill Ford preferred an intimate conversation as opposed to a crowd with microphones stuffed in his face, yet there he was, becoming the leader of the people and a sought-after spokesman of the company by accident. And the more easy attention Ford drew, the harder and faster Nasser worked to bring in outsiders who did not have the loyalty and understanding of the Ford family name and history—perhaps further alienating the majority of Ford Motor Company's longtime employees. Meanwhile, Bill Ford continued to publicly support Nasser, but was growing increasingly frustrated by the CEO's flagrant use of his empowerment by the board of directors to change and grow the company and his apparent disregard for the company's time-tested culture.

Ford and Nasser occupied neighboring offices at World Headquarters. Ford's quarters were warm and detailed with all recyclable materials, while Nasser's were brushed-chrome finish and filled with the latest electronics, from flat-screened televisions to a well-used Blackberry that never rested far from its user. The two men frequently talked back and forth about the latest developments of some issue or another. Rumors circulated throughout Detroit about a tense hallway confrontation between Ford and Nasser in which security was supposedly called, but insiders say published reports of an altercation were untrue.

What actually occurred was a heated argument between

Ford and vice president of public affairs Jason Vines, who had been brought to Ford from Nissan by Nasser to replace Vaughn Koshkarian. It started after Ford gave input during a meeting about information to be included in an upcoming annual report. When Ford walked out, Vines suggested to the group that Ford's suggestion would be a logistical nightmare. "Don't worry about Bill," he said. "I'll talk to him." Dan Murray was in the room and heard the comment. He called Ford, who called Vines into his office. Ford held nothing back verbally, nor did Vines, but blows were not exchanged.

The tension in Dearborn was growing.

It did not help that Nasser's personal life was making negative headlines, beginning with stories that his wife, Jennifer, was filing for divorce after 30 years of marriage. The couple was seen as being among Detroit's A-list: she, the brassy, civic-minded leading lady, working tirelessly for various charities; he, the work-all-night, super-achieving auto executive, dashing around town in luxury sports cars and expensive suits to make an appearance at various crowd-pleasing functions and cocktail parties. Nasser earned so much money at Ford Motor Company—almost $14 million in 1999 and more than $17 million in 2000, in salary, bonuses, and options—that his wife said she had become "accustomed to an extraordinary standard of living . . . enjoyed only by the rich and powerful," and she wanted a divorce from Jac because he was "controlling" and an "absentee" parent.

As Nasser sensed Bill Ford's growing frustration with his antics, the CEO worked increasingly hard to close his self-built inner circle tighter, keeping pertinent information from the chairman, who was becoming more interested in operations in light of Nasser's erratic behavior. Ford worried that the company's core Ford Division—the auto industry's number-one-selling brand that accounted for nearly 80 percent of Ford Motor Company's total vehicle sales in 2001—might be losing ground in quality and profits due to a lack of focus on the basics from the hurried activity on e-business and an emphasis on luxury car development. When he went looking for detailed answers in operations, he was met with executive roadblocks. Upon hearing about Bill Ford's more frequent in-quiries for details, Nasser routinely walked across the hallway to the chairman's office to try to smooth things over with glossy management answers that everything was fine and that the plan was being executed to perfection. Publicly, though, Bill Ford continued to try to dispel the growing rumors of dis-content, showing he supported Nasser, because he felt doing anything less might damage the company's reputation on Wall Street and cause more stress internally than what al-ready existed.

"This company," Ford said, "has always loved to form camps around its top players. We're trying to avoid that."

Despite the top-level stress, Ford Motor Company continued marching on, receiving rave reviews on Wall Street and in multiple business publications for its radical transformation plan led by Nasser. Following the CEO's lead, the company was doing everything possible to show there was no longer merely one Ford brand under the blue oval, for and about middle-class Americans. The new Ford Motor Company was now so much more, led by luxury brands Jaguar, Land Rover, and Volvo. To emphasize this shift, not long after the com-pany purchased Land Rover, Nasser aides ordered taken down the two large Ford blue oval logo signs that adorned the top of World Headquarters on its north and south sides.

Weighing six tons each, the signs were giant versions of the trademark blue oval that was the company's global identity. All over the world, the blue Ford oval was one of the most recognizable corporate identities, along with McDonald's golden arches and Coca-Cola's "Coke" insignia. Ford Motor Company had first used the blue oval in 1927 on its Model A, and the logos had been placed on top of the "Glass House" in 1968.

But in Ford's new era of diversified business, Nasser and his top aides—especially Jim Schroer, Nasser's handpicked global marketing chieftain—saw the Ford Motor Company as much more than the blue oval, which was a nagging reminder of Henry Ford's original plan of building affordable cars for all Americans. They replaced the oval with an all-brand logo showing "Ford Motor Company" in script. Known as the company's "trust mark," it was placed on the top of both sides of the building where the blue ovals had long been displayed. The oval was relegated to Ford Division and its products; the new trust mark would become the company's overall identity.

"I couldn't believe it," said Michigan resident Art Schaaf, an 81-year-old retired Ford employee, on the day the blue ovals came down. "It is one of the best brand names, right up there with Coca-Cola. I think it's a big mistake."

Dark Days
in Dearborn

In the months just before and after the new millennium, Ford Motor Company's heady successes had many ironic underpinnings. Every step the company tried to make away from its smokestack, nuts-and-bolts heritage was greeted with a hard yank back from the core of manufacturing reality, beginning with the tragic Rouge accident in the first month of the new leadership roles for Jac Nasser and Bill Ford. But the Rouge tragedy, serious as it was, was only the beginning of dark clouds gathering over Dearborn during its transformation from old-economy business to new. One year and one week after the explosion had rocked the company, a Houston, Texas, television news story about shredding tires served as the catalyst of a rapidly developing perfect corporate storm that would completely engulf Ford Motor Company.

The American economy was still raging and the technology bubble still rapidly expanding on February 7, 2000. Ford, the automaker, was in the midst of its whirlwind transformation tour, guided by Jac Nasser, desperately trying to be part of the next big thing. Despite numerous acquisitions, the company still sat on $20 billion in cash, due in large part to heavy profits delivered by SUVs born of the trendsetting Explorer.

Ford Motor Company had introduced this wildly popular product in 1990 as an improved, four-door version of its segment-building but phased-out Bronco II. Fit with Firestone tires as standard equipment, the Explorer quickly became America's best-selling SUV, contributing more than $500 million in profits to Ford in 1991 alone. No SUV, manufactured by any company, sold more units than the Explorer did in the 1990s, and the product led the company to unprecedented success, inspiring competitive knockoffs along the way.

The fast-paced times at Ford, however, were about to take a significant blow when KHOU television station in Houston opened its 10 P.M. newscast with a breathless story regarding safety concerns about the Explorer and its Firestone tires. It was the kind of consumer action story favored by local television stations during the all-important February "sweeps."

"They are among the most popular vehicles in Texas," the news anchor intoned as he opened the broadcast, "Ford Explorers. But if you're driving one, you could be in danger."

The KHOU news team reported that Firestone Radial ATX tires, for many years standard equipment on Ford Explorers, could be a dangerous common denominator to a number of Explorer rollover accidents that had occurred nationwide and resulted in some deaths and serious injuries. The reporter cited one crash involving a Ford Explorer, saying police speculated that a Firestone tire on the SUV came apart at highway speed, causing the Explorer to flip three times, killing a passenger. The news broadcast led to a barrage of calls and e-mails to the station from Texas viewers who said they had experienced similar problems. By May, the National Highway Traffic Safety Administration (NHTSA), which governs automobile safety, had opened an investigation into the numerous complaints in response to the broadcast and the ensuing consumer outcry.

The primary targets of the investigation, Ford Motor Company and Firestone, had one of the longest-lasting and most valued relationships in all of American business. Henry Ford and Harvey Firestone had met and become friends and occasional fishing buddies in 1896, before either had made a fortune selling cars or tires. By 1906, the Akron-based tire manufacturer was supplying the majority of tires put on Ford Motor Company cars, and the success of the Model T, which sold thousands of units in no time, led to riches for both. The friendship and business partnership of Henry Ford and Harvey Firestone flourished through the years as they traveled the countryside together, their families co-mingling as friends. In 1948, Firestone's granddaughter, Martha Parke Firestone, married Henry Ford's grandson, William Clay Ford. Who could have guessed then that 52 years later, the oldest son of Bill and Martha Ford would be the chairman of Ford and the company would be involved with Firestone in a national transportation crisis?

The Firestone family, of course, was long gone from its namesake company when the Houston television station broke the story about Firestone tires possibly causing Ford Explorers to roll over. The tire maker had been owned by parent Bridgestone, a Japan-based manufacturer, since 1988. Still, Bill Ford and other Ford Motor Company executives were used to a warm relationship with Firestone and found no comfort in the contentious tone quickly developing between the corporations.

In the beginning of the crisis, Firestone relied heavily on Ford for spin control as the rollover saga rapidly turned into a disaster, making newspaper headlines throughout the country and serving as lead stories for Tom Brokaw, Peter Jennings, and Dan Rather on national evening news broadcasts. Under the public relations guidance of Jason Vines, Nasser's hand-picked aide, the automaker's management worked initially to protect the tire maker while internal investigations were under way at Ford to try to determine the specific causes of Explorer rollover accidents. Ford had previously recalled Firestone tires in Venezuela, the Middle East, and Southeast

Asia, and when this piece of news became public, media attention increased further and relations between Ford Motor Company and Firestone grew even testier. By August 2000, the NHTSA had more than doubled the number of fatalities attributed to Firestone tread separations on Ford Explorers from 21 to 46 with 80 injuries and 270 complaints. In response, national retailers, most notably Sears, dropped Firestone tires. Over the course of a long, tense weekend summit at Ford World Headquarters, Ford and Firestone management and lawyers confronted data freshly crunched by Ford quality assurance engineers that showed an alarmingly higher accident claim rate on Explorers equipped with Firestone tires that had been made at Firestone's Decatur, Illinois, plant.

Firestone and Ford agreed to meet with NHTSA in the coming days to declare a recall of 6.5 million on-the-road tires. Firestone officials wanted to announce the recall by means of a one-way satellite feed, keeping inquiring reporters at a distance, but at Ford Motor's insistence a press conference was held in Washington, D.C., instead and the biggest media outlets in the country attended. More than two months of daily news headlines followed.

The tire recall, though, was disastrous. Firestone's plan, reliant on replacement tire availability, would take almost a year to complete. Consumers, fearful of tread separation after numerous media accounts of the problem, loudly complained through hotlines and the airwaves of not being able to get replacements fast enough. Following Nasser's lead, Ford Motor Company closed production at three factories to free up more tires, making 70,000 additional replacements available for immediate recall use. Ford even allowed other tire brands to be used as replacements at Ford dealerships, costing the company hundreds of millions of dollars.

It was Nasser who filled the visible public role during this public relations nightmare, appearing in up-close television commercials as the company tried to hold on to public trust. Nasser also agreed to a one-on-one interview with USA To-

day at the height of the problems and sparred with Ted Koppel on *Nightline* before appearing before the U.S. Congress to answer pointed questions about the debacle. Sitting silently in the background was difficult for Bill Ford, who in the early stages of the crisis never imagined the level of destruction it would ultimately cause. Ford knew recalls were an unfortunate part of the business of making a complicated product like an automobile. The chairman—the one participant tied to both companies by blood—considered attending a Firestone anniversary celebration in August 2000 commemorating the company's 100th anniversary, before a Ford senior legal counselor strongly advised against it, knowing that the legal wrangling between the two companies was only just beginning.

Ford Motor Company had begun to prepare for a 100th anniversary celebration itself, to be held three years later. The Ford family had worked for almost a century to build a reputation of trust with the American people, but in one sudden stroke it was being devoured by a controversy involving a product bearing the chairman's mother's maiden name, Firestone. Once Bill Ford realized the catastrophic nature of the Explorer/Firestone crisis, he met with his most trusted advisers as his instincts told him to take a more public role in the worsening events. He was "dying to jump in," said one. Ultimately, he followed the advice of others inside the company who believed it best for Nasser, the CEO, to be the lead Ford spokesperson and take any heat or heroism that came along with it. If Bill Ford, the non-operations man, suddenly stepped forward during a recall crisis, would it not undermine the leadership of Nasser, his chief executive?

Behind the scenes, aides say Ford was showing increasing strength and assertiveness as Ford Motor Company's problems continued to mount and to grow in severity. He was in the midst of a "long period of frustration," watching the names of his father and mother—Ford and Firestone—leading newscasts and newspapers with ongoing negative headlines.

This growing aggressiveness, says Dan Murray, corresponded

with his advancement in martial arts, the place Bill Ford could channel his frustration and get through his days of growing agony. After almost three years of lessons, the chairman tested for his black belt in Tae Kwon Do on June 14, 2000, in Dearborn. Ford tested solo for two and a half hours before a panel that included Murray, his immediate instructor, and a grand master. Ford underwent an "exhaustive period of sparring and fighting single and multiple attackers" and demonstrated breaking techniques by chopping in half a stack of cement blocks.

"I was meaner," says Murray, "and tougher on him than I was on anyone else I've ever trained. I made sure that there would never be a question as to whether or not he earned it."

While Bill Ford maintained a low public profile during the developing Firestone crisis, Nasser, to his credit, aggressively took the role of company spokesperson and charged with valor, delivering sincerity in moments that those close to him had never seen before. It was not easy, as Nasser was undergoing personal problems at the peak of the controversy, with his wife of almost 30 years filing for divorce. The couple's split made headlines and served as leading watercooler gossip fodder throughout Detroit. Nonetheless, Nasser worked tirelessly during the peak of the crisis, manning company crisis hotline phones in Ford's 11th floor Firestone war room, promising customers on phone lines that he would personally fix their problem, and telling them where to find replacement tires at area dealerships.

The damage, however, was severe and beyond repair for the hardworking Aussie. BusinessWeek ran a cover story with Nasser's picture and the daunting headline: "Ford: It's Worse Than You Think." By May 2001, Ford Motor Company had announced the recall of more than 13 million additional Firestone tires from a range of company products because of safety concerns. The total recalls cost Ford Motor Company far in excess of $100 million and ultimately severely strained the longtime relationship with its oldest supplier as Ford and Firestone formally, painfully, and publicly ended the business association between the companies.

As the number of recalled tires grew, Bill Ford instructed the company's internal environmentalists to find means of reuse. Many tires were ground and incorporated into the construction of numerous projects, including mats for children's playgrounds and even the playing surface at Detroit's new Ford Field football stadium. The ground rubber was also made into mulch and donated to parks around the country. Due largely to evidence linking the problem exclusively to Firestone's tires, the Explorer survived the damaging rollover crisis publicity, and a new version of the SUV was released in 2001. Explorer set a June sales record in 2001 with 42,833 units sold, eclipsing that with 50,000 units sold in September.

But Ford Motor Company was also having quality problems, albeit not life-threatening, with many of its other products. The company's famous slogan, "Quality Is Job One," had become a pledge and an important part of Ford's culture as a result of groundbreaking 1982 UAW negotiations. Now Ford was unwittingly sending to dealerships some cars, trucks, and SUVs that operated below traditional company standards, a sign of increasing internal distractions caused by the consumer-driven diversification blitz. Ford Motor Company's lack of core product focus adversely affected product launches, the backbone of any good car company. Ford would hype a new product but fail to deliver it to market properly, lessening its chances of marquee success. The best example of this failure might have been the return of the Thunderbird to the company's car lineup.

Ford Motor Company had turned heads at 1999 auto shows with its retro concept car, a remake of the original 1955 Thunderbird. Designer J Mays, Ford's prize recruit, had car enthusiasts and industry watchers abuzz over the design of the new Thunderbird. Searching for a Ford halo car, Nasser made production a reality, believing the revamped Thunderbird would invigorate the Ford brand, which suffered from a weaker car lineup as trucks and SUVs dominated and the success of the Taurus wound down. The Thunderbird was launched by Ford Motor Company in August 2001 after two years of fever-pitched hype from product appearances at auto shows, on magazine covers, and on popular television shows. The car was initially sold through the Neiman Marcus 2000 Christmas holiday catalog, selling out 200 pricey special editions in just two hours. The special-order cars were to be delivered to catalog buyers in June, one month before standard editions of the new Thunderbird went on sale publicly at dealerships.

The Thunderbird, however, faced multiple production problems just as it was scheduled to come to market. A cooling system flaw delayed on-time delivery by one month for dealers and two months for the special orders—making the Neiman Marcus Christmas cars deliver a full month after standard edition cars hit the streets. It did not help that Ford Motor Company did little to manage the launch gaffes, either. Flashing his trademark haste, Nasser announced at a Dearborn press conference to kick off Thunderbird sales in the summer of 2001 that the company was "filling the pipeline" with the cars, despite repeated warnings from Ford team members that production was running behind and having problems, dealer delivery was late, and "no mention" should be made of current availability. Known to often be overcome by his own enthusiasm, Nasser only made matters worse for the Thunderbird-seeking public that was having trouble finding the product on showroom floors.

The poor launch hurt the much-hyped Thunderbird, with first year sales totaling just 19,000, some 25 percent less than the company had projected, thus eliminating any prospects that the heavily invested program would halo Ford Motor

Company. If anything, the Thunderbird fiasco underscored what company and industry insiders had been surmising ever since Jac Nasser took office as CEO: Ford seemed to be rapidly losing its industry-leading touch, and the facts were there to back it up. In 1999, the company had botched aspects of the launch of its small car Focus, designed to replace the once-popular Escort, and had to recall 31,000 due to a defect with the speed control cable. The small SUV Escape fared no better with its launch as a 2001 model, facing multiple recalls. The problems sent Ford Motor Company consumer purchase consideration numbers, key industry determinations that reflect brand worth, dramatically lower.

Once a global leader, Ford Motor Company was sinking closer to its second tier competitors. The company that had pioneered the moving assembly line and later restored America's confidence in quality domestic-built products appeared no longer capable of effectively designing, building, and manufacturing a new product in one uninterrupted, successful sequence. Ford Motor Company, wrote Mark Truby in the *Detroit News*, had placed "cyber-savviness" above engineering prowess and paid the price, slipping dramatically away from quality being "Job One."

Many employees felt product quality was not the only tradition that Ford Motor Company was leaving behind. Employee lawsuits were filed, resulting from what was said to be a pattern of discrimination against white males. Disgruntled employees complained they were passed over for promotions under the PMP plan and other initiatives to increase management diversity instituted under Nasser and human resources vice president David Murphy. The employees said the plan, which ranked Ford's 18,000 top managers against their peers, favored women and minorities and gave management too much leeway to manipulate the unpopular A-B-C scoring system. In

June 2001, lawyer Sue Ellen Eisenberg filed a suit on behalf of 75 Ford managers who had received a C grade under the evaluation system the year before. In an organizational meeting of the managers, Eisenberg suggested that signing up to join the complaint was like giving Nasser a grade of F.

"We all know sadly enough that under the leadership of Jacques Nasser brother has been pitted against brother, sister against sister," Eisenberg said. "A house divided against itself will fall."

Sensing deep internal stress from the ongoing Firestone crisis, the developing employee crisis and lawsuits, and the widespread discontent with Nasser, Bill Ford sent an eight-paragraph memo to employees, explaining the company's position in the Firestone recall and offering support for the embattled Nasser: "The Board of Directors and I," he wrote, "were involved in this decision [to recall Firestone tires from Ford vehicles] and fully support the efforts of Jacques Nasser and our team to resolve this issue and ensure the safety of our customers.

"It is clear this is a defining moment for Ford Motor Company."

―――――――

Dating back to the earliest days, one of Ford Motor Company's strengths has been its Ford and Lincoln-Mercury retailers, but the group as a whole grew increasingly frustrated with Nasser and the automaker, and by 2001 became more vocal in their displeasure just as everything else seemed to be unraveling in Dearborn. Ford Motor Company's entry into the retail market, by purchasing close to 50 dealerships in select markets, had not gone over well in leadership circles of the dealer network. Sure, Ford owned just 50 dealerships out of almost 4,000 in the United States, but independent retailers who had invested millions of dollars, years of service, and generations of ownership to support their dealerships felt threatened by the move. They also did not like Ford's global entry into service centers, a profit source for dealerships, and felt Nasser had plans to eventually push them out of the car selling and servicing business in his quest to take more of the profits from the life cycle of the car for the automaker.

The president of the Ford Division at the time, Jim O'Connor, had been with the company for more than 30 years, and most of that time had been spent on the sales and marketing side, up close and personal with Ford and Lincoln-Mercury dealers. A New York native, O'Connor had married a girl whose father was a longtime Ford employee. "The only paycheck she's ever known," he says, "has been from Ford." O'Connor briefly left the company once, to co-own dealerships with longtime Ford dealer Bob Kelly. He returned with a better understanding of the importance of good relations between manufacturer and retailer and developed a reputation through the years, within the company and among dealers, as one of the strongest executive links between the two.

When Ford dealers complained so loudly about changes under Nasser that the complaints began reaching Bill Ford and the Ford family, Nasser ordered O'Connor to fix the problem.

"Jac said, 'You better get this fixed,'" O'Connor remembers. "I said, 'They are talking about you, not me.'"

Believing his help was no longer needed in the new Ford Motor Company, O'Connor considered resigning. He was prepared to leave the company he had lived with and loved since going to work after graduating from college in 1964. O'Connor's plan was to leave Ford and buy a dealership. He even went so far as to make a handshake agreement with a dealer on a price for buying a specific one. O'Connor talked about his plans with Kelly, his friend, fellow Ford dealer, and former business partner. Kelly was fully aware of the turmoil at Ford and far from shocked at the division president's plans, but he urged his friend to stay.

"Wouldn't you make a better contribution to the company if you stayed?" Kelly asked O'Connor.

Nasser wanted nothing of O'Connor leaving, either. Losing O'Connor, one of the last remaining executives with whom the dealers talked openly, would have fanned into flame an already smoldering fire, proving to Bill Ford and members of the board once and for all that Nasser had absolutely lost control of the company. Nasser invited O'Connor to lunch in the Magnolia dining room in the penthouse of Ford's World Headquarters and pleaded.

"I can't have you leave," he said.

O'Connor agreed to stay, but found no more support from those at the top.

"I was on a limb by myself," he says, "but they kept me because I guess they thought I had some value. But there were a lot of memos written not supporting what was being done. The Ford brand has the strongest retail system in the world and our dealers are absolutely our strongest assets, but we were not showing it."

Nasser knew he and Ford Motor Company had major dealer problems because a National Automotive Dealers Association (NADA) satisfaction survey found that Ford, once a leader, was viewed by retailers as the worst in the industry to work with. To counter, Nasser himself began traveling the country to meet face-to-face with retailers, pledging to open lines of communication. The dealers' concerns, however, continued and some significant complaints got past Nasser, despite his strongest efforts, to members of Ford's board of directors, who became increasingly concerned about the deteriorating relationships. For board member Carl Reichardt, a crowning moment in the downfall of Nasser came when one major dealer looked him in the eye, delivering a questioning plea for help.

Reichardt remembers: "He said, 'Do you guys know what the hell you are doing? You are killing [your dealers].'"

Rumors swirled throughout Detroit in July 2001 that Ford's board of directors would pull back on Nasser's power by reducing the number of executives that reported directly to him. In fact the board set a two-day meeting to grill the company's CEO about the range of issues troubling the company, including declining profits, quality, and productivity; increasing costs; and unhappy employees and dealers. In response, Nasser sent a letter to employees just before the meeting to announce that the company was dropping its controversial A-B-C grading scheme.

The man who liked to don a Santa Claus hat at Christmas and prance around the 12th floor of Ford's World Headquarters serenading executives, including Bill Ford, was not as jolly as the summer dragged on and speculation about his future intensified. Publicly, the CEO acted generally unfazed by the trouble, stating that he knew how to survive tough times. But the pressure was mounting and the rumors about board discontent were true. In July, Ford Motor Company's board officially formed the Office of the Chairman and CEO, giving Bill Ford operational authority while limiting Nasser's. It was essentially a formalization of a day-to-day working relationship between the two. The PR line on the reasoning for the move was to "improve decision-making efficiency" and to give both "a formal opportunity for an earlier review in policy, strategy, and business proposals," but everyone close to the situation knew exactly what it meant: Bill Ford would officially be in the operational loop, making it much more difficult for Nasser to hide information from him and keep him away from decision-making meetings. Ford assumed a position on the company's executive operating committee and quickly learned through biweekly meetings that the vital signs of Ford Motor Company were worse than he even suspected. The automaker was in deep trouble, as all indications were that sales, quality, and profitability were in rapid decline.

Changes in the organization were begun immediately. With involvement from Bill Ford and the board of directors, the company announced plans to sell its retail dealer collections despite major investments and imminent profits. Executives admitted in the process that the company had made a mistake, pushing years of trust with dealers to the limits by its retail entry.

"It says a lot," said Ford Dealer Council Chairman Jerry Reynolds of Texas, "for their dedication to dealer relations that they'd do this at this time. It would make a lot more sense for them to hang in there, sell some cars and recoup some revenue. That tells me a lot about their sincerity."

The quick, decisive move rescued the company's precious dealer relations in the nick of time, but it did not help restore the dealers' trust in Nasser—the man they believed at the heart of the company's diversion.

As if Nasser's and Ford Motor Company's problems were not bad enough, the perfect corporate storm got its final elements of rapidly developing strength when America's economic bubble burst and the dot-coms and technology companies tumbled down, along with American stock markets. Coupled with September 11, 2001, the day terrorists attacked the country, destroying the World Trade Center Twin Towers, thousands of lives, and hopes for a rebounding U.S. economy, the downturn and domestic uneasiness rattled Ford Motor Company's shaky foundation even more.

Like its domestic competitors, Ford had enjoyed three consecutive record years of blistering sales and profits. As recently as March 2001, the company had come close to slipping past General Motors as the world's sales leader. But Nasser and others at Ford suspected, in the hours and days after the terrorist attacks, that the American economy, already in recession, would suffer greatly. The widely held theory from Washington to Detroit: Slumping auto sales would result as the country's flagship manufacturing companies watched scared consumers hold on tightly to precious dollars.

Nasser and Ford Motor Company prepared to take lumps with other suffering businesses in America and do the inevitable—cut back. On September 20, 2001, however, startling news reached Dearborn from crosstown rival General Motors. GM would "Keep America Rolling" by offering unprecedented zero-percent financing on a wide range of GM products. Nasser was furious and perhaps even embarrassed at being one-upped by General Motors. Here was Ford, preparing to slow down as the nation mourned, and there was General Motors, waving red, white, and blue colors, pledging a patriotic theme and customer giveaways so it could gather more market share. Along with crosstown rival Chrysler, Ford Motor Company quickly followed suit with incentive campaigns of its own. Instead of reducing capacity, Ford followed GM's lead, offering consumers its own set of zero-percent financing deals on Ford and Lincoln-Mercury products.

"Single-handedly," said auto industry consultant George Petersen, "GM stimulated the economy and forced other manufacturers to go along with it."

In the business world, it was known as a fire sale. Ford had deeply incentivized products before 9/11, propping up cars like the Ford Taurus or Mercury Sable with low financing. Now, though, it was following GM's lead in discounting the best and most profitable it had, including SUVs and F-150 pickup trucks, to move product out of plants and off dealers' hands. Despite predictions of North American market doom after 9/11, auto sales did more than remain strong in response to the deep incentives—October sales across the industry set all-time highs.

The strategy could not help the Thunderbird, though. Ford's award-winning-design sports car, back-ordered due to prelaunch hype, was sitting idle on production lines in the days after 9/11 because overseas parts could not get through tightened security for shipment, damaging the car's already rocky launch even more. Other, more significant problems continued springing up at Ford Motor Company in the final months of 2001, as well, doing more damage to Nasser's cause. One in particular, the rapid demise of Ford's traditionally staunch financing division, Ford Motor Credit Company, caused particular concern for Bill Ford and members of the board.

———

For 40 years and 160 consecutive reporting financial quarters, Ford Credit had been a conservative, reliable, and significant profit center for its parent company. Edsel Ford II retired as president of the division in 1998, and Nasser seized control of it in 1999 when he took over as CEO of Ford Motor Company, hiring flamboyant banker Donald Winkler to run the credit company. The 51-year-old Winkler was a hot-tempered, travel-budget-busting wheeler-dealer who was reportedly on the outs as an executive at Bank One when Nasser picked him as CEO of Ford's sterling credit division. Winkler was a poster-child dyslexic who told anyone who would listen how he went to the office at 3 A.M. to do "mental warm-ups" in preparation for the workday.

Like his boss, Winkler was a business aggressor. He followed Nasser's lead and pledged to remake the traditionally conservative Ford Credit into a global financial superpower through aggressive lending and expansion. In 1999 Ford Credit acquired the sub-prime lending unit Triad Financial and also expanded its own sub-prime lending efforts through in-house Fairlane Credit.

Oddly, considering his banker background, Winkler was a free spender known for liberally handing out company-funded "Wink Bucks" as rewards to employees, suppliers, dealers, and even executives. The fake dollars, containing his picture, could be redeemed at restaurants, hotels, and retail establishments, and he gave them away freely as perks designed to motivate those around him, handing out almost $350,000 worth in two years. Winkler, who lived in a big house on the grounds of the Tournament Players Club in Dearborn, was not shy about spending on himself, either, often using a company jet and taking employees, friends, and Ford dealers on overseas trips, including golf jaunts to Ireland. His reputation at Ford Motor Company became suspect outside of Nasser's close circle as questions arose about an internal explosion of sub-prime auto loans to customers with credit problems. As a result of those loans, Ford Credit's lending portfolio grew dramatically under Winkler's leadership, but losses doubled. It was becoming obvious by the fourth quarter of 2001 that Ford's prime money-making credit division would post its first-ever loss.

Nothing was going right for Ford Motor Company or Jac Nasser. Employees were riled, dealers distrusting, consumers wary, and profits evaporating. Nasser's dream of remaking Ford Motor Company and positioning himself in the process as an all-powerful, global corporate leader above all others was rapidly coming to an end.

Taking Charge

Beginning with his roots, Joe Laymon has seemingly little in common with his friend and boss Bill Ford. A black man from the South, Laymon is the son of migrant farm workers. He grew up in tiny Enterprise, Mississippi, working in fields as a teen. Laymon picked tobacco and cotton in the summer to earn money, and read the newspaper at breaks and at night to older fellow workers for a nickel.

A middle-aged man with a big laugh and a passion for golf and people, Laymon was one of 13 children born to Tom Laymon, a civil rights activist and occasional Southern bootlegger. Joe Laymon earned a bachelor of science in economics and accounting from urban, mostly black, Jackson State University in Mississippi before earning a master's degree in economics from the University of Wisconsin. He worked for the U.S. State Department in Zaire and Washington, D.C., after spending 17 years in senior human resources management at Xerox. He was working for the Eastman Kodak Company when the opportunity came to move to Michigan.

Laymon and his family were comfortable in New York in 2000 when he was a top human resources executive at Eastman Kodak, but Laymon transplanted his family to Michigan in the early spring. An economist by training, he knew how important the automotive industry is to America's economy and believed that managing people resources at

Ford Motor Company would be one of the most important assignments he could take in his field. Laymon joined Ford as executive director of the human resources business division, working under David Murphy, Jac Nasser's vice president of human resources.

From the start, Murphy and Laymon did not click professionally or personally. Murphy gave Laymon the toughest HR assignment in all of Ford Motor Company, naming him to lead the controversial Performance Management Program (PMP) launched in 1999. When Laymon took over PMP, the program was already under attack throughout the company from many longtime employees who did not appreciate the shift in hiring and promotional tactics. Working with a team of company managers from multiple disciplines, Laymon tried to fine-tune and relaunch the program, but saw evidence as early as August of 2000, the first month he put a new and improved PMP in place, that the program was "the most divisive thing you ever could imagine" among Ford Motor Company employees.

Laymon continued, however, to do the best he could with the job he was given until a moment in January 2001 when he could not take it anymore. Bill Ford was addressing Ford Motor Company's top 250 executives and managers during a town hall–style leadership meeting in the auditorium of the company's Product Development Center (PDC) in Dearborn. After talking about such issues as commitment to a better world and corporate responsibility, Ford opened the floor for questions. In the audience was Laymon, who had never before met Bill Ford. There was no media in attendance and no obvious reasons the top leaders of the company, given free rein to fire away at the chairman of the board in an open, frank forum, would sit silent—but they did. Moments passed. No questions. Finally, one hand went up and a single, innocent question was asked. Bill Ford answered, and waited for more. Nobody stood, no hands were raised. Ford paused, waiting awkwardly, before turning and walking out of the auditorium as the crowd continued to sit in silence.

Laymon was awestruck by the silence and lack of participation from Ford Motor Company's top leaders and realized at that moment the automaker had serious problems. He wrote Bill Ford a note, explaining it was his opinion that PMP was killing the company by cutting out its heart. Ford's employees were scared, he said, too scared to speak up for fear of retribution. Bill Ford read Laymon's note and called him to meet in his office.

"He said, 'Joe, do you understand? *You* are PMP,' " Laymon says. "But I reminded him I did not develop PMP or ask to supervise it. I told him that what I saw in that room was a level of fear. These people were afraid to ask the chairman a question for fear of insulting Jac. I told him, 'I think you and Jac have lost your people.' He listened closely and said he wanted to continue to talk."

When Laymon opened the door to leave Bill Ford's office, he saw Jac Nasser sitting in the waiting area outside. Laymon nodded to Nasser and walked on, while Nasser nonchalantly made his way into Ford's office. He did not have an appointment and apparently did not want anything of an urgent nature so Laymon thought little of it. That is, until he was called back again to meet with Bill Ford to talk more about his concerns. In the subsequent meeting, Laymon told Ford more about how he felt the company was losing its employees over its controversial human resources scheme. When he left Ford's office, it was not Nasser sitting outside waiting, but David Murphy, Laymon's boss and Nasser's right-hand man. Murphy, Ford Motor Company's VP of human resources, had worked for Nasser in Australia in the early 1990s when the hard-driving executive sliced Ford of Australia's 15,000-person workforce in half and improved productivity by 40 percent.

The offices of Bill Ford and Jac Nasser were across the 12th floor hallway from one another at World Headquarters. Nasser's secretary could see who came and went from the chairman's office and was alerting her boss about Laymon's entrance, and certainly the entrance of others. If he felt threatened by the announced visitor, Nasser could run over to see what was happening or, if he was busy, send one of his top lieutenants to run over and determine what the problem might be.

Even amid such erratic behavior, Bill Ford wanted Jac Nasser to succeed as CEO because he knew that a change in power would signal failure by all, including the company, its chairman, and the board of directors. The damage, however, from more than two years of mistakes, bad timing, arrogance, and misfortune was beginning to give him a feeling that something had to change in regard to the company's leadership. Even though he chaired the board and shared the company name, knowing where to turn to voice such concerns was a difficult proposition because as pressure increased, Nasser closed the circle around him at the top tighter and tighter. Ford was finding it increasingly difficult to get standard operational information as Nasser let flow through only what he thought would be palatable to the chairman and board. The shroud of secrecy, and the fact that Nasser had surrounded himself with almost 200 handselected executives and senior managers, made knowing where to turn a challenge. But Bill Ford did not want to disrupt already fragile operations.

Ford and Jim Vella had forged a trusting, professional relationship during the Rouge crisis in 1999, and Vella had since then come into more frequent contact with the chairman. Disturbed by what Laymon told him about the company and its leaders losing the people, Bill Ford called Vella to his office in early 2001 to discuss the rash of problems involving Nasser's leadership, from employee alienation to concern about information flow and his ability to lead the company into the future amid poor corporate morale and investments. Ford thought out loud with Vella about how a transition in leadership might occur, if one, in fact, ever became necessary. Vella took careful notes during the meeting and promised to maintain utter confidentiality and return with a full report. He came back the next day with a strategy paper, a "what to do in case" document, and presented it to Ford. Days passed after the second meeting, and although Vella and the chairman met to conduct company business on other subjects, no mention was made of the paper by either until two weeks later, when they were again in private and Ford brought up the subject.

"You remember that paper you gave me?" Ford said. "Make sure you keep a copy."

––––––––––

Joe Laymon was buoyed by Ford's response to his insight about the internal problems he saw at Ford Motor Company, but working under the pressure of Nasser loyalist David Murphy took its toll. In July 2001, Laymon submitted his resignation from the automaker. The long road he had traveled from the cotton fields of Mississippi to the near-top of America's tall corporate ladder was coming to an abrupt end in Dearborn. Laymon's family—including his oldest son, Kiese, by then a 26-year-old professor at Vassar College, and two school-age children at home—were comforted by his departure from the stress and the family's impending return to New York. The younger children were excited about returning to a familiar school, and the family planned to make an offer on its old New York home, which was back on the market again. Two weeks after resigning, Laymon returned to Ford Motor Company to gather his personal belongings from his office when Bill Ford happened by, wanting to know where he was going.

"I'm moving," Laymon said.

"Moving?" Ford asked. "Are you moving upstairs? Getting promoted? What?"

"No," Laymon said. "I quit. Two weeks ago. I can't do this job anymore."

"Give me 45 days," said Ford, who left and climbed the stairs to the 12th floor, where he walked down the hall and into Jac Nasser's office to tell the CEO the company was making a big mistake in letting a valuable employee walk out the door when the human resources department was in such disarray.

Nasser summoned Laymon to his first lunch in the plush World Headquarters penthouse executive dining room. David Murphy was out of the office, in California on business, but rather than hesitate and wait for his return, Nasser begged Laymon to stay on the job at Ford Motor Company. Nasser promised that he and Murphy would sign off on significant changes to PMP in short measure.

"To his credit," Laymon says, "Jac offered me the job on his watch."

A new and improved PMP was put in place that month, scrapping the A-B-C grading system in favor of three new designations: top achiever, achiever, and improvement required. The lowest rating was only required to be given to 5 percent of the workforce instead of the original 10 percent. But the changes did not help the deteriorating situation much since so much damage had already been done that the blood pressure of employees jumped at the mere mention of PMP. Laymon's efforts and frankness, though, helped him unwittingly emerge into Bill Ford's small inner circle, becoming the human resources team leader in the plan to oust Jac Nasser as CEO of the company if operations and leadership did not improve.

By fall 2001 morale had so deeply deteriorated in Dearborn, particularly in departments like engineering, where severe cuts had been made by the freewheeling taskmaster Nasser, that Ford employees had taped or tacked many sarcastic Nasser cartoons and degrading quotes ripped from newspaper and magazine stories to office cubicle walls—so many, in fact, that public affairs employees who saw them stopped taking them down. There was little that could be done to stem the tide of negative feeling swelling against Nasser and his plan to change Ford.

The company's dealer network grew increasingly dissatisfied as well. They harshly criticized Nasser to the board in a 14-page internal memo dated October 4, 2001. The memo was written by Ralph Seekins, incoming chairman of the Ford Division National Dealer Council. The owner of Seekins Ford-Lincoln-Mercury in Fairbanks, Alaska, Seekins conducted an information survey of 200 Ford dealers, who responded by saying flat out such things as they believed Nasser spent too much time with Jaguar, Volvo, and Land Rover—Ford's premier brands—and needed to focus instead on building and producing Ford brand vehicles in North America. Dealers said in the memo that they considered Nasser arrogant and aloof, and that he was competing directly with the retailers by engaging in e-commerce and customer satisfaction ventures they viewed as intrusive.

"[Dealers] thought we were starting to take them for granted," Carl Reichardt says, "and I guess we had forgotten how important they are to us. That was a major part of [Nasser's downfall]."

Nasser was so busy trying to emulate companies like Cisco and Microsoft that he became mesmerized with how easy it was for them during the technology and dot-com bubble, and in the process lost vision and discipline throughout Ford Motor Company. As the automaker

continued in decline, Bill Ford put a plan in motion to begin the ouster of Jac Nasser.

In the first week of October 2001, he met with family members. The Ford family holds periodic meetings to stay unified
and on focus, but this meeting had a much more serious tone,
serving as confirmation and support of drastic action ahead.
Most members of the family were thrilled about the prospects
of a Ford returning to the operational helm of the Ford Motor
Company, the one exception being Martha Ford, Bill's
mother. She was predictably "worried about my life, or lack
thereof," says Ford. He also met with select board members,
seeking direction on how they wanted to deal with the management crisis and trying to determine their pulse on the
leadership future of the company. Ford concluded that the
reign of Nasser was beyond the point of successful repair, and
that there was no alternative other than to personally shoulder the burden of returning the company to respectability
among dealers, employees, shareholders, and consumers.

Assuming the full-time duties of CEO had not been high
on his personal priority list, if on it at all. With four children
still at home, he knew the job would take a toll on his family
life. He also did not want to be seen as taking over the company. Ford had signed on as chairman, and chairman was the
only position he wanted. But clearly, Nasser was not getting
the job done, much less earning the salary that would total
more than $17 million in bonuses and options in 2001. A
change had to be made. If Ford Motor Company gambled and
turned outside for a replacement, the risk was high that further alienation might occur. There only seemed to be one log-
ical choice. Family members and board members Bill Ford
talked with agreed that the company was in desperate need of
a management change and that he, the great-grandson of
Henry Ford, should take over CEO responsibilities.

"Bill made his feelings known," Reichardt says. "He met
with several directors initially and then canvassed the board.
Everybody supported him because it was fairly obvious some-

thing had to be done. We'd given management a lot of room and made a mistake."

Nasser was in Japan attending the Tokyo Auto Show during the last week of October 2001, and it was during his absence that Bill Ford put into full motion the plan to oust Ford Motor Company's standing CEO. He made calls outside the company, reassuring valued friends and allies that the company had not forgotten them, and pledged to restore their faith and trust through actions and hard work.

Ford asked Reichardt, a longtime family friend, if he would consider leaving retirement to help him turn the ailing company around by serving as vice chairman and head of the finance committee—jobs to which Reichardt agreed. Bill Ford also met with key outside figures, like Ford dealer and friend Roger Penske, chairman of Penske Corporation, and Ron Gettelfinger, a former Ford employee who had risen to lead the powerful United Auto Workers union. Support, Bill Ford determined, existed in every direction, from fellow board members to top dealers to labor leaders. He had never sought the job of CEO, but it was about to become his.

On Monday morning, October 29, 2001, Nasser's first day back in the office after his trip to Tokyo, Ford asked Nasser to a private, afternoon meeting with him. Nasser had a morning speaking engagement at a press conference in Detroit earlier in the day, where he announced, ironically, that Ford Motor Company would soon begin building zero-emission electric vehicles—a pet Bill Ford project. A report in the *Detroit Free Press* the next day said that "Nasser departed almost immediately after that event, curtly answering one question before leaving."

Just after the lunch hour, Nasser was summoned and walked the few steps from his office on the 12th floor of World Headquarters, across the hallway to Bill Ford's wood-paneled, plant-filled office. Ford, who had first experienced a high-profile termination in 1995 when he let then–Detroit Lions coach Wayne Fontes go, told Nasser in a face-to-face, somewhat lengthy meeting that he was out of the job immediately and that Ford would take operational control of the company.

"It was a very normal conversation," Ford told *Newsweek* Detroit bureau reporter Keith Naughton the day after he fired Nasser. "We both realized that the pounding that the company had taken and the divisiveness that had ensued and the paralysis that was about to set in really made clear to both Jac and to me that this was probably the right thing to have happen."

Even today Ford refuses to cast blame on Nasser, saying the 30-year company employee gave everything he had to Ford Motor Company but got caught in the end by a strategy that did not work.

"The pace of change," he says, "was too much for the Ford culture to handle. But Jac gave his life to the company and to this day he loves Ford Motor Company."

Reichardt was the first person to see Nasser after his termination meeting with Bill Ford. He, too, respected Nasser's wit and commitment and, while he knew the company needed a change, found the end of his tenure difficult.

"Jac was one of the most competent guys I have known," says Reichardt. "His modus operandi was fast-forward. Add to that this feeding frenzy we had and the fact that in many people's minds, the auto industry had to change. We had to be more than a manufacturing company . . . and we had a lot of cash. We just had the wrong strategy.

"I supported Jac," Reichardt says. "We all supported Jac, including Bill. But we forgot that most acquisitions don't work. In fact, numbers we have seen say 75 percent don't work. We made a lot of mistakes because our acquisitions were generally not good and the prices paid were so huge compared to underlying value.

"You could justify it at the time because everything was moving so rapidly. The technology was much more complicated than we understood, and we started getting quarterly results and realized this is not working."

———

Nasser's public affairs leader, Jason Vines, was working in his 11th floor office on the day Nasser was fired. He suspected something was up, but could not get anyone on the telephone to tell him what. Jim Vella was part of Bill Ford's transition team but did not have the authority to tell Vines, still technically his boss, that a power change was under way. Later in the day, Nasser met with Vines and Murphy to tell them the news.

The termination meetings were known by only board members and the small number of executives needed to plan and execute the immediate management transition. Rumors, however, swirled from floor to floor, office to office, and computer to computer throughout Ford's World Headquarters. E-mails containing slivers of leaked details and speculation were excitedly fired one after the other, employees stringing together pieces of information that led to the realization and an excited buzz—"Nasser's out! Ford's in!"—that some say they had never experienced at work and may never experience again.

The rumors were confirmed the next morning when word circulated throughout World Headquarters that a special press conference would be held in the first floor auditorium at 10 A.M. announcing a management change. Ford Motor Company was ailing and Bill Ford was taking over the company. Ford met early in the morning with Ford Motor Company's corporate officers in the penthouse at World Headquarters, discussing transition plans. By 9:30 A.M. the auditorium was full, employees making sure they had a seat or standing room for the historic event.

The public-address announcer opened the meeting: "Ladies and gentleman, Bill Ford." The company's new CEO walked in wearing a sharp gray suit, blue shirt, and red tie. He was greeted with a robust, standing ovation from a standing-room-only crowd. Spectators lined the walls, stood in the aisles, and cheered. Thousands of other Ford Motor Company employees, from the nearby Rouge plant to the Louisville, Kentucky, truck plant, watched by closed-circuit, satellite television broadcast via the company's in-house communications network.

When Bill Ford reached the podium and finally quieted the crowd, he was filled with emotion and caught slightly off guard by the hero's welcome.

"Gee, you'd think the Lions won a game or something," he said of the applause, spontaneously drawing more.

Politely, Ford asked for a round of applause for Nasser, who had served the company for more than 30 years. Then he quickly got down to business, telling the world that Ford Motor Company's board of directors had officially approved management changes earlier in the morning and that he, effective immediately, would serve as chairman and CEO of the company. This drew another standing ovation. Sitting in the front row was Joe Laymon, who looked over his shoulder and saw three Ford employees crying, overwhelmed with satisfying emotion brought on by the legacy and leadership before them.

"I've never seen anything like it," Laymon says.

Ford announced his new management team, built around experienced automotive executives familiar with the long traditions of Ford Motor Company, including an appreciation of valued, time-tested employees and automotive business fundamentals. The idea was not to build a team loyal to Bill Ford, but to build one capable of leading the company's back-to-basics strategy, founded solely on the nuts and bolts of designing, building, and marketing quality cars, trucks, and SUVs. No more Internet-savvy, jet-setting, loyal-at-all-costs, next-big-thing dreamers. Bill Ford wanted sensibility, reliability, and tradition on his team above all else.

"I was brand-new," Ford says, "and I knew there were a lot of skeptics. I thought it was extremely important to have people around with stature to be advisers to me with no axe to grind."

———

Nick Scheele (pronounced *SHAY-luh*) was installed to head up the operational management team as chief operating officer. An Englishman, Scheele had joined Ford of Europe in 1966 because he thought it was a wonderful "British company." In the mid-1970s, the rising-star manager was sitting in economy class on a flight from Great Britain to Detroit when, 10 minutes into the flight, a stewardess told him a gentleman in first class wanted to meet him and have a drink. To Scheele's surprise, it was Henry Ford II.

"He was a great guy," Scheele says. "We chatted and he was very open. He wanted input about the company."

Less than 20 years later Scheele was credited with miraculously turning around Ford's Jaguar division when the luxury car unit was bleeding money and suffering due to limited and out-of-date products in the early 1990s. He cut costs, invigorated the lineup, and increased productivity, restoring profitability and earning himself knighthood from the Queen of England in the process. Scheele, who briefly ran Ford of Europe before moving to the United States and World Headquarters, was known for his laid-back style—the antithesis of Jac Nasser—and commitment to building the company through "fantastic product." Scheele was also appointed to Ford Motor Company's board of directors.

Scheele had been brought to Dearborn the year before to lead Ford North America in what many speculated was a move by the company's board to groom an operational replacement for Nasser if he could not get the job done.

Scheele was the first executive to pick up on and start using the line "back to basics," which had been spoken by a senior public affairs manager.

"He's the ideal person," Bill Ford said, "to lead the company in the primary mission of building quality cars and trucks."

Responding to the call of "a close personal friend," Reichardt agreed to increase his post–Wells Fargo retirement workload and serve as Ford's vice chairman and as chairman of the finance committee, paying particularly close attention to the ailing Ford Credit division and the company's worsening financial situation. Ford said the choice of Reichardt was natural, as long as the longtime banker was willing.

"We had a guy sitting on our board," Ford said, "who, if there was a banking hall of fame, he would be in it."

Living on a ranch in northern California, Reichardt would commute to Dearborn on a regular basis until he was "no longer needed," giving the automaker much-needed credibility on Wall Street, where concerns over its financial future were growing. Reichardt planned to "take the credit and financial side so that Nick and Bill can have time to run the business."

A Detroit native who joined Ford Motor Company in 1966 as a quality control engineer, Jim Padilla was appointed group vice president of North American operations by Bill Ford. Padilla had teamed with Nick Scheele during Jaguar's revival, directing engineering and manufacturing from 1992 to 1994 during the company's critical turnaround. With master's degrees in engineering and economics, Padilla's leadership-by-example demeanor and blend of technical and management expertise summed up Bill Ford's commitment to assemble a management team that did not necessarily reflect his idealistic world, but one that reflected the reality of what Ford Motor Company needed: reasonable, seasoned, respected executives to lead the company out of troubled times.

With an internal transition team including Joe Laymon and Jim Vella—the executives Ford had trusted to help plan and execute Nasser's departure—Ford built his management team around people he believed able to help Ford Motor Company, not people to blindly follow him. He defined his style from the start as one based more on coaching than dictatorship. He would rely more on focus, openness, and free-flowing information from top team members than on a yes-sir approach, but would step in and make tough calls when necessary.

"When assembling a team," Joe Laymon says, "you should not use loyalty as the gate of entry. Bill Ford used competency and skill [as his leading criteria]. It did not matter if they were part of his inner circle. Bill did not know me that long, but he said, 'I'm not looking for loyalty to Bill Ford. I'm looking for the best people to run Ford Motor Company.'"

———

In his to-the-point, eight-minute talk in the auditorium at World Headquarters when announcing his replacement of Jac Nasser, Ford explained to employees the basis of what would become his driving foundation of creating great products, a strong company, and a better world.

"The sole reason for these changes," he said, "is to ensure the ongoing success of the Ford Motor Company, and that's what matters most to me. We need to focus on the basics of our business, which is building great products. We need to be a company that employees want to work for and are proud of. We need to be a company that has quality products that customers want to buy and feel they can trust. We need to be a company that investors want to invest in. We need to be a company that dealers and suppliers want to do business with. And finally, we need to be a company that the world looks to in doing things right."

He talked about the legacy of Ford Motor Company that he was inheriting and promised to leave "an even greater one." And, with a wide smile and looking straight at the audience, he told employees why he believed he was the right person to lead the company.

"I love this place," Bill Ford said. "I bleed Ford blue."

———————

Flanked by Scheele and Reichardt, Ford met with members of the media during a standing-room-only press conference following the announcement that he would lead the company. He opened it up by saying he "had a prepared statement," but was "not gonna do it," instead getting straight to a free-flowing question-and-answer session.

Ford had shown during speeches in his term as chairman that he was not most comfortable delivering the presidential type of prepared speech before a crowd. He learned early on that he is at his best when speaking in direct response to issues or to an audience in a straight-from-the-heart manner. The first questions fired during his initial appearance as CEO, with the world's top automotive and financial journalists in attendance, centered around the external belief that Bill Ford had just taken a job that he did not want. Reporters wondered out loud if he was just offering a temporary answer to a terrible situation or planning to lead the automaker for the foreseeable future.

"Yes," said Ford. "I'm willing to do whatever it takes to take this company forward. This is not something I sought, but I'm glad to be able to step in and do it, and plan to do it as long as the board would like me to serve.

"I just got here," he added. "I can't announce my replacement today. I do plan to do this for the foreseeable future. I can't give you a time. Who knows how it is going to work?"

Ford said he would surround himself "with as many good people as possible" and looked to "Nick and Carl as sort of an easygoing partnership," adding, "I've stepped back [from the Detroit Lions], unless they need me to play quarterback."

The management changes, Ford said, had been speculated about in the press for "a long time," but it was not until recently that the "cacophony of noise and the overwhelming pressures from our constituents and from the media got to the point where to say we were distracted would be an understatement."

"It was reaching," Ford said, "almost a paralysis point for a lot of our management and a lot of our employees, and it was clear to Jac and me we needed to make a move."

Ford Motor Company's new CEO put three years of acquisitions, diversions, and new visions aside in one day, saying that all aspects of the business were up for review.

"Every asset, every piece of geography," he said. "There is no point in keeping any part of our business that is not adding strength to our business. We lost our focus in several areas. Some of it may have been chasing a [wrong] strategy, but some of it came from outside events like Firestone. But there is no question we are going to have a renewed interest in the car and truck business. We have done it before and we just have to get back to it."

Ford talked about his name, the legacy, and the internal pressure of taking over a company founded by Henry Ford and run for decades by Henry Ford II with continued Ford involvement as board members, shareholders, and even employees (Elena Ford, from the fifth generation, is a Ford Motor Company employee). With active participation from "13 cousins and my dad and my uncle," the Ford family is a small but strong unit that meets on a regular basis and offers unified support on endorsed decisions.

"My last name," he said, "you can look at as either burden or opportunity. Nobody is going to care more about this company and more about the future. . . . I happen to think those are strengths.

"I don't approach this," Ford said, "like I'm a family member going to a job. I approach it like somebody who loves this company."

The euphoria from the dramatic change in leadership quickly wore off in the top levels of Ford Motor Company as Bill Ford and his new team of executives plowed into the myriad issues plaguing the automaker. They obviously had known there were major problems, prompting the change in the first place. What they did not know was exactly how much trouble Ford Motor Company was in, since the previous leadership team had kept such a tight lid on pertinent operational information during the period of rapid decline. Their findings revealed a giant, mismanaged pile of trouble, with multiple problems resulting in an enormous and mounting financial dilemma.

Jac Nasser walked out the door of Ford, following his ouster, on a company that would lose $5.5 billion for the fiscal year, including one-time write-offs. Bill Ford, who refused any salary or bonuses in accepting the job—he asked only to be paid in stock options, saying that relying solely on success and upside share price movement for compensation was a risk he wanted to take—found problems in almost every division at Ford Motor Company. His executive office was "like a triage unit" during his first weeks and months on the job, facing a new crisis every single day, from recalls to declining consumer purchase considerations to the news that a huge corporate investment in a precious metal was mostly worthless.

Palladium is used in catalytic converters, vital components of vehicle exhaust systems. Since it is a precious metal and supplies can prove unreliable, Ford Motor Company began buying large quantities of palladium from Russian sources. Most automakers relying on palladium secured it through contracts, but Ford Motor Company was actually buying it and driving up prices along the way, as palladium soared from just under $100 an ounce in the late 1980s to more than $1,000 in 2000. Better technology, however, reduced the need for large quantities of palladium. Prices drastically dropped, costing Ford millions. There was also the little matter of locating all the palladium it supposedly owned in Russia.

Bill Ford's only solution was to fix the daily rash of major problems as quickly as possible in order to stabilize the company and restore internal and external faith. Ford Motor Company's legal team worked quickly to settle employee discrimination suits; the company announced a $1 billion write-off on its palladium investment; and Bill Ford began meeting with analysts, suppliers, and dealers to rebuild trust. As for the ailing Ford Credit, he sent in the best he had.

Carl Reichardt's first task in his new role as vice chairman was a complete audit and review of the financing unit. Well-versed in finance from his legendary days leading Wells Fargo Bank, Reichardt shared Bill Ford's concerns about Don Winkler's reckless management style.

"Ford Credit," Ford says, "was in real disarray. I knew I did not have the skill set to fix it. Carl needed this like he needed a hole in his head, but [when asked] he did not hesitate and stepped right in."

What Reichardt discovered was financial weakness throughout the division and a Ford Credit CEO he believed was in over his head and out of touch with core lending values that had traditionally been the heart of the division. Reichardt delivered the bad news to Bill Ford that Ford Credit would lose more than $200 million in the fourth quarter of 2001 and that Winkler was absolutely not the man for the job. Just as he had done with Nasser, Bill Ford fired Ford Credit CEO Don Winkler, despite his personal pleas to stay on the job: "What does Reichardt know? He's just a numbers guy." An irritated Bill Ford stuck to his plan of cleaning up and restructuring Ford Motor Company and its ailing parts.

The mood among employees and insiders close to Ford Motor Company, however, took a dramatic, overnight swing and remained intact during the leadership transition despite the numerous and ongoing problems in Dearborn. One moment the automaker was being sued by employees and the CEO was pinup-joke fodder. The next moment, employees were cheering wildly and pledging to follow the lead of the company's new CEO.

"Bill Ford," said one Ford manager, "rescued the employees from Jac Nasser. It would have been a lot easier for him to just run the Lions . . . and a lot more fun. He stepped in for the job when he knew we needed him."

But it was more than a rescue leading to brighter days among the people in Dearborn. It had as much to do with the fact that the man running the company—a Ford—represented everything the automaker had revolved around since its inception in 1903: the founder, the family, the legacy of leadership, nameplate signage atop World Headquarters—and products bearing the same name.

Exactly how close to home Bill Ford's presence hit at Ford Motor Company was shown in December, just over a month after he accepted the job of CEO. Like most large American corporations, Ford is followed on a regular basis by an entourage of regional and national media. The company holds an annual Christmas party in early December for journalists to mingle with the top executives and public affairs managers they deal with throughout the year on a daily basis. Following a particularly tense year between the company and the media, due to Firestone and mounting financial problems, the 2001 party was held at Fair Lane, the famous Dearborn estate built by Henry and Clara Ford in the early 1900s. Fair Lane sits on 1,300 acres and originally included such lavish features as a $30,000 organ, a bowling alley, a gigantic indoor swimming pool, heated marble benches, and an underground tunnel to a then state-of-the-art, Thomas Edison–designed powerhouse.

At the party, Bill Ford greeted the gazing media attendees who admired the National Historic Register mansion. He stood up on a chair to give a short welcome speech and thank the guests for coming. The moment was not lost on attendees, aware of the historic implications: Henry Ford's great-grandson, in the founder's home, hosting a Ford Motor Company Christmas party. The scene was not lost on Bill Ford, either, who could not resist displaying his sense of proprietorship.

"This is my family's house," he said. "If you have a drink, make sure you use a coaster."

CHAPTER

6

The New
Face of Ford

Thousands of automotive and business print and broadcast journalists from around the world flock to Detroit in the first days of January each year to mingle with company executives and to see, touch, and feel the hottest new car and truck products global automakers have to offer. From Honda to Toyota, Chrysler, and Ford, all companies participate in the world's most important auto show, giving vehicles a rock star treatment with splashy entrances and accompanying silky smooth promotional materials. Journalists quickly discern the handful of winners and losers of this annual product warfare, in spite of the best spit-shine PR efforts from every company, and rapidly relay the vibes throughout the world, shaping the thoughts of consumers, Wall Street analysts, and investors. The result is that tomorrow's winning products are rarely a surprise, having been detected typically one to two years before during preproduction viewings at the Detroit show.

When Ford Motor Company revealed its best and brightest at the 2002 North American International Auto Show—less than three months after Bill Ford and team took over operations—its overall upcoming product lineup was so depressing in comparison with competitive products, particularly those shown by foreign automakers Nissan and Toyota, that top tier journalists began to suggest out loud that perhaps the day of American doom had come—the end of Detroit. Chrysler was long gone, gobbled up by German automaker Daimler in what was called a "merger of equals" but everybody knew was an outright foreign acquisition. With little to show and in financial distress, Ford Motor Company appeared headed down a difficult road, the biggest thing it had to reveal being a long-awaited operations restructuring plan instead of a stable of cutting-edge, future products.

The one product that turned heads was a high-priced concept car, a modern version of Ford's historic GT40. That super sports car had made Ford Motor Company the international racing manufacturing leader in the 1960s with its stunning first-second-third sweep of the 24-hour Le Mans race in France in 1966 and its repeat victory in 1967. The modern concept car version unveiled in 2002 was a spectacle for auto enthusiasts, but it did not signal a turn in fortunes for the beleaguered automaker because nobody thought the money-losing company could afford to actually engineer and manufacture a roadworthy version of the car for sale. The GT40 is cool, they said, a real novelty. But Ford won't be able to do anything with it because they've got no money to spend on product development.

Ford Motor Company was hurting financially, and the world was waiting to see Bill Ford's plans for reviving the automaker. The widespread assumption was that risky, expensive research and development had no place in the company's short-term future. The best Bill Ford and company could do was to slash expenses to restore bottom-line results quickly. Of course, the problems at Ford Motor Company in the first year of Bill Ford's reign as chairman and CEO had more to do with a lack of focus for the previous three years than with overcapacity and a bloated budget, but these by-products of trouble were crippling the company and had to be immediately fixed if the automaker was to avoid slipping to the level of second tier.

Times at Ford had gotten so bad, so fast that nobody could believe how far the automaker had fallen in just a few short years. The company that two years earlier had seemed poised to become the world's biggest and best was, in the early days of 2002, a near disaster and on display for the entire world to see. Ford Motor Company was poorly invested from its diversionary plans, core auto operations were losing money, and product development had few immediate hits in the pipeline. So ailing was Ford that the company even had to tinker with its hands-off dividend, lowering the payout for Class B and common shares, and find the means to save its way to near-term survival. The only choice for Bill Ford was to formulate a long-term restructuring plan in a very short time, unveiling it during the auto show where the thousands of interested journalists were gathered.

Automotive management models were available to study during the two-month revitalization blueprint planning process, since Nissan's Carlos Ghosn was in the midst of a much-publicized and highly successful turnaround of the Japanese automaker. That company had been in no better shape in 1999 than Ford was in 2002, but, through its Nissan Revival Plan, had returned to respectability in less than two years. Ford Motor Company had also undergone a turnaround of its own in 1991 and 1992 when Bill Ford was on the company's board, offering vital lessons to learn from experience. Ford says he and the company's management team studied "a few pages from Ghosn's playbook" and looked back over Ford's history for previously used strategies in formulating a restructuring plan, but ultimately did not rely heavily on any one source.

Ford Motor Company, due to its size, history, and the unique issues faced in 2002, was unlike any available automotive case study. The company was big and global, with multiple brands and 340,000 employees spread over six continents. It was also very American, bound by decades of employee legacy costs and 1999 union labor agreements that provided extensive job and income protections for UAW member employees.

Nick Scheele, who had previously helped put a restructuring plan in place for the ailing Ford of Europe, directed the plan effort. He and the Ford executive team decided the plan should span five years, ultimately resulting in Ford Motor Company's return to world-leading automotive profitability. The heart of the blueprint involved cutting from company payroll 35,000 employees, closing five plants, and eliminating four low-market car models, including the Mercury Cougar and the Ford Escort. Ford Motor Company also cut roughly 330,000 vehicles from its production lineup by eliminating shifts and slowing assembly lines; eliminated white-collar jobs in North America through early retirement; and aimed to eliminate $1 billion in noncore assets, including an assortment of companies like Kwik-Fit as well as dot-com shares acquired by Nasser during his remake of the company. Ford Motor Company also said it would reduce general and supply costs by $3 billion.

The Ford Revitalization Plan, aimed at boosting profits a lofty $9 billion by the middle of the decade (management committed to generating $7 billion in annual pretax profit within five years), was, however, built almost completely around the one big thing missing from the 2002 auto show—product. Bill Ford was troubled that all his company had to talk about at a car show was its restructuring plan and vowed to his management team it would not happen again under his leadership. He announced a product-led program designed to result in dozens of new or significantly freshened products in the United States during the restructuring plan.

"If you look at Ford's history," Bill Ford said, "one of the most obvious lessons it teaches is that great products are what drive success in our industry."

Instead of taking the easy road, restoring short-term profitability by slashing bottom-line product development investments, Ford Motor Company would more than double the money spent on creating new and exciting products while costs were reduced in every other area of the business. New computers on the desks of employees could wait. New product could not. A billion dollars was added to the capital expenditure line.

"The easiest thing we could have done," Ford says, "is cut capital expenditures on product, but we actually stepped it up. Today, we are spending more than General Motors and they are one-third bigger. We're building for the long-term."

Scheele, who once revived Jaguar through head-turning new product and coined the "back to basics" phrase at Ford Motor Company despite the objection of then-boss Jac Nasser, could not have agreed more with Ford's approach. "We are a car and truck company," Scheele says. "A car and truck company designs, builds, and sells great product."

A simple statement, but one that the thousands of people associated with Ford Motor Company wanted, and needed, to hear. The American car manufacturing industry is unique in that most executives, managers, and people who work on manufacturing lines or in dealerships are romanced by the automobile. It is a passion they all share, no matter what level of hierarchy they occupy in the company. They may specialize in design, engines, or product development—but most of them love finished cars and trucks. At Ford Motor Company, this passion often runs even deeper, perhaps because of a century of lineage, product, and family continuity. Say "Mustang" to a room full of Ford employees and attention quickly moves to the center.

The employees needed a leader to stand before them and say that the company was once again staking its future on providing innovative, well-built vehicles for the masses. They could live without a free computer or low-priced Internet service or company-owned European service centers and junkyards. They could not, however, bear working for a product-starved Ford Motor Company that was built on the back of a legacy involving some of the world's greatest automotive names, including the Model T, the Thunderbird, the Mustang, the Taurus, and the F-150.

"We do have icon products to build on," says Bill Ford, "and that is an incredible advantage."

Bill Ford and his new management team took this message—that the company was putting excitement back into its North American product lineup—to the same dealers that were alienated during the three years of turmoil in Dearborn. A leader in delivering the good news was longtime executive and dealer ally Jim O'Connor. Ford had approached O'Connor in late 2001 and asked him to serve as the company's vice president of sales and marketing, his primary charge being to rebuild dealer trust and relationships. O'Connor's locker at Grosse Pointe Country Club in the suburban Detroit area is next to Bill Ford's, and he often runs into Bill Ford Sr. on the golf course.

"He'll say, 'Hey, man,' " O'Connor says, " 'what's going on down at the shop?' "

O'Connor was going on 40 years with the company and not far removed from seriously considering an exit during the company decline under Nasser when Ford called, but when given the opportunity to stay at Ford and help, there was only one answer to give.

"I told my wife," O'Connor says, "this is Bill Ford saying 'I need you on my team.' "

O'Connor began visiting with dealers, promising new waves of upcoming products and pledging a renewed spirit of cooperation under the company's new leadership team. He took fellow executives, including Bill Ford and Jim Padilla, to meet with individuals and groups of dealers to show commitment to North American auto operations, hoping to ease escalated tensions.

"Some of our best dealers," Padilla says, "did not feel we treated them as valued members of our team. Ford [Motor

Company] is personality, and it was not good for the face of Ford to be pissed off."

Executives held a closed-door meeting with the owners of 900 franchises at the 2002 NADA convention, admitting mistakes and pledging more openness and respect. And by February 2002, Ford Motor Company had only five of its almost 50 dealerships remaining and was close to selling those.

"They realize," said Fernando Garcia, president of Fall River (Mass.) Ford, "they took the wrong course. They told us at the meeting that it's their job to build quality cars and it's our job to sell them. That goes a long way to improving relations."

As a sign the focus was back on the products, the company also made a surprise announcement. Just one month after the GT40 concept car was unveiled at the Detroit Auto Show among whispers that Ford Motor Company could never afford to build it, O'Connor announced on a stage at World Headquarters that the automaker would in fact put the GT40 into production. His words drew cheers from a standing-room-only crowd of Ford Motor Company employees. Broadcast live to dealers by satellite, the announcement was a message from the company's new leadership team that product investment was a top priority and romance was very much a part of Ford's vehicle affairs. It was also a commitment to building new, exciting products faster than ever before, as O'Connor committed that the car would be ready in time for the company's 2003 centennial celebration—just 15 months away.

"When O'Connor said, 'We're gonna build it,'" a Ford employee remembers, "it was almost as big as when Bill Ford took over. You knew things were different."

While product development raced into place, Ford Motor Company's human resources department's three-year rush of activity was coming to a grinding halt—in new initiatives, that is. Under the new leadership of Joe Laymon, Ford's single new HR policy for 2002 was that no new policies would be put in place internally during the entire fiscal year. As the company worked to settle lawsuits resulting from previous turmoil, Laymon stopped initiatives so employees could relax and focus on the important tasks at hand—designing, building, selling, and financing cars and trucks.

"We had too many people involved in strategy," Laymon says. "We did not take the time to find out if new policies and procedures worked. I put a moratorium on it. My point was that this will not result in us selling one fewer vehicle."

Laymon says much of what was being done in people management at Ford Motor Company was good, but "few gave it a chance to work" before seeking more change, and therefore the company was in constant churn with employees, its most prized possession.

"If you take the time," Laymon says, "to get to know the people and the products and understand . . . that we have the best dealer body in the country, this culture will take you in and embrace you."

The company, Jim Padilla says, had "effectively pissed off" three out of four employees with multiple and rapidly changing personnel policies since 1999. "We took our biggest asset and juxtapositioned the thing," he says. "It was nonsense, the whole thing about A players and B players—thank God we have B players, because we could not stand having all A players.

"B players [at Ford] are making a comeback," Padilla says. "We've thrown all those processes out and gone back to seeing people as people. Even though times have been tougher, we've had more with us."

The realization by Bill Ford and other Ford executives during the 2002 auto show that the focus was on the pains of business rather than the company, its products, and its heritage was a harsh reality that needed to be dealt with in short measure. Ford Motor Company was an automaker and, despite its problems, still produced some of the best-selling vehicles in the world, including the perennially best-selling F-150, the Explorer, and the increasingly popular Focus. Something had to be done to remind the American people that the company was more than a nuts-and-bolts business story on the financial pages.

It had become apparent from the swell of pride among employees and dealers during Bill Ford's ascension to CEO that having a Ford at the helm of the company was one of its strongest assets at the moment—a stabilizing blend of past, present, and future that gave Ford Motor Company a competitive advantage. General Motors was a big, strong auto company, but *who* was GM? Ford Motor Company's strength was the legacy it shared with American history.

"We needed to take back the voice of Ford," said Rich Stoddart, Ford Division's advertising manager. "Lawyers [and] the media were being heard louder than we were."

Another Ford insider put it more bluntly: "We had no fucking product. All we had to sell was Bill."

Working with the company's advertising agency, J. Walter Thompson, Ford executive and marketing team members came up with an idea, suggesting to Bill Ford that he should be the center of an advertising campaign designed to "rearticulate" Ford Motor Company values. Because Ford is uncomfortable in heavily scripted settings and had no desire to be seen as an attention-seeking CEO, he heartily resisted the idea at first. Longtime Ford executive–turned–Chrysler CEO Lee Iacocca had become an American celebrity in the early 1980s because of commercials he starred in, personally urging consumers to buy from him. Ford had no interest in looking into a camera and saying, "Buy from me." But close aides worked to convince him that it was in the company's best interest because the face of Ford needed to be a Ford. He agreed to participate in an advertising campaign, but only if he got to do it his way, relaxed and unscripted.

However, when Ford went for the ad shoot, he found a Hollywood-style setting with hundreds of bright lights, a teleprompter, a stool to sit on, and a script-hugging director. Despite the efforts made to set up the studio for Ford Motor Company's "No Boundaries" campaign star, Bill Ford was so uncomfortable with the sterile setting that he walked out.

"I can't do this," he told Jim Vella.

Realizing that Ford is more comfortable in an intimate and off-the-cuff setting, Vella asked him to try it another day, another way. This time it was Bill Ford talking for two hours to a rolling camera about what he knows best: the history and heritage of the company, its products, and its founding family. The ad agency easily got four commercials out of the one-take, from-the-heart footage.

In the first 60-second spot, titled "Legacy" (it aired nationally in February 2002), the camera zooms in tight to Ford's face, revealing new lines from three years of stress, but eyes that glisten when he talks about the company's past relating to family knowledge.

"My great-grandfather Henry Ford," Bill Ford says in the commercial, "really redefined what it meant to live in this country. 'No boundaries' applied to everything he did, and that's the part of him that really inspires me. It's a wonderful legacy.

"For me, it's really a great honor to be able to try and advance that legacy and redefine it in the 21st century. This company has always been about looking forward and anticipating the future and actually helping shape that future . . . and that's what gets me up in the morning."

In another spot, pictures are shown of Ford's great-grandfather on one of his well-documented camping trips with Harvey Firestone.

"They used to take these camping trips every year," Ford says, "with Thomas Edison and whoever the President was. They called themselves the vagabonds. They sort of invented SUVs.

"I love the outdoors. . . . I won't even stay in a hotel if I can't open the windows, and so our SUVs provide a great deal of freedom. You can't accept limitations. . . . SUVs are what people want, and we do them better than anybody else."

In "Family," he talks about how the automaker was not "just another nameless, faceless company," suggesting Ford Motor Company has a soul.

"[Employees and dealers] are third, fourth, fifth generation," Ford says, "and people have stories. The stories are, 'My grandfather worked with your grandfather' or 'My aunt, my uncle, my cousins, my brothers, my sisters . . . they all work here.' That really sets us apart from other corporations.

"To me, the litmus test of whether we've done a good job here really is going to be the stories the next generation is going to tell."

The ads were an immediate national hit, scoring strong results in advertising consumer polls that interpret viewer likeability. Auto company ads, because of their frequency, typically rate low in positive response, but *USA Today* reported through its Ad Track poll in 2002 that 21 percent of consumers familiar with Ford Motor Company's ads "liked them a lot."

"We were not trying," says Ford's Jim O'Connor, "to make Bill Ford a celebrity. But the dealers really got behind it, and it allowed us to break through all the clutter at the time."

But interwoven among the successes were frustrating lessons in celebrity for Bill Ford to learn. Like any youth worth their salt, his children found the television commercials intriguing and half-jokingly asked their father about appearing in one. Ford promised his daughters a gig in an upcoming ad if their team won a state soccer championship. They did, earning a background-only appearance in a commercial with a soccer mom minivan and a minimal paycheck. And even in such an innocent incident, Bill Ford attracted controversy. Ford's children wore practice sweats instead of uniforms in the commercial, and positively identifying them during the brief spot is almost impossible. Yet when a parent from a rival team heard about the commercials, he called the sanctioning soccer association in Michigan to complain that by appearing in a paid commercial wearing soccer uniforms, they had violated amateur rules and should have to forfeit their championship and be barred from further participation. The matter was resolved, but only after Bill Ford was forced to engage a lawyer and deal with the reality that he was no longer just a parent with children who could easily involve them in fun and interesting parts of his job without heavy scrutiny.

In every way possible, Bill and Lisa Ford have tried to avoid such situations and keep normalcy at home by giving their children advantages without entitlement. When his oldest daughter, Eleanor, got her driver's license, Ford could not bring himself to bestow her with a flashy new vehicle, despite having a stash of products from Aston Martins to Land Rovers, Volvos, and Lincolns at his immediate disposal. But as a straight-A student and a multisport athlete constantly on the go, she needed transportation. The Fords compromised by getting a "pretty stripped down" Mercury Mountaineer as a third family car, saying she could drive it on an as-needed basis. Ultimately, it was always needed and her regular use made the SUV essentially hers. Ford said that was fine, but he hoped the point was driven home with his children: that very few things in life—like keys to a car when your father is head of the world's second largest automaker—are given automatically. They may be due an inheritance, but that does not relieve them from sweat equity in their chosen fields, especially later in life.

"I hope," Ford says, "that I have been able to impart to my children that not working is not an option."

Getting
Back to Basics

W hen Bill Ford was seeking the best base strategy to use in rebuilding Ford Motor Company, he simply looked at glaring corporate weaknesses and moved in the opposite direction for solutions. A freewheeling style had been detrimental for almost three years. Sweeping plans for change and new strategies had been talked about in such broad and dreamy terms that getting employees to rally behind yet another big plan would prove difficult if the perfect approach was not taken.

He turned to a theme that had first emerged in late 2001 before the departure of Nasser and continued to resonate through Ford's most hard-core loyalists as a drumbeat reminder: that the strength of a manufacturing company should be its ability to design, build, and deliver exciting products based on value and quality. Having determined by a long history that Ford Motor Company is at its worst when "we are fat, dumb, and happy" and not concentrating on the fundamentals of good automotive design and manufacturing, Bill Ford put a team and a plan in place with firm instructions to repeatedly drive home the importance of operational basics.

"In the short term," Ford said, "we have to be focused on

the core business and we have to have the fundamentals right. In the past, this company has not done well when it has lost focus, and it is my job to keep the focus on the basics so we don't lose sight again."

Executive vice president Jim Padilla could not have been happier with Ford's commitment to staying true to the company's heart: auto manufacturing built around good design, quality, and profitability. Having directed manufacturing and quality through some of the automaker's best years, Padilla would become the backbone of a significant movement at Ford North America where business fundamentals took priority over all else. The "Back to Basics" campaign, launched internally in 2002, would be the passion and primary mission of Padilla, who articulated goals and priorities on small blue handout cards that he began distributing more liberally than Don Winkler had distributed Wink Bucks. Padilla's cards were similar in shape and color to the ones Nasser used to give out, but his cards contained a much different message, driving home a theme he takes daily to all ends of Ford's North American operations. Padilla's "Vital Few Priorities," listed atop the pyramid of the "Back to Basics" strategy, include these five:

1. Improve Quality

2. Improve Quality

3. Develop Exciting New Products

4. Achieve Competitive Cost and Revenue

5. Build Relationships

With the exhortation to "go simple, go common, and go fast," the cards and Padilla's warm form of message delivery have been the basis of hundreds of face-to-face departmental meetings and larger town hall–style sessions he holds with employees in an attempt to keep them on task so the company, at all levels, can avoid the types of distractions that were so costly before. Some mornings, Padilla is in the office before 7:00 to deliver an early session. Some days he'll do two or even three, repeating the same message with the same cadence.

"I tend," Padilla says, "to be a little anal, but when you are looking for direction, the most important thing is the consistency of message."

The "Back to Basics" concept was actually introduced informally while Jac Nasser was still in power. Scheele, now the number two executive at Ford, was speaking in a town hall meeting at the Product Development Center in September 2001 when he made a plea to North American employees to refocus on the basics of business.

"I knew [the situation] was fairly bad," Scheele says, "and we did not have an option. I said, 'This is what we have to do.'"

The comments flew in the face of Nasser's entire strategy, and when he heard about what Scheele had said, he was outraged. When Padilla launched a Ford North America corporate strategy around the "Back to Basics" theme months later, Bill Ford was in full agreement, particularly since the campaign supported the most crucial elements of Ford Motor Company's automotive business, including the key areas it slumped in during the Nasser era, like productivity, quality, and efficiency. It only made sense to adopt the core strategy companywide as the basis of Bill Ford's five-year plan.

"In the prior administration," Padilla says, "we certainly lost focus on quality and delivering exciting products and delivering revenue. [Nasser] was smart, but he was a Hail Mary specialist. Fishes and loaves happened years ago. . . . What is important is to be realistic about the company and the people. This is not magic we are talking about."

There is irony in the fact that Scheele and Padilla led Ford Motor Company's "Back to Basics" effort, presumably with strategies the executives employed while reviving Jaguar. Scheele says, however, the reality is that Ford's systems have traditionally been good. In fact, when he and Padilla were teaching Jaguar employees how to get it right, they often did so by sending them to Ford for training or handing them Ford manuals to read. In its brief but severe period of distraction, Ford Motor Company's processes had scattered and program development had become "anarchic in a sense," keeping the once-proud automaker from getting programs out on time or with Ford's traditional quality.

"Our development process was broken," says Scheele. "We could not launch product without a lot of difficulties, and this had to be fixed."

Scheele says it was evident in his return to World Headquarters that, even amid the chaos, Ford "had good, bright people" and if you "bring people back to the prescriptive manual, it tends to work."

One of Ford Motor Company's biggest challenges, Padilla says, was to eliminate poor quality, "because you pay for it in so many ways." When quality slips, like it did when Ford launched its Focus car in 1999 and experienced numerous subsequent recalls, Ford loses "loyalty, sales, and residual values." The move away from "Quality Is Job One" from 1999 through 2001 was painful for many longtime Ford Motor Company employees who had lived by the slogan at work, and the new management team knew the focus had to be restored for the automaker to escape mediocrity. In response, they openly attacked quality issues by removing barriers in place from previous regimes that often fragmented engineering and manufacturing, causing divisions to "go in different directions." Through a steady cadence that reinforced daily the importance of such mundane work chores as "focusing on vital few priorities," "keeping the message simple," and "communicating with team members consistently," the company began to make progress by the end of 2002, removing hundreds of millions in waste from North American operations and learning lessons applicable globally.

"It may not be evident [to the public] for a while," Padilla says, "but it will be, because we are making headway."

Bill Ford in Brazil during a 1995 Conservation International trip.

Jac Nasser wanted to remake Ford Motor Company into a consumer company.

Nick Scheele, Bill Ford, and Carl Reichardt address the media in October 2001 during a press conference announcing Ford Motor Company's management changes.

Jim O'Connor tells employees Ford Motor Company will build the GT40 supercar.

Jim Padilla preaches Ford Motor Company's "back to basics" at a town hall meeting.

William Clay (Bill) Ford Jr. is flanked by his father, William Clay Ford, during Ford's 2003 shareholders meeting, held on the company's 100th anniversary.

Bill Ford draws a crowd during Ford Motor Company's centennial celebration.

Steve Lyons introduces Ford's all-new F-150 at the Detroit Auto Show.

Bill and Lisa Ford first met when they were students at Princeton.

Bill Ford introduces the all-new Mustang at the 2004 auto show in Detroit.

Carroll Shelby and Bill Ford officially reestablish relations between the racing legend and Ford Motor Company.

Allan Gilmour, Bill Ford, and Nick Scheele discuss Ford Motor Company's improving business.

Getting back to basics also meant streamlining and speeding up product creation at Ford, particularly in North America—the one area crucial to success under Bill Ford's vision of a product-led recovery. Ford Motor Company had traditionally been one of the slower companies to get new cars and trucks to market, a serious problem when facing increased competition from fast-moving, foreign automakers like Toyota and Nissan. If Ford takes 30 months to get a product to market, Toyota and Nissan take 24, time that is critical when seeking attention from customers constantly searching for the newest and hottest products available. Not only does speed deliver market excitement, but trendy products demand a higher market premium, delivering higher profits.

To make product creation faster and more efficient, Ford put 43-year-old Phil Martens in charge of product creation for North America. Martens had earned a reputation as a rising star within the company during a stint in Japan at Mazda, where, as managing director of product planning, design, and development, he reenergized the brand with the return of the rotary engine for the RX-8 sports car and developed the wildly popular Mazda 6 sedan, hatchback, and wagon and the smaller Mazda 3. So influential had Martens been in Mazda's ongoing industry surge that Bill Ford, Jim Padilla, and fellow executives believed he could do the same for Ford, pushing, pulling, and searching for commonality and reusability.

The young, sharp-dressed Martens reveals in conversation a hungry and aggressive style. Unlike Nasser's bullying approach, Martens uses positive encouragement to motivate his product development teams. But anyone who sees him as soft is making a serious mistake.

"You have got to have the mind-set to win," Martens says. "This is a serious damn business. [Nissan's Carlos] Ghosn, [DaimlerChrysler's Jürgen] Schrempp ... these guys are killers, they'll slit your throat. If you blink, it's over."

At Ford, Martens' job was daunting, considering that product development had been pushed into individual cells at the company years before, when globalization efforts achieved more isolation than symmetry. To combat this, Martens was given license to move faster than the company had ever moved before. He received a big budget, empowerment—and the heavy burden of delivering the goods destined to turn the fortunes of the company. In fact, product development was so important to Ford Motor Company that Bill Ford signed off on a remarkable increase of $1 billion in capital expenditures in the midst of such fine-line cost cutting throughout the company as the elimination of magazine subscriptions to ensure the viable future of the automaker. The money was to be spent globally, but a lion's share went to North America and Martens.

"He has the power to go," Scheele said.

Martens' job has been to overcome traditional barriers that keep product at a company with the size and tradition of Ford from getting to market fast enough. Along the way, he must integrate sensibility that emphasizes and enforces such things as commonality of platforms—the backbone of a car or truck—and rationality in terms of product cost. It is a tricky formula that, if not managed just right, can throw millions of dollars to waste. If a product launches late, or poorly, the company pays for years to come, just as it did with product problems under Nasser.

"[The pressure] could crush you," Martens says, "if you allow yourself to let down and become overwhelmed with the burden."

Like Padilla, his immediate boss, Martens began the process of pushing dozens of new North American Ford, Lincoln, and Mercury products through by maintaining a relentless, structured sequence that includes a weekly review of ongoing programs and costs, engineering solutions, plant reviews, and advances in companywide benefits derived from global commonality. He restructured personnel to provide more emphasis on development and allowed for open decision making, reducing time-consuming bureaucracy.

"Before," Martens says, "we had 50 percent of our people working on support and 50 percent working on program design. Now we have 75 percent working on programs and 25 percent in support. We need some support, but we now have 25 percent more people than before focusing on program delivery."

———————

Not only did Ford's new management team have to improve product creation efficiency, but there was also the significant challenge of reinvigorating Ford's sagging car lineup and properly aligning its brands. The automaker that gave America the Model T, the Mustang, and the Taurus had transformed in the 1990s from a car company selling some trucks into a truck company selling some cars. Lower-margin vehicles like cars, for obvious reasons, did not hold top priorities at Ford or elsewhere in Detroit when hot-selling SUVs and trucks delivered record profits for almost a decade. But as competition in those segments increased—with Nissan and Toyota entering the full-size truck market, taking Ford's F-150 head-on, and all automakers unveiling eye-catching crossovers and SUVs—Ford executives realized the need to restore excitement, innovation, and quality into car markets. When the new management team took over, the car products in existence contained strengths but were dated and in need of major overhauls. Elements of the Mustang, for example, dated back to 1978, while the Crown Victoria dated to 1979. The outdated Ford Taurus and Mercury Sable were also in decline.

"It is amazing we did as well as we did," Martens says. "All our cars have different front ends and they look like they were made by different people at different times. Frankly, they were."

The decision was made to retemplate the car lineup. For Ford Motor Company, that meant determining exactly what should distinguish products displaying the blue oval from others, including characteristics such as dependability, desirability, affordability, and driving enjoyment. A company, Martens says, can't be all things to all buyers. That's why Ford has such luxury divisions as Jaguar and Volvo—to offer a broader range of choices. The approach for Ford is to align the products together, benefiting from sequence and cohesion, while drawing on company strengths—an ability to combine toughness with comfort and design.

The Lincoln-Mercury Division was also brought back into Ford's North American operations, giving hope to the division that had been alienated during its Nasser-led move to California, where Lincoln-Mercury was supposed to have become a sparkling part of the company's Premier Auto Group. When focus was lost and money got tight during Ford's decline, Lincoln-Mercury suffered with limited products and little in the pipeline, and many wondered if the ailing division had any future in Ford Motor Company. So devastated was Lincoln by its lack of direction that the division dropped from the top-selling luxury car brand in the United States in 1998 to fifth, behind Mercedes, Lexus, BMW, and Cadillac. Not only was the focus gone, but also the brand's identity. Continual turnover in Lincoln-Mercury's top executives brought ever-changing ideas about what consumers wanted. Some even began to wonder if Lincoln-Mercury should have a life at all.

But Ford's new leadership recognized that the brands had decades of customer loyalty behind them and deserved to be revived and supported by Ford's North American strengths, rather than being killed with a swift blow or left to drown with little support. As plans were made for multiple new products in a short time—including the Lincoln Mark LT, a luxury truck to be based on an all-new 2004 model of the popular F-150—commitments were made to Lincoln-Mercury dealers as well, the principle being that Ford Division product hits would get upmarket styling and extras as Lincoln-Mercury offerings, capitalizing on proven successes. In other words, Lincoln-Mercury products should be more along the lines of "Ford plus a lot more" than an independent luxury line free-wheeling and hoping to find success.

"We used to think," Padilla says, "that we needed all new vehicles [in the Lincoln-Mercury division]."

But the division had learned a tough lesson in 2001 with the ill-fated Blackwood, an upscale truck that cost $50,000 but did not have four-wheel drive. Now, new Lincoln-Mercury products would be upscale, sexier versions of popular Ford hits.

"Mountaineer versus Explorer is the best way to look at it," Padilla says.

The Mercury Mountaineer shares its underpinnings with the best-selling Ford Explorer. But a very different front end treatment, unique colors and trim, and a stylized interior give the Mountaineer affordable differentiation.

When he talks during one of the dozens of town hall meetings he conducts each year throughout North America, Padilla pulls no punches with employees seeking answers during frank sessions about how the company will succeed in its race to win the product development war. During one such meeting in the auditorium at Ford Motor Company's Product Development Center in Dearborn in November 2003, before hundreds of engineers, Padilla was asked why Ford, with such a broad global lineup, couldn't implement more commonality faster. He responded by saying previous company administrations set up product development processes involving independent teams that resulted in "everybody either doing their own thing or freewheeling." He said Ford engineering had lost its control and the company was working overtime to get its arms around the massive singularity that resulted.

"We're trying to bring that back together," Padilla said, "but we can't be allowed to go out and freewheel. We must follow what North American engineering says has to be done."

When questions turned to battling product development costs, Padilla reminded his audience that Ford must restore profitability to its North American auto operations by finding more solutions to cost challenges without sacrificing quality. But he closed with a stern warning.

"Don't screw the customer," he said.

The "Back to Basics" philosophy has the ring of a management style that easily fits Padilla but is the opposite of what one might assume an idealist like Bill Ford would joyfully embrace. Ford made no secret, when Jac Nasser was charged with running Ford Motor Company, that he was energized by chairman duties that allowed him to focus on long-term planning and noble causes like corporate citizenship and global responsibility. Rebuilding the Rouge, for example, was an enormous chore due to the project's size and the strong objections from many who doubted the huge investment would really be environmentally friendly and cost-effective in the long term, but the potential rewards aligned completely with his better-world philosophies. Dealing with the daily grind of manufacturing, however, can prove much less invigorating for a man wanting to lead industrial change through innovation.

Ford never hesitated, though, in espousing the cause, staking the company's future on a return to core principles from day one. He emphasized the importance of basics during his first appearance as CEO and built the company's management team with specific skill sets to make it happen, adding by early 2002 more time-tested executives to the team. He talked the highly respected former Ford executive Allan Gilmour out of retirement to lead the company's financial restructuring efforts as chief financial officer, adding more external insurance that Ford Motor Company was in experienced hands.

Gilmour is a former Ford vice chairman who retired in 1995 after a career and industry reputation as one of the sharpest minds ever to work at the company. He returned at the age of 67 because Bill Ford asked him to and the company needed his help.

"Allan had been gone for seven years," Ford says. "He was a legend. His reputation preceded him."

A native of Vermont with degrees from Harvard and the University of Michigan, Gilmour had joined Ford Motor Company in 1960 and, with his quick wit and no-nonsense approach to numbers, quickly became a star in finance, serving as president of Ford Credit, president of the Ford Automotive Group, and as a vice chairman of the company. So respected was Gilmour in his previous stint at Ford that some inside the company had wanted him to succeed Donald Petersen as CEO in the early 1990s. But, as a measure of how much the company had changed since he had left, just before the arrival of Jac Nasser, many top managers and executives in place upon his return only knew *of* Gilmour. They quickly learned that Gilmour's style was an uninhibited frankness, colored by experience, that extended directly through to Bill Ford.

"He will tell me exactly what he thinks," Ford says. "We don't always agree, but I love getting his opinion. I ask for it. Allan loves this company. He came back because he knew how badly we needed his leadership."

Bill Ford also brought to World Headquarters David Thursfield, group vice president of international operations. An Englishman, Thursfield was elevated from his job as CEO of Ford of Europe to help the company invigorate its global brands. At Ford Credit, company veteran Greg Smith was named president and chief operating officer. Ford's team was in no way a group of trailblazers cutting a path to the revolutionary future in transportation that he had eloquently and often referred to during his chairmanship. Instead, Ford's commitment as chairman and CEO was to build a team that could get the core business right, restoring productivity, pride, and, most important, profitability. Only then would he have the flexibility behind the financial strength to push Ford Motor Company toward a future as a leading global corporate citizen, providing his measures of success: great products resulting in a strong business and ultimately a better world.

"If we don't fix the business," Ford said, "it won't matter."

Ford reluctantly stepped back for a time from his publicly outspoken role as an iconoclastic Detroit executive making waves about global warming and the end of the gas combustion engine. Ford Motor Company's resources were under such enormous pressure and its fundamentals so weak that talking about anything other than the basics did not seem to make sense.

"We have to have the fundamentals right," Ford said, "before we move forward. Right now it's just three yards and a cloud of dust and it is not sexy, not fun. But I don't want the organization to get distracted, and in the past Ford has been easily distracted."

Instead of dreaming about solutions for the future, Ford spent much of his time in the trenches of the moment, personally poring over company budgets line by line and item by item, searching for cuts that would save the company and protect must-have product development.

"We are absolutely going to make money in the car business," Ford said. "That is why you have seen this enormous focus on cost."

When company leaders found $2 billion of waste to eliminate in one year, Bill Ford personally identified and pushed for another billion in cuts. Company fleet car use was reduced and departmental fluff attacked. He met periodically with small groups of employees, reminding them that waste occurs large and small, and urged them to spend company money like it was their own. All available money, he said, needed to go toward product development.

"There is a lot of waste at a company this size," Ford said. "We've gotten a lot out, but you can find it every day. If there is still 5 percent slop, you've got a lot to go after at a company this size."

While Ford was cutting costs and learning more about the

daily nuances of running a giant automaker, he repeatedly asked a lot of questions about what he did not consider his areas of expertise, like product design. Ford does not get involved in the intricacies of design like Nasser did or other auto executives do—suggesting a different placement for a piece of trim here or a different line there—but he likes to pay attention and keep pressure applied to areas that count most.

"I did ask myself every day if we were doing the right things," Ford says. "I was new. Padilla and Scheele were in the biggest jobs they had ever had. Thursfield was in the biggest job he had ever had. We were all new, but I believed in our ability and knew we were on the right path."

Ford crystallized his guiding vision for the automaker, recognizing that Ford Motor Company was not a consumer company or an Internet company or a technology company. Since 1903, the company has been a leader in transportation, putting the world on wheels and keeping it there. The fundamental goal, Bill Ford determined, should be for Ford Motor Company to continue its leadership in transportation, finding innovative solutions and meeting developing needs in a rapidly changing global environment.

"Longer term," Ford says, "we are in the transportation business. What I don't want to do is rule anything out. Ultimately, if you define us as a transportation business, that can lead us into the future."

The belt-tightening led by Ford was helping the company's bottom line in 2002 but forcing it to slow down in some areas. Ford had envisioned the automaker becoming "more of an environmental leader" by then, but its poor financial situation briefly took precedence. If the company is not strong, Ford said, it cannot lead in the future. The company had to be fixed first. Publicly he stepped back—but behind the scenes he agonized.

"He was still pushing [for environmental issues]," a close aide says, "just not as visibly."

Environmental organizations that had once embraced Bill Ford showed no sympathy to Ford Motor Company's short-term plight, nor appreciation of his long-term vision. Taking full advantage of his high profile and outspoken role as a self-professed environmentalist leading one of America's largest industrial companies, some now portrayed him as the environment's public enemy number one among American corporate leaders. The environmental lobbying group Sierra Club was the most aggressive, launching a three-year advertising campaign in June 2002 that tied vehicle fuel economy to patriotism and specifically called for action by Bill Ford in radio and television spots that ran in a dozen states. The ads targeted Ford by name.

"Now more than ever," the narrator said, "America needs cars that get better gas mileage. That's why we're asking Bill Ford, head of Ford Motor Company, to do his part and to produce more fuel-efficient cars, SUVs, and pickups."

Detroit-area radio stations declined to run the spot, suggesting that attacking one individual over a global issue was not fair. Still, the Sierra Club did not let up its national attacks on Ford, and held protests at select Ford dealerships with signs including such sayings as "Henry Ford would have loved hybrids." The Sierra Club asked members to send form letters to Ford demanding that the automaker help reduce America's dependence on oil, and provided his fax number and e-mail address to its membership.

Publicly, Bill Ford stood strong, dismissing the attacks as misguided.

"The Sierra Club," he said at the time in a prepared statement, "chose to target Ford and me personally because we are seen as leaders. I think it is ironic, because I have often been criticized for being too far out front on this issue."

Privately, friends say he was stung by the attacks, which hit at the heart of what he desires most—for Ford Motor Company to one day build environmentally friendly vehicles that consumers want to buy.

"It hurt him," says Dan Murray, Ford's former Tae Kwon Do instructor. "Sure it did. He's not the type to back down from what he believes."

———

Bill Ford's entire first year as chairman and CEO had its personal lessons to be learned. He often dropped by the main cafeteria at World Headquarters, avoiding the plush, executive dining room in favor of a chance to mingle with employees. Some approached him, but others did not, too surprised by the unusual sight of a top Ford Motor Company executive hanging out on the first floor. He was sometimes confused by this reaction, wanting to be viewed as simply an employee who is the leader of the company, not an isolated executive above all others.

Ford currently spends office time at World Headquarters in Dearborn daily but does not hold normal work hours, preferring to find snippets of time outside the office to meditate over company needs. He does, however, have weekly sequences that he follows routinely. Mondays, for example, are for operating committee meetings and review of European and Premier Auto Group operations.

In meetings he is usually informal, and in one-on-one dialogue in the office he is engaging, but he likes to get to the point. In interviews, for example, Ford speaks with candor and easily invokes camaraderie, but he prefers not to sit still for more than an hour and is known to leap from his chair to chase down such verifiable items as his driver's license, to confirm that it is commercial, or pictures drawn by his younger children. He exercises daily, at whatever available time he can find, either at home or at World Headquarters, and gets stressed when his daily schedule leaves no room for moments in which he can get a clear head to do what he believes is becoming a lost art of the

American chief executive: thinking in quiet. At the office, Ford nearly always wears a suit, usually gray, sometimes blue. Ford tried dressing down when the company had casual days, but found it did not work because at home he typically wears jeans, and he had nothing in between to wear to work.

His new job does not leave much time for the many hobbies he loves. After earning the black belt, Ford dropped "almost everything," including regular Tae Kwon Do workouts. He keeps in periodic touch with former instructor Murray and has become an annual visitor to the company photo department Christmas party, held in the cavernous studio on the first floor of World Headquarters. Eating off a paper plate with photo department employees, Ford trades verbal jabs with Murray.

"Every now and then," Ford says, "he'll say something to me like, 'Hey, you looked stupid when you said that,' or 'Come on, you've got to get tougher, more like when we are fighting.'"

Ford's assistant, Ann, keeps his daily and weekly schedule—he has a general rule that, for the sake of flexibility, no company appointments can be scheduled more than six weeks out. That includes sporting events, parent-teacher conferences, and other activities related to his four children, ages 7 to 17. If a child has a game—they all play multiple sports—he wants to be there and usually is, even if it means driving from Dearborn to Ann Arbor and then back for more work appointments.

"I've pretty much given up hobbies," he says. "I'm okay with that. It is not a hardship but a reality of people in my situation at this stage in life [a working parent with school-age children].

"Two things drive me: my family's happiness and the success of Ford Motor Company. That does not leave time for much else."

Despite progress in cost cutting and morale, Ford Motor Company's bottom-line results were not improving rapidly. Its 2002 auto sales dropped almost 9 percent, despite deep customer incentives. The company's stock price plummeted as well, falling a staggering 60 percent and into single digits. Market share dropped and concern was widespread over the fact that the automaker could not turn a profit in North American automotive operations despite Ford Division unit sales of almost 3 million.

Reasons for continuing sales declines amid tighter management strategies were many. Most notably, Ford's product lineup, particularly in the car area, was outdated and unable to deliver premium prices on dealer lots. Capacity and costs were still too high, even with ongoing cuts. And then there was crosstown rival General Motors. Conventional wisdom in Dearborn was that GM, the world's largest automaker and Ford's biggest competitor with its Chevrolet division, saw an opening with Ford's floundering and went for the jugular. The competitor kicked at its downtrodden counterpart, pouring on incentives at previously unheard-of levels to take precious points of market share from Ford.

"GM," says a Ford executive, "saw our weakened posture and came after us."

The strategy worked, for a while. Ford offered deep incentives of its own in response, but in 2002 GM still made more money per vehicle sold than did Ford and was closing the sales gap in North America with its chief rival brand. The Chevrolet division had sold 850,000 fewer vehicles than Ford Division in 2000, but got to within a differentiation of 350,000 in 2002 by applying incentive pressure to its struggling competitor with the force of a vice grip. Ford Motor Company posted a loss of $980 million on sales of $162 billion in 2002, despite having 3 of the 10 top-selling vehicles in North America, including the number one F-Series (813,701 sold), the fourth-best-selling Explorer (433,847), and the seventh-ranked Taurus (332,690).

"I liken it to the airline business," says Ford Division president Steve Lyons. "Almost every time you get on a plane it is full, but [airline companies] are not making any money. In the car business, it only takes one competitor to make business pretty tough."

The company's 2002 problems were not confined to the difficult auto business, either. The funding status of its pension funds was adversely affected by low interest rates and declines in equity markets following the burst of the technology bubble. By the end of the year, worldwide pension plans were underfunded by more than $15 billion. Also raising concerns were staggering health benefits costs of $2.8 billion, almost $2 billion of which was linked directly to retired company employees—a legacy liability resulting from Ford's size and corporate longevity. Forecasts were for the automaker's retiree health care and life insurance costs to rise 14 percent, more than a half billion dollars, in 2003 alone.

To compensate for the company's difficult 2002, Bill Ford and other top executives did not receive bonuses or merit raises while they worked to cut costs throughout. Ford, in fact, took no pay at all—he received options on 408,247 shares in lieu of a cash salary, and options on another 4 million shares in place of other long-term pay. Top executives signed noncompete agreements during the year, earning additional restricted stock awards. Ford signed the noncompete agreement but refused the additional options, figuring it was not worth much since the chances of him working for another automaker were zero.

Ford Motor employees were working tirelessly to turn the company around and stop the negative trends. After layoffs initiated by the restructuring plan, many were carrying one-third or even two-thirds more than their previous workload. As a result, lights were seen burning in many of Ford Motor Company's Dearborn offices seven nights a week. Still, tough days continued to mount as the weak economy and ultracompetitive, incentive-driven auto environment drove on.

"We had younger employees," Scheele says, "who have never lived through a downturn. I've lived through three of these. During the first one I was terrified. I remember thinking . . . this is going to be it, forever."

Like the rest of Ford's experienced team of executives, Scheele focused on the industry signs of recovery he's learned to look for, reminding company employees that by working hard on the jobs at hand—designing, building, and marketing good products—Ford Motor Company would survive its crisis and eventually emerge more lean, productive, and profitable than ever before.

"Detroit," Scheele said, "has proven itself to be reasonably resilient. At Ford, we've always come back through great product. We've got the people to do it again."

The end of the year held many frustrations for Bill Ford. He was confident the company was on the right track to recovery, but weary from a continuing lack of confidence among some investors, media, and analysts voicing concern over whether the company was moving far enough fast enough. Every company goal outlined in its five-year revitalization plan was being met, but naysayers lined up nonetheless. A top automotive journalist wrote that the company was "beleaguered," while a New York broadcast journalist who polled national business reporters for background on Bill Ford found all considered him "likeable," but most wondered if he was "tough enough" to get the job done.

His heightened public profile was also making life difficult, particularly in the form of negative publicity: Questions were raised over his 1999 purchase of 400,000 shares of Goldman Sachs' IPO stock. The transaction showed up in late 2002 during reviews of Goldman documents, showing that Ford was allowed to buy a bigger block of Goldman's lucrative public offering than anyone outside of the investment banking firm. Ford Motor Company's board voted to review whether the purchase, which yielded Ford $8 million in paper profits, was proper.

Connections between Ford the leader, Ford the company, and Goldman are strong and run deep. Goldman COO John Thornton is a Ford Motor Company board member, as is

Robert Rubin, a former Goldman chairman. The automaker also has a history of doing significant business with Goldman Sachs dating back to the days of Henry Ford II. The practice of letting outside executives buy blocks of IPO shares was common practice at the height of the bubble when Wall Street's freewheeling ways were not closely scrutinized. While the transaction broke no security laws, it was embarrassing for Ford, who accepted no salary as CEO and said the last thing he wanted to do was profit improperly off Ford.

"There is nothing," he wrote in a memo to employees, "more important to me than the success and reputation of Ford Motor Company. I would never do anything to hurt this company or violate the trust all of you have placed in me."

The board's internal investigation found no wrongdoing, and Ford sold his Goldman shares. He donated all profits to charity and ended the brief but troubling controversy.

The story that did not reach the press, though, was Bill Ford's brief run-in with the law. He was on vacation with his family, visiting his parents at their winter home in Florida, near Naples. He wanted some morning exercise and set out on a solo Rollerblading excursion in the streets, near the beachfront. Ford was stopped by a policeman, who told him that Rollerblading off the sidewalk was against the law. The area had no sidewalks, but Ford Motor Company's chairman and CEO was still in violation of the municipal law. The police officer refused to let Ford Rollerblade back in the streets, in further violation, so he put him in the back of the squad car and delivered him to a household of amused family members.

"My children," Ford says, "thought it was so funny. They loved it. Their dad, arrested for skating."

By the early days of the New Year, Bill Ford was laughing and smiling, too. The 2003 Detroit auto show was the first opportunity the management team had to show the results of 14 months of work centered on the premise that product would lead the automaker's recovery. Ford luxury division Volvo kicked the show off by winning the prestigious North American Truck of the Year award with its new XC90. Sporting an SUV-like body on a station wagon frame, the crossover vehicle was a testament to the auto world for perhaps the first time that Ford Motor Company's diverse brands could stand independent and thrive, and that Ford Motor Company was beginning to effectively manage its multiple divisions.

But finding a hit with Volvo, while important, would not show the world that Ford Motor Company was back in full force. Bill Ford and everyone else in Dearborn knew world journalists had been disappointed with 2002 Ford Division show wares. The company may have upscale diversity with its range of global brands, but it still lives or dies under the blue oval and North American sales and profits, or lack thereof. With less than two months to prepare after Nasser's forced departure, there had been few options in 2002. But 12 months of intense focus and a product development license to go made all the difference one year later.

Journalists who joined company employees in filling the seats of Detroit's downtown Cobo Arena for the unveiling of Ford's newest and best at the 2003 auto show watched Bill Ford walk onstage to the tune of Louis Armstrong's "What a Wonderful World," accompanied by a video montage of historic company photos (including Bill Ford on his first day of work at the company in 1979). Then the automaker showed its future in pillars of its past, among the highlight glimpses of more than a half dozen new models.

Ford Motor Company showed commitment to its Lincoln and Mercury brands with new concept cars and created a buzz with a new, retro-style Mustang. Bill Ford's self-professed all-time favorite, the Mustang was shown as a concept car that promised production the following year. With styling that relied on its heyday from the 1960s and early 1970s, the new Mustang rekindled images of Steve McQueen's Mustang GT in the popular 1968 film *Bullitt* and promised to put some life into Ford's lagging car lineup.

The star of the show, however, was the production-ready version of the company's flagship product, the Ford F-150 pickup. The F-Series, America's best-selling vehicle, had accounted for almost a quarter of Ford Motor Company's sales in 2002, but numbers began to lag with a design in need of update. Chevy's Silverado was catching up and the competition was getting stiff, with foreign automakers entering the full-size truck market. Ford needed a winner with its all-new 2004 version of the F-150, and few who saw the new truck for the first time were disappointed, making note of its luxury interior and tougher exterior.

In addition to new product, numbers being compiled from the previous 2002 fiscal year were markedly better than the year before. Ford Motor Company had turned a profit before special items, earning roughly $750 million; improved 12 percent in JD Power product quality numbers; and reduced recalls by 46 percent.

When Ford met with journalists in the early days and weeks of 2003, many noted a decided mood shift. He talked about feeling "very different" and "much more confident." Why not? Finally, there were subjects at Ford Motor Company to talk about besides problems. The balance sheet was in the black. A killer new truck was on the way. The Mustang was making a comeback. And Volvo, one of the automaker's 1990s acquisitions, was drawing headline-grabbing attention.

CHAPTER

8

Surviving the Cold of Winter

D earborn, Michigan, can feel dreadful in winter. On one particularly cold day in February 2003, it's beginning to look as dreadful as it feels. The temperature is in the low teens and the ground frozen hard enough that precious remaining moisture makes each step another loud crunch. A steady wind blowing in from upstate still carries a lake chill for extra measure. The blanket of clouds is high, but thick enough to snuff out any hopes of warming sun, and tiny ice pellets racing in the wind feel like sandpaper against a cheek. The view is not much better. The trees and ground are the same color as the road and sky—a flat, hopeless gray.

It is a Tuesday, mid-morning, but area activity is slight. A young taxicab driver making his way down deserted Michigan Avenue to Ford Motor Company World Headquarters talks about the legacy of leadership at Dearborn's original industry. His father worked at Ford, as did his father before him.

"Everything we have," the driver says, "is tied up in that company."

The driver suspects Bill Ford is out of the office, attending a press conference in downtown Detroit, where former San Francisco 49er football coach Steve Mariucci will be named the new head coach of Fords' pro football team, the Detroit Lions. Two days before, the driver is told, Ford was in San Francisco at the annual National Automotive Dealers Association (NADA) conference, delivering a keynote speech and walking the convention floor with first cousin Edsel Ford, talking casually with company retailers and reminding them he cared.

"He's trying hard," the driver says.

The taxi stops in the front parking lot at World Headquarters, where flags bearing the logos of the global brands whip in the cold wind. The driver walks around to the side of the vehicle, opening the door to let his passenger out. A stiff breeze hits the driver's back with the grace of a hairpin turn.

"Gee," he says, grimacing. "It can't get much worse up here than this."

Three weeks later, it got worse.

A previously little-known credit rating analyst named Sean Egan, of the small Egan-Jones firm in Wynnewood, Pennsylvania, suggested in a February 28, 2003, piece in *Grant's Interest Rate Observer* that Ford Motor Company's debt was so high and its auto sales so sluggish that "if it didn't have the name Ford, it would be in bankruptcy." The quote was picked up the next week by the London *Daily Telegraph*, and unjustified rumors began flying worldwide that Ford Motor Company, one of America's oldest, signature corporations, with more than $160 billion in global sales, could be a candidate for bankruptcy.

That same week, more negative rumors involving the company became daily news in the mainstream press. These accounts, hinting at a rift between Thursfield and Scheele, had Ford executives battling at the top. The stories talked about growing pressure internally as Bill Ford, unsatisfied with 14 months of restructuring results, pushed harder from the top for better bottom-line results faster.

In response to this barrage of bad press, Nick Scheele, Ford's president and chief operating officer, sent a memo to company officers, urging that any rumors about discontent in executive offices should be stopped at the source immediately. A couple of days later, the company announced a surprising 17 percent cut in second quarter fiscal year production, signaling that demand for its products was in continued decline and the automaker was still running at overcapacity.

The general gloom and combination of negative news sent Ford Motor Company's stock price downward to a 15-year low of $6.58. Tremors from the fall shook both internal confidence that had just begun to steady and company foundations that were finally solidifying after three consecutive turbulent years. Much of the euphoria from the successful auto show and improved year-end financial results in January was now gone, and the national media sensed the stress.

"A century ago," wrote Danny Hakim in the *New York Times* on March 14, "American car companies were nearly as plentiful as 1990s Internet start-ups. Now there are just two independents left, General Motors and Ford Motor, and some prominent analysts rate their prospects as not much better than a dot-com's."

Three days later, *BusinessWeek* countered with its own story about doom in Dearborn, suggesting under the title "Ford Rides the Low Road" that the company's stock prices could "bump along at their current depressed levels for quite a while" since it "has yet to prove that better cars and trucks are on the way."

Ford Motor Company was just months away from its much-anticipated centennial celebration, and Bill Ford was hoping that the year and the major event would be a turning point for the automaker. The pieces were all in place for a decisive move. Cost reductions were ahead of schedule, totaling more than $2 billion since the revitalization plan had been launched. The new F-150 pickup truck was going to be launched on time, and automotive operations, as Ford had promised, appeared on track for breakeven. Never mind that the company had more than $25 billion in stockpiled cash available to pay bills in troubled times and 100 years of experience behind it.

"When people look back on 2003," Bill Ford said, "I want them to remember it as a turning point."

Ford believed the company was making legitimate progress, and he was eagerly pointing toward brighter days. But the dreariness in Dearborn held a firm, seasonal grip that only appeared to grow tighter with each passing day. Winter was taking a harsh toll on the automaker as residual effects of almost three previous years of mistakes, combined with difficult economic conditions, continued to plague the company. Doubt about Ford Motor Company's short- and long-term future was rampant.

"The reality," said longtime auto analyst Maryann Keller, "is that Ford is very bad."

Much was at stake when the barometer quivered and violently shook near the end of the company's 100th year in business, but there was not much Bill Ford or other company employees could do but roll up their shirtsleeves and keep fighting to make progress, hoping ultimately to turn improving reality into improved perception. Their biggest battle in winning back analysts, investors, and internal confidence was fought in the trenches of North America against rival General Motors. The world's largest automaker had become the domestic benchmark during Ford's demise, with lower production costs and higher per-unit profit. If Ford Motor Company simply chased GM's giveaway incentives launched after 9/11, it would suffer great pains, losing millions in potential profits and ultimately billions in market capitalization due to ongoing doubt from special interest onlookers.

Vice president Lloyd Hansen had held many positions in his 28-year career at Ford Motor Company, from his very first job as a financial analyst to company controller. But no job had been as important to the automaker as the one Hansen assumed in late 2001. A new office of revenue management was created, and Hansen was charged with running it, searching for ways the company could increase profitability by managing incentives and customer information better than competitors.

With a bachelor's degree in economics from Brigham Young and an MBA in finance from Northwestern University, Hansen is a numbers-driven executive romanced by the ability to impact small percentage numbers that resulted in gigantic savings of hundreds of millions of dollars. He had been doing work in revenue management at Ford Motor in the 1990s, but it was not until the company's Ford Division in 2001 found itself at such a significant disadvantage with competitor Chevrolet in the area of retail incentive spending per unit—the amount of money discounted from a product to entice a customer—that Hansen's effort mattered most. In August 2001, Ford Motor Company spent an average of $565 more in incentives per vehicle sold than did Chevrolet—a primary reason GM made money in North America and Ford Motor Company did not.

The problem then was that Ford, like most automakers, built cars and shipped them to dealers, placing incentives—marketing cost—on them in a follow-the-leader manner, without truly knowing which finer points of transaction price, financing, and product extras meant the most to customers. If GM, for instance, rolled out heavy incentives on its Cavalier, Ford followed suit with matched incentives on its comparable product, the Focus. This strategy allowed the company to keep plants running and hold on to share, but it proved costly on the bottom line.

"When the market started to soften," Hansen says, "we should have taken production out and kept our profit."

Market share is important because once it is lost it can be hard to get back. The incentive war developed into a years-long industry epidemic, but in 2002 Ford had to abandon a "hold on at all costs" strategy, adopting instead a more conservative approach to keeping valuable segments of the market share. This resulted in 1.6 points less of U.S. market share but, more important, increased profitability versus GM and Chrysler.

Hansen and Ford recognized they had to learn how to give customers what they need and want, while holding on to what they don't. To do this, Ford Motor Company needed tools that would enable Hansen to better understand the true cost of chasing market share. Ford's traditional system of gathering sales data was not sufficient. It was spotty from dealer to dealer and did not provide detailed information about the minor differences in transaction prices or customer desires that ultimately impact such vital measures as the time a vehicle spends on a dealer lot.

When Hansen ran into David Power of JD Power and Associates at a conference and shared Ford Motor Company's problems, the data tracking company custom-built a five-year, exclusive software system for the automaker that gathered specific Ford sales figures week by week and region by region. The data allowed Ford to determine its own marketing incentives, vehicle by vehicle and region by region, avoiding carte blanche discounts or simply following the lead of GM. If buyers of Ford's Crown Victoria, for example, were typically older and paid for their car with cash, then enticing such buyers with deeper manufacturer rebates made more sense than offering low financing.

"My father," Hansen says, "is 82 and drives a Crown Vic. He is from that generation of people who hate to be in debt and would rather get $1,000 off than zero-percent financing, even though his cost is actually higher."

Another example Hansen uses to show the importance of knowing what Ford buyers want involves antilock brakes. GM, he says, made antilock brakes standard "across the board a few years ago." However, Ford Motor Company found one-third of its buyers were willing to pay for antilock brakes, one-third would take them if they were free, and one-third (mostly in the South) did not want them at all, even if they were free. "So we never made this standard," saving the company millions.

By learning more about what customers wanted, earlier, Ford Motor Company could avoid making standard costly equipment that customers didn't care about—like adjustable pedals (which data showed only 10 percent of customers wanted), third row seats, or antilock brakes. Ford could also determine by region which dealerships needed certain extras, like more expensive four-wheel-drive trucks and SUVs.

"At the factory," says Hansen, "we say, 'They don't need four-wheel drive in Florida,' so we don't ship as many there because we've determined there is no snow in Florida. But the data we are getting now says something different. We send more four-wheel-drive vehicles to Florida and our [sale] close rates are higher.

"For years," Hansen says, "we sold vehicles . . . but did not know years later if customers even liked them. Now we are learning more about what they want earlier in the process."

The data also helped Hansen and Ford Motor Company improve profitability by determining which products were moving off dealer lots the fastest—allowing advance production decisions to be made that could reduce the average inventory churn. This figure was important because, despite Jac Nasser's view that car sales at traditional retailers would diminish, Ford still sold 85 percent of its vehicles through dealer inventory, and the average time products spent on lots was 70 days. Hansen said 40 percent of the vehicles on domestic lots were 90 days old. Calling it a "terrible" number, Hansen said that if Ford Motor Company could save $500 per unit in marketing costs by reducing the number of slow-moving vehicles, the company could save more than $1 billion.

"We're trying," he says, "to identify and improve availability of fast-moving vehicles."

Ford Motor Company also began using its new Web-based tool, Smart Order System, which helped dealers make better order choices for optimum inventory. In doing so, Ford could increase availability, while reducing the production of vehicles that sell more slowly due to less-favorable colors or extras.

"There is nothing," Hansen says, "like looking at real customer demand."

There was also nothing more important at Ford Motor Company than increased profitability. Within months of putting the revenue management effort into high gear, Ford had turned its retail spending-per-unit disadvantage against Chevrolet into a significant advantage, spending an average of $300 less per vehicle than its competitor in the first half of 2003. In an industry that typically has a return-on-sales margin of just 3 percent, the benefits of effective revenue management were staggering. Hansen said that if Ford, or any other automaker, figured out how to make another penny on every available dollar, the 3 percent margin would turn to 4 percent—yielding a 33 percent increase in profits.

"It is taking demand signals," Hansen says, "and turning them into revenue."

Hansen's department was the only one of its type among U.S. automakers, but he was hoping others would catch on to Ford Motor Company's advances, because he believed the entire industry would benefit from increased profitability and a move away from obtaining share for share's sake. GM, for example, was so entrenched in the chase of market share in 2003 that it sold a bundle of fleet cars for Ford's rental division, Hertz, at prices Ford would not touch, even for its own division. Selling the cars at a loss just to keep market share did not make sense in Dearborn.

"GM," Padilla says, "has a cost advantage over us, but they are giving more away."

Ford executives decided that in a tight business environment, profitability should come first, and that bigger did not necessarily mean better.

"It cost us share," Hansen says, "but it was share we could not afford [anyway]."

Revenue management as a corporate discipline was first embraced by the airline industry when established carriers needed effective pricing strategies to combat discount carriers. While Hansen hopes the entire auto industry will catch on, he has no plans of slowing Ford's progress if it does not.

"We're just at the beginning," he says, "and believe we can provide a lot of value [for the company] going forward."

Coinciding with revenue management were increased efforts at Ford Motor Company to learn more about its customers so it could meet needs better. The U.S. auto industry had long been derided for its hubris and unwillingness to step down from an all-knowing pedestal, but this automaker proved that notion to be largely myth when the new management team took over. Ford recognized it needed a better customer database and better processes for identifying leads and closing sales on a large-scale level. Some individual dealerships had particularly good information and excelled at selling cars and trucks, but a franchise network as a whole can only be as good as its parent company.

Ford Motor Company looked to FordDirect.com for sales leads, merging this information with data taken from its financing arm, Ford Credit, to better predict when customers with affections for Ford products would be likely to buy again. The automaker also took cues from its brief entry into the retail market, where managers and executives learned more about the unique nature of automobile selling.

"It is no longer a job," Hansen says, "of salespeople waiting on the floor for someone to come in. We are constantly looking for ways to focus our leads, finding the ones that want to buy."

Ford Motor Company's progress in gathering mass sales data and sharing it with dealers eased frustrations over the company's previous entry into the retail market, as the mistakes that had been made often led to learning.

"Would I have preferred," said dealer Jerry Reynolds, "[Ford's Auto Collections] hadn't happened? Sure. But since they did, we did learn a lot."

———

That Ford Motor Company was able to reverse pricing ground so quickly with its chief competitors in North America was one of a handful of reasons that Bill Ford's optimism for a short-term recovery increased as winter turned to spring in Michigan and the automaker's much-anticipated centennial celebration approached.

Ford Credit, under the leadership of Carl Reichardt and the direction of Greg Smith, was also reversing its troubled trend by focusing on the basics of good finance. The division was concentrating on supporting Ford's new and used vehicle sales while reducing other high-risk loans. Profitability at Ford Credit returned and was a primary reason parent company shares jumped dramatically in April 2003 on stronger-than-expected profit for the year's first quarter.

"What Carl and Greg did at Ford Credit so quickly was remarkable," Ford says.

Ford Motor Company stock surged 15 percent the day it announced earnings of 45 cents a share ($896 million) for the first quarter of 2003, double the average analyst estimates. It was just the second quarter out of the previous eight that Ford Motor Company had posted a profit, and it was much larger than anyone had expected. Contributing to the upsurge was $442 million in earnings from Ford Credit, along with strong vehicle pricing due to the company's revenue management efforts. Sales continued to decline slightly, partly because of the company's aging car lineup, but also because of Ford's new strategy of not chasing unprofitable market share, and the bottom line was improved as a result.

"Ford," said Goldman Sachs analyst Gary Lapidus in a research note, "is holding the line on vehicle prices more successfully than GM."

Ford Motor Company's forward progress continued with the mid-April initiation of a 100-city anniversary tour across the United States and Canada, timed to spark enthusiasm for its centennial celebration and raise awareness that the company was reaching a milestone. Executives and employees traveled the country, visiting dealers, consumers, and Ford car and truck enthusiasts. From New York City to San Francisco to Shreveport, Louisiana, to Jackson, Mississippi, the tour took the heart of the company to the people who had made it strong for a century of business.

Near Los Angeles, some 25,000 people turned out with Ford president and chief operating officer Nick Scheele for the 18th Annual Fabulous Fords Forever event, one of the largest single-make car shows in America. In Mississippi, vice president of human resources Joe Laymon threw out the opening pitch for a minor league baseball game and was hailed in the state's largest newspaper in a front page feature honoring the native sharecropper's son, while in Atlanta, company board member and Ford family heir Edsel Ford gave Model T-100 rides. And in Lancaster, California, a Model T tour started in May, with 42 cars of "rolling ambassadors" who began the 3,000-mile trip to Dearborn in hopes of arriving in time for the kickoff of Ford's massive 100th anniversary celebration in June.

"This company," Bill Ford says, "means so much to so many

people. When they started to talk about what Ford means to them . . . it was easy to listen."

Hundreds of warm generational stories from around the country about Ford Motor Company and its products began to reach World Headquarters, giving employees and executives a much-needed boost following three hard years filled with too many long days and negative headlines. The management team, with guidance from Bill Ford and outside coaching, quieted external distractions and continued focusing on the enormous task of cutting costs and developing can't-miss products. Meeting twice a week with key operating committee executives, Bill Ford listened to advice and asked for more from top executives, including Allan Gilmour, Nick Scheele, Jim Padilla, and David Thursfield.

"The meetings," Padilla said, "are usually held in a small, informal setting where he gets unsolicited feedback. Bill does not like big meeting rooms where he is surrounded by executives. He is definitely a nontraditional auto guy in that regard. Number one, Bill is not a top-down leader. He's not a big-ego guy. He does not like big meetings and he does not tell you what to do. He listens well, seeks a lot of input, pulls out the consensus view, and goes forward. When he needs to make the tough decision, he makes it."

Padilla said not having dominant personalities on the management team allowed the group to rely on experience and facts.

"We don't need dominant personalities," he said. "Look at Toyota. Toyota is a benchmark because Toyota is so consistently over the top with fundamentals."

Bill Ford's leadership within the Ford family was developing in a similar way. His father had been the torchbearer of the family for many years, but as Ford's leadership within the company increased, so did his voice within the family. Members typically meet a couple of times each year for business discussions to maintain communication and cohesion.

"Bill Sr.," says Steve Hamp, "has been a revered man in this group. For Bill [Jr.], there is clearly a growth process. He was not exactly a shrinking violet prior, but when he became chairman he began to take on a bigger leadership role within the family. He took another step forward when Jac left. There is no question that a quiet, unacknowledged passing of the torch has begun."

Ford's children, as well as Hamp's children and others from the fifth generation in the Ford family line, showed increasing interest in Ford Motor Company as the centennial celebration approached and stories about the automaker's rich past increased. Bill Ford tried to integrate the company into his family's life "as much as possible" without making them feel like one day they must join the business. But he also knew they valued the legacy and were interested in what he did at the office.

"I don't want them feeling any pressure to work here," he said. "I want my kids to be proud of their heritage, not burdened by it."

Ford felt the same about the company he was running. The automaker's history, as it neared its 100th anniversary, was so compelling that it could sometimes be overwhelming. Few companies, for example, have had a longer or more interesting relationship between labor and management than Ford, yet its legacy health care costs were near crippling. But rather than distance the company from its sometimes burdening past, Bill Ford chose to embrace the best as guiding lights to a future of innovation. That's why Ford made the call just before the centennial celebration to return the blue oval to the top of the company's World Headquarters.

Replaced with a script "Ford Motor Company" logo under Nasser in 2000 to reflect the automaker's global breadth, the blue oval's return to the company's main stage was a sign to all that the emphasis in Dearborn was back on the flagship

Ford Division. The famous symbol returned in early June, just as the centennial celebration was about to begin, replacing the company's so-called "trust mark." Nasser had removed the previous blue ovals because he felt they were too blue-collar in nature and did not adequately represent the company's other brands, like Land Rover and Aston Martin. But Bill Ford had the newly designed blue ovals—the company's logo for the next 100 years—placed back on World Headquarters because "it never felt right to have the oval missing" and he considered it more representative of the company's heritage and its people. The new blue ovals were unveiled before a cheering crowd of current and former employees, just days before the centennial celebration was to begin.

"Frankly," Ford said at the unveiling, "it's back where God intended it to be."

CHAPTER

9

Momentum

Rare is the American company that celebrates 100 years in business. Even rarer is the company with an executive bearing the founder's name running the same business a century after its inception. But in the days before the kickoff of Ford Motor Company's most important week ever—its five-day centennial celebration—the biggest story about Bill Ford was not that he had the job or how he was doing at it. Rather, the strong suggestion was that he did not really want to be Ford's leader in the first place.

Ford had been dubbed "the reluctant CEO" before, mostly because when taking over for Jac Nasser, he made it clear to anyone listening that the job was not one he had sought. Ford said he would have much preferred that the company prosper under Nasser than fail, but, when faced with few options, he stepped in with commitment as CEO. However, the spin in *Newsweek* magazine as Ford Motor Company's celebration began was decidedly different. Journalist Keith Naughton suggested in an article that Bill Ford "revealed himself" in candid interviews "as the reluctant CEO, with misgivings about the toll his job was taking on his time, his hobbies, and even his passions outside of work." The story also suggested that Bill Ford did not like his level of responsibility at the automaker or such nagging vagaries as having to make small talk with strangers at functions.

Ford and Naughton had for years been professional acquaintances, if not friends. As the Detroit bureau chief for *Newsweek*, Naughton had earned exclusive interviews with Ford since he became chairman in 1999, including one the day after Ford fired Nasser. *Newsweek* had pitched the centennial story to Ford company officials as "a day in the life" of Bill Ford. The reporter, it was suggested, would spend time with Ford and write about what it is like to be a fourth generation heir running one of the world's largest companies. The story would be timed to run just before the important centennial celebration, when the eyes of the world were on Ford Motor Company and Bill Ford.

For the basis of the story, Naughton was allowed to follow Ford around, traveling with him on the company jet to Michigan's Mackinac Island for a Governor's Conference speaking engagement and reception in May. The problem, according to Bill Ford, was that as the day wore on, he sometimes responded to Naughton's leading questions in a jesting, even sarcastic manner, like someone might jibe with his wife or friends on the golf course. If, for example, Naughton asked, "Don't you get tired of all this?" Ford responded, "Hell yeah, I do."

Ford, though, said he was glad to represent the company and enjoyed doing his job, including the occasional greeting, speaking, and shaking hands with a variety of people. He admitted that he got tired and weary at times, and missed his wife, children, and hobbies—particularly at the end of a long, hard day. But, if led at the right, or wrong, moment, it is easy for anyone to offer sarcasm about the less enjoyable daily parts of a life they actually love.

The story came off with a tone of a spoiled CEO complaining about his lot in life. Ford's wife, Lisa, read the story and was angry—not with Naughton, but with her husband, for letting his guard down and forgetting to remember that when you are CEO of one of the world's largest companies, nothing is ever off the record and sarcasm can always be played against you. Ford agreed with his wife, not blaming the writer, whom he considered a friend, but blamed himself instead for falling into the casual conversation trap.

"I really like Keith," Ford said in a recent interview, looking off to the side and cracking a slight smile. "Or, at least, I did."

Ford looked back, staring straight ahead, and sat up in his chair.

"The problem," he continued, "is that story was the antithesis of who I am. I do want to do this job. Yes, there are pressures. But everybody has them. I'm no different than anybody else with a job to do. It's tough.

"But the last thing I want to be seen as is a poor little rich kid who is not getting his way. That's bullshit."

It was a hard-learned lesson for Ford, who has worked at protecting his privacy, closely guarded by those around him. He couldn't, however, help being overtly friendly with guests, even journalists, once he let them into his space, becoming intellectually playful with a sometimes nonstop dry sense of humor that, if played wrong in print, could easily backfire. If prodded with a line, "You sick of all of this?" a joking Ford was almost sure to respond with a wisecrack before giving his real answer.

"There are moments," he said, "when I get tired. But I'm energized by the pressure and bound and determined to succeed."

It is just that kind of common occurrence with journalists and executives during off-guard moments that has led repeatedly to suggestions by some that he does not want the job he holds. Ford freely admitted that he did not want it at first. What he wanted, when taking over as chairman in 1999, was for Jac Nasser and Ford Motor Company to reach new heights and uncharted success. Any other thoughts would have been foolish, considering that he personally owned more than 2.5 million shares of Ford Motor Company stock, which lost millions in market share during the company's downward spiral—not to mention that as chairman he had been living what many would consider an idyllic life.

As chairman of the world's second-largest automaker, Bill Ford had a net worth of more than $100 million and lived in a plush area on the outskirts of picture-perfect college town Ann Arbor, Michigan, with a striking wife and four beautiful children. He could avoid the headaches of daily operation and never *had* to be at work unless there was a board meeting. He could champion noble world causes and check daily on the happenings involving the family's NFL team, with time left over for hobbies including fly-fishing at some of the world's best and most remote locations, skating (in-line and ice), martial arts, and traveling wherever he wanted, whenever he wanted, via a fleet of corporate jets available for his use (though he has always reimbursed the company for personal trips). Who would want to give all that up for the daily grind of operations responsibility? But once he took the job as Ford Motor Company's CEO, Bill Ford committed to it willingly, not reluctantly—a fact that he emphasized on the eve of the kickoff of the centennial celebration.

"I was only reluctant," Ford said, "in that I never was looking for it to happen."

It did not help the situation that Ford did not respond greedily in interviews like most executives when asked how long he envisioned staying on the job. Just as his six-week rule reveals, Ford lives his life without mapping out his long-term future when it comes to work. His actions in the office today are for Ford Motor Company tomorrow, but contemplating what his job at the automaker will be in 10 years does not hold his interest.

"It is hard," he says, "for me to look that far down the road. Part of it is just my personality. I have never wanted to plan my life that far in advance. I have always taken this place a year at a time."

Mark Truby, who covered Ford Motor Company during its tumultuous period for the *Detroit News*, sensed at the beginning of the centennial that Bill Ford was sick and tired of his "reluctant CEO" label and having to constantly explain himself, particularly in light of the *Newsweek* article. When journalists gathered on the morning of June 12, 2003, for a sneak preview of the reconstructed Rouge complex as a prelude to first-day celebration events, Truby gave Ford a chance to publicly respond to his critics during a brief question-and-answer session.

"Are you tired of people saying you don't want the job?" Truby asked.

"I'm annoyed," Ford replied, "because there is nothing I would rather be doing than this job. When I get out of the bed in the morning, I'm fired up. This is what I choose to do.

"I'd be kidding, if I said every day is a bed of roses, but this 'reluctant CEO' stuff is for the birds. It's a privilege and an honor to run the company. There is nothing I would rather be doing. I could have done anything I wanted with my life."

Ford was at the forefront of the business world as Ford Motor Company's centennial celebration kicked off in June 2003 with 100,000 guests, including dealers, suppliers, auto enthusiasts—and former executives. The five-day celebration was seen as a time to reflect on the past and launch into the future by mending fences and building bridges. Bill Ford and event organizers wanted just about everyone who had been a part of the automaker's 100-year history to participate in the momentous celebration.

When invitations were sent for the chairman's dinner in association with the centennial to all living former directors, Jac Nasser was included on the guest list at Bill Ford's request. When Nasser had not responded to an RSVP a few days before the dinner, Ford personally called to invite him. The next day, Jim Vella got a call back from Nasser, asking if Bill really wanted him to come. "Absolutely," Vella said.

"[Nasser] was a valued company employee for 30 years," Ford said. "He loves this company and I appreciate his service."

Nasser attended, as did former CEO Red Poling; Nasser spoke with Ford one-on-one for 15 minutes before the dinner started. He agreed to come back the next day for a golf-cart tour of event grounds, which included displays of Ford's global brands that he had fought so hard to get, including Land Rover and Volvo.

For Bill Ford, the centennial celebration was a shift away from the difficult year-and-a-half grind with media, analysts, and executives, where problems were typically the topic of the day. From the moment the five-day celebration began, he was given rock star treatment and admiration from thousands of Ford enthusiasts. A Ford running the Ford Motor Company during its 100th year had obvious appeal.

The centennial's opening day was marred by daylong heavy rains that caused the cancelation of a concert by the band Earth, Wind and Fire, and muddied the massive 150-acre grounds of Ford Motor Company's Henry Ford II World Center, making for a sloppy entry by Model Ts completing the 3,000-mile caravan. In fact, the weather conditions were so bad that Bill Ford confided to an aide his doubt that anyone would attend the opening ceremony he was scheduled to preside over. To his surprise, umbrella-holding fans standing in heel-deep mud lined the entrance, waving adoringly and asking for autographs as he arrived in an all-new, red F-150 pickup truck.

"We love you!"

"Keep up the good work!"

The frustrations and fears haunting Bill Ford, that Ford Motor Company was not moving far enough or fast enough in its rebuilding effort, were alleviated by the sight of 3,200 cars and trucks covering the centennial grounds (bigger than Disney's Magic Kingdom); the hundreds of journalists (more than typically cover the World Series) who traveled from all corners of the world to attend and file stories; the thousands of Ford employees, past and present; and consumers who came to share their love of the company, its products, and even its founding family for five days.

Attacks on Ford from environmental organizations like the Sierra Club and Global Exchange grew louder, however, as the company's centennial approached and publicity opportunities increased, bringing the threat of massive protests during the event. But so successful was Ford Motor Company's festival that anticipated protestors were hardly noticed, if at all. Only a few representatives of Global Exchange even showed up, staging a minor protest in a roped-off area along Michigan Avenue. Set up directly across from World Headquarters on the centennial's second day, news cameras rolled, but not more than two dozen sign-holders protested at once. Still, by boldly displaying such slogans as "Ford: Oil Addiction Is Job One," protestors made it clear that Bill Ford and the company he runs were the primary focus of their attention.

According to Global Exchange communications director Jason Mark, "We are focusing our grassroots effort on Ford Motor Company because we think William Clay Ford [Jr.] could be the guy who goes to Washington, D.C., and says something has to change. We want to hold him to his rhetoric."

Bill Ford did not back down from the critics. He said their accusations were wrong.

"My vision," he said, "has not changed one bit. It gives them instant headlines to shoot at us, but the more responsible ones are working *with* us."

Despite the minor protests, the enormous 100th anniversary celebration came off as smoothly as a big corporation hosting 100,000 guests on its grounds can expect. There was no alcohol sold, even at the major concert events, creating a family-style atmosphere. The only long lines were for rides on a historic Model T or at the handful of Ford memorabilia souvenir stands. And outside of main-stage music by Beyoncé

Knowles on one night and America's "Ford Truck Man," Toby Keith, on another, the entire event revolved around the automobile. Parking lots were filled with Model Ts, Mustangs, Edsels, Lincolns, F-series pickups, Thunderbirds, Volvos, Aston Martins, and more, while Land Rovers climbed up, down, and around a new man-made dirt hill in front of World Headquarters. Ford employees and executives walked the grounds, admiring decades of work. When Edsel Ford II stopped in front of World Headquarters to see a rare 1956 Lincoln Mark II hardtop convertible, owned by Barry Wolk of Farmington Hills, he was followed by a crowd happier to see him than to see the rolling art before them.

"I have been asked," Bill Ford said, "what I thought my great-grandfather would think if he could come back here and see this all 100 years later. My answer is that he would be thrilled.

"It was electric to feel the enthusiasm and soak it all in."

———————

The culmination of Ford Motor Company's centennial celebration was the 48th annual shareholders meeting—held exactly 100 years after its founders first met in Detroit to fill out incorporation forms for the automaker. This would be the first time in 10 years that the annual meeting was held in Dearborn.

"To fully appreciate the impact Ford Motor Company has had on people's lives around the world," Bill Ford said, "you have to understand what life was like 100 years ago. In 1903, there were only 8,000 cars in the United States and only 144 miles of paved road. The average life expectancy was 47 years. The average wage was 22 cents an hour. Most people never traveled more than 20 miles from home in their entire lifetime."

Exactly 100 years and millions of automobiles after Ford Motor Company's founding by Henry Ford, almost 70 members of the extended Ford family, including children, walked into the auditorium just before the shareholder meeting began, and sat together in reserved front rows. Presiding before them was family member, company chairman, and CEO Bill Ford. Seated beside him were his cousin, Edsel Ford II, and father, Bill Ford Sr.

"Very few companies," Ford said, "make it to a 100th anniversary, and very few founding family members are still involved when they do in day-to-day operations. How has the Ford family stayed together? The answer is simple: pride and a love of the company. Each generation has devoted their lives to this company, and now the fifth generation is coming along."

Ford talked at the meeting about the company's revitalization strategy, assuring shareholders it was on track and working. He talked about its backbone, building better products that would ultimately result in a stronger company and a better world. He mentioned the Escape Hybrid, to be available in 2004, and the plans to make hydrogen fuel cell–powered vehicles available to commercial fleets.

"Many people," he said, "are becoming impatient. But I believe our industry is poised to take real leadership in this area."

Ford introduced his father, age 78, who offered to the audience a unique grandson-to-grandfather perspective on Henry Ford.

"He spoiled me rotten," Bill Ford Sr. said.

The elder Ford told a story about how his grandfather had taught him to drive at the age of 10. He would do the steering, while Henry Ford would control the pedals. Bill Ford Sr. said he remembers being pulled over by a policeman when they were going 70 miles per hour.

"[The policeman] gave us a lecture," he said, "and sent us on our way."

The policeman never asked for Henry Ford's driver's license, and it was a good thing.

"No driver's license [with him], no money. . . . He [even]

made his own hair tonic. There are the stories you won't read about. Another I remember, he took me on my first ride in an airplane. I met the pilot—his name was Charles Lindbergh. I got a pretty good start [in] flying."

Before relinquishing the floor, Bill Ford Sr. closed with an irresistible, fatherly plug on behalf of the company's leadership.

"I do know," he said, "the company is in very good hands. Presently, it is tough . . . but I'm sure it will prevail. That's despite the doomsayers on Wall Street. Don't believe them for a second. This company . . . is going to do just fine."

Bill Ford Jr. glided through the shareholders meeting as the company and family spokesperson with ease, despite the typical attacks from a small handful of complaining shareholders found at most any annual meeting. When they complained—like suggesting Ford Motor Company should do more for the environment, or that Ford had slighted the company through his Goldman Sachs stock purchase—he felt compelled to respond and did, offering personal and passionate explanations.

"Business as usual is not acceptable."

"An independent board found there were no corporate profits usurped."

"I gave the profits to charity just to get the thing offstage."

After the shareholders meeting, Ford family members privately gathered across the street for a reunion at Greenfield Village, the Dearborn grounds dedicated by Henry Ford in 1928 as a repository for his artifacts. Organized by Edsel Ford and Steve Hamp, the reunion was the largest gathering of the Ford family anyone could remember and included the family's wide-eyed, rising fifth generation. Family members toured the Rouge, saw firsthand Bill Ford's pride—its new, living roof—and had lunch on the grounds at Green-field Village. The just-renovated, 88-acre complex includes buildings reflecting 300 years of American life and The Henry Ford, its nationally recognized museum. Opened in 1929, The Henry Ford contains such original pieces as the theater chair in which President Lincoln was shot and the convertible that President Kennedy was riding in when he was assassinated in Dallas.

The day was as much a centennial celebration for the Ford family as it was for the company. The Fords have faced some public and private ups and downs through the years, but few families connected through such wealth and social power have remained so steadfastly loyal for such a long time, de-spite periodic dustups. One reason for the time-tested unity is that Henry and Clara Ford had only one son, Edsel, which kept the family very small for half a century. Another is that the family (with some historic, notable exceptions) has typi-cally respected the decision making of its leaders, avoiding bloody rifts. The family has also respected its Class B stock ownership, maintaining an active, long-term view regarding Ford Motor Company.

"Each generation," Bill Ford said, "has devoted their lives to this company."

In the days and weeks after the demands and euphoria sur-rounding the centennial died down, Bill Ford was back to business as the chairman and CEO, trying to guide a global corporation while maintaining an approachable air. One morning, while driving to work on the daily commute, he heard personalities on a favorite rock station discussing plans to raffle off a souped-up Ford Mustang for charity. En route from Ann Arbor to Dearborn, Bill Ford could not resist jump-ing into the conversation.

JJ and Lynne of Detroit's popular 94.7 WCSX, "the classic rock station," conceived of and organized the Stone Soup Mustang fund-raiser, in which a classic muscle car was being rebuilt through donations of parts and talent from the community and raffled off, with benefits ($100,000) going to the Children's Leukemia Foundation of Michigan.

"Morning, JJ, this is Bill Ford calling," Ford said on the air.

"Mr. Ford, chairman of the board, the big kahuna of Ford Motor Company. To what do we owe the honor of this?" JJ said.

"Well," Ford said, "I was just listening and heard about the Mustang and it sounds terrific. It is one of the coolest things I've ever heard. I'm driving to World Headquarters this morning in my Mustang."

"Is it a convertible Mustang car?" JJ asked.

"It is a convertible," Ford said, "a convertible GT."

"Is it the yellow one?" Lynne asked.

"It's almost a bluish purple one with a black interior," Ford replied.

"Well, wait a minute, Bill. We'll move on to that in a minute. But I think people would be interested in knowing, thinking about Bill Ford Jr. driving in to work each day. You could drive almost any car you want."

"Pretty much, yeah," Ford said, laughing. "I keep the Mustang all summer. I've always loved Mustangs, and pretty much every summer that is what I drive to and from work. Then in the winter I usually switch into a pickup truck."

"Do people sometimes whip their heads around and go, oh, it's you?" Lynne asked.

"They do," Ford said, "and it's funny because with the top down, people sort of have instant access to you. When I pull up at stop lights a lot of people want to talk about either cars or football, and sometimes it is tough to get away from the light."

"We will talk later, if you have some time, about the Detroit Lions, if you wish," JJ said.

The ease with which Ford talks with acquaintances, strangers—anyone—is one of his strengths, but it is also a quality that works against him now as public recognition of him has increased. He likes people and enjoys conversations on a range of topics, soaking up the information that others have to offer. But as the CEO of a $160 billion global corporation, a husband, and the father of four active children, he is not blessed with an abundance of extra time, and he finds the increasing demands of a well-meaning public a challenge.

When Ford first moved to Ann Arbor, for example, he could drop in at a neighborhood Starbucks before or after going for a run in shorts, with bed-head hair, and go unnoticed. Now he feels the need to freshen up and be on his toes because, after being the centerpiece of national commercials and a high-profile centennial, Ford's anonymity in the college town—and everywhere in America—has virtually vanished. Sure, he grew up in one of America's higher-profile families, but a year and a half into his dual leadership role at Ford Motor Company, the chairman and CEO found he was working and living in a much bigger public arena than he might have imagined.

"Bill," says Steve Hamp, "is still working through his modus operandi in accessibility and exposure. He's a private guy, but he does enjoy a lot of his public dimension, particularly where it benefits the company. It does not happen overnight—he's still evolving."

The main thing, Hamp says, is that Ford can sense the automaker is progressing, making the price of higher public demands more palatable. "He's got the company moving," Hamp says. "There's traction. You can see and feel the movement."

Ford adjusts to the change of life that allows for less personal time outside of his Ann Arbor house and 17-acre spread by taking advantage of opportunities for playtime at home with his children whenever possible. He is building a "sports barn" on his property, with half-court basketball, a track, indoor hockey, a weight room, ping pong . . . anything allowing him to compete among his children and their friends.

"In the winter," he says, "we are bouncing off the walls [in Michigan]."

He skated a couple of times with the company's notoriously tough hockey league during the centennial summer and held his own on the ice, but couldn't find time to play in weeknight games due to a rigorous schedule.

"Surprisingly," Ford says, "I did fine. I just can't find the time. So in the summers I'll get my boys and their friends and we play."

Ford also works out daily because he feels he can't function well without the exercise.

"This place," he says, "does not leave time for much else. I have to [work out regularly] just for my peace of mind and energy level."

———————

At the office, Bill Ford and Ford Motor Company's challenges were far from over at the conclusion of the centennial, despite some much-needed reputational momentum gained from the celebration. In the month of June 2003 alone, the company benefited from an incredible media response, including hundreds of magazine and newspaper stories, evening news clips, and television and radio features around the world. The result was a significant bounce in public opinion, translating into higher consumer purchase considerations, which helped support Ford Motor Company's brand value and ultimately its more balanced pricing efforts during the heat of the incentive battle. In the first half of 2003, Ford's corporate reputation grew favorably by more than five percentage points following the centennial—reaching levels not seen since the automaker's peak days in 2000.

Problems, however, remained. Most notably, the anticipated turnaround at Ford of Europe was behind schedule as losses continued despite significant cost-cutting measures under a revitalization plan. Ford's European business, which excluded its London-based luxury brands that were part of the company's Premier Auto Group, lost $525 million before taxes in the second quarter of the year, despite a rise in revenues. The parent company, at the same time, reported a decline in second quarter earnings, as incentives gobbled up profits from weaker auto sales and the drag of such weak spots as Ford of Europe took a toll.

"Red Poling, when he was [Ford's] CEO, said it's a tough old world out there," said Ford vice chairman Allan Gilmour. "And that's what it is in the auto industry these days."

So difficult was the situation in Europe that Martin Leach abruptly resigned as president and CEO of Ford's European operation in August. The company replaced him with Lewis Booth, 54, who had been president and CEO of Ford affiliate Mazda, and began lending more corporate assistance in the cost-cutting strategy to battle the ailing division's financial woes.

Domestically, Ford was still plagued by price wars, which, even though it was holding the line on incentives in North America better than rivals GM and Chrysler, were still costing the company $700 million for the quarter, eliminating most automotive profit. The good news was that the cost cutting done by Ford Motor Company's leadership, combined with strong results from Ford Credit and improving profits from its Premier Auto Group, resulted in the majority of its $417 million second quarter profit.

The balance of progress weighted by problems as the automaker emerged from its successful centennial celebration signaled an important crossroads for the 100-year-old manufacturing company. A tip was all it would take to send Ford Motor Company in either direction, and the months ahead contained multiple, crucial opportunities. UAW negotiations were set to begin in August as the four-year national contract was about to expire. Obtaining a palatable new contract became imperative in light of escalating employee costs. If talks went off course and manufacturing was interrupted, Ford's forward progress would be wiped out. Also, in September the most important product in the company's history would launch. The automaker had made a bet-the-farm investment in a full makeover of its best-selling product, the F-series pickup. If the all-new 2004 F-150 launched smoothly and found success, bingo! Ford's forthcoming new-product onslaught would be off to a running start. But if the launch found trouble, Ford Motor Company's second century of business would be off to a rough beginning that could derail Bill Ford's five-year, product-led recovery plan.

10

America's Best-Selling Truck Is New Again

When country music star Toby Keith comes calling, you never know what to expect. The man from Oklahoma has a reputation for saying what's on his mind, no matter what is at stake. So Ford Motor Company designers held their breath when the singer/songwriter known for crooning number one hits about bars and trucks and the "good ol' US of A" dropped by the design studio in response to an invitation to see development of the all-new, 2004 F-150 pickup.

Keith first got involved with Ford Motor Company in 2001 after word had spread to executives in Dearborn that he was an avid, third generation Ford truck man. It all started, he says, when a Ford dealer in Phoenix approached him at his annual charity golf tournament, asking about his passion for the company's trucks.

"I got my first one," Keith said, "when I was fifteen and a half. I had just gotten my driver's permit. My dad worked in an oil field in Oklahoma and bought it at an auction there."

They paid $600 for the truck, investing another $600 to spice it up. "It was a '74 model Ford pickup," Keith said, "three-speed on the column, six cylinder."

The Phoenix Ford dealer told Keith that if he loved Ford trucks so much, the company could use his help selling them. The dealer notified Ford Division president Steve Lyons and top marketing executives in Dearborn, and the effort was under way to land the country music star as the F-150's pitchman. Ford Motor Company's advertising agency, J. Walter Thompson, got involved, suggesting to Keith that he craft an F-150 theme song from his 1999 number one hit, "How Do You Like Me Now?!" Toby had a different idea.

"For years," Keith says, "advertisers have used hit songs that people already recognize. I stepped out on a limb and said, 'Hey, you've got to give me a shot at writing an all-new song.'"

Fine, the agency said. Write two: one the way you want to do it and one based on "How Do You Like Me Now?!" But Keith was so confident he could deliver a winner with his original "Ford Truck Man" that he never worked on the other. When he presented the new song to ad agency and Ford Motor Company officials during a visit to World Headquarters, they loved it. But when the agency asked him to play the other based on his former hit, he could not.

"I didn't bring it," he told them.

Ford Motor Company had its man.

When Keith met in Dearborn in July 2002 with Lyons and company marketing executives, they presented him with his "Ford" guitar and gave him a behind-the-scenes look at the company and the development of its all-important, new F-150. They took him into the company's design studio, allowing a rare view of the truck's design in progress. Designers were interested in input from the man who knows something about the importance of headroom and dashboards in pickups.

"I'm a truck guy," Keith says. "I was not afraid to tell them my opinions."

At the very least, Ford designers figured Keith's response to the truck would be a good predictor of America's reaction to it. If the new F-150 was tough enough for Toby, the truck should have no problem finding success.

Craig Metros was the chief exterior designer on the F-150 remake and was in the studio during Keith's look-and-see visit. Metros is a soft-spoken Detroit native who prefers versions of metropolitan garage rock to country music. He met Keith's manager, who came along for the studio visit. The manager was armed with Toby Keith CDs and prepared to give the handful away.

"You like country music?"

Metros thought about the right answer to give. He knew nothing about country music and had little interest in uncovering its seductive secrets. What Metros wanted was an honest response from Keith about the truck. Metros had worked for several years on F-150 design, taking over an entire studio to create what he called an "F-150 land" where he and fellow designers could immerse themselves into the feeling of the product. The truck's final designs—several versions were still in consideration at the time—were based on honest reflections of its passionate users.

"No," he said. "Not really."

It did not matter. When Keith saw the new versions under consideration for the best-selling truck in America, he could not contain his all-out enthusiasm.

"*That's* what I'm talking about. *That* is a pickup truck."

For Ford Motor Company, that was a good thing. The F-Series truck has been America's best-selling pickup for 26 years, and for 20 years has been the country's best-selling vehicle, period. So important is the product to Ford that it accounted in 2002 for about a fifth of the company's U.S. sales and roughly half its profits. If the company was to meet its goal of earning $7 billion a year in pretax profit by 2006, it could only do so with a grand-slam launch of its single best vehicle. What's more, the competition was getting tougher. Japanese automaker Nissan planned to launch in October the first full-size pickup ever by a foreign automaker, while Toyota had broken ground on a U.S. truck plant to build a full-size product. Its Tundra had gone on sale in 1999, billed as a full-size truck, but it was actually smaller than American pickups and never had become a serious threat. Things were changing, though.

"The F-150 is certainly the make-it or break-it vehicle for Ford," said Dennis Virag, president of the Ann Arbor–based Automotive Consulting Group Inc. "Ford needs to hit a home run."

In 2002 Ford Motor Company sold more than 800,000 F-150 units, including 90,000 in Texas, 50,000 in California, 31,000 in Florida, 22,000 in Michigan, and almost 20,000 in Georgia. But the truck had last been redesigned in 1997 and, while it remained number one in popularity, its dated style was contributing to a decline in the closely watched nameplate loyalty rates. Internal surveys showed the F-150's loyalty rate of 53 percent in 1997 had dropped to just above 40 percent in 2002. Field studies showed some hard-core truck buyers considered it "a sissy truck" due to its rounded body lines and dated demeanor. To find solutions, Ford designers and engineers went to the source—truck buyers in pickup country—to try to create a more "rugged but refined" look in keeping with Ford's "tough truck" philosophy.

"How do you challenge yourself when you are already the leader?" asked Frank Davis, chief engineer of the F-150 team.

The pressure was on. When the F-series team began planning for the remake of the popular truck in 1999, members knew it could not be just a little better. To stay on top, it would have to be a full generation ahead of the oncoming competition. Ford Motor Company had been building tough trucks for more than half a century, selling more than any manufacturer in the world. In Dearborn, they set the bar on pickup trucks, in both quantity and quality (JD Power surveys ranked the F-150 tops in reliability). The directive from on high was to push the bar out of reach with the 2004 model, showing the world that Ford Motor Company could make its best better.

"We looked," Davis said, "at unmet customer needs."

The truck team conducted field tests in key markets like Houston, Texas, and Atlanta, Georgia. They found that American truck buyers covered the widest range of all vehicle buyers. Most want tough looks and high performance, but many also want the added look and feel of luxury, enabling an executive to drive clients to lunch on weekdays and haul full loads on his or her weekend farm on Saturdays. The decision was made to launch a tough truck segment within a segment. The five truck models in the F-Series would allow Ford Motor Company to serve all buyers with a variable lineup, ranging from the base XL to the Lariat, which would feature luxury previously found only in cars.

"Clearly," Bill Ford said, "one size does not fit all."

The look of the 2004 F-150 was altered on the inside and out, including a hood that sits two inches higher than before and a longer body. The interior was made to reflect today's upscale tastes.

"It was the first vehicle," says vice president of group design J Mays, "that we decided to triple the investment on interior. When sitting in that vehicle, you need to see and feel like it is nine times better."

But the truck's drastically improved functionality was what gave those inside the company such high hopes for its success, simply because the new F-150 exceeded all previous parameters of power.

"This," said F-series marketing manager Todd Eckert, "is not a sissy truck."

The new F-150 engine delivers 15 percent more peak horsepower than its predecessor; has a frame nine times stiffer than its predecessor, providing significantly smoother and quieter rides; has newly designed rear suspension with outboard shocks, allowing for easier handling; and has easier access and more cargo capacity. Details meant for brochures, yes, but details that made the difference between just another product update or a smashing success that would lead the way to recovery. Pulling off a big birthday party was one thing. Building a truck above all trucks is another. So, serious about ensuring the 2004 F-150 was a cut above all oncoming competition, the company modestly announced an anticipated best-in-class towing capacity for the new truck as bait, hoping to unearth rival information. When Nissan countered, saying its new truck would match the reported F-150's pull power, Ford restated the F-150's strength, saying it would actually be higher.

"Having the highest towing rating means a lot to many of our customers," Ford Division president Steve Lyons said. "It's a very competitive world out there and sometimes you find yourself in a high-stakes game of poker. We knew we hadn't showed all our cards. We had some reserve in our towing capacity and now . . . we are clearly best-in-class."

In many ways, the new F-150 is head and shoulders above the competition's trucks. And there couldn't have been a better time for a home run—or a better product to lead the way than America's best-selling vehicle. "In terms of sheer impact," Bill Ford said, "on a product-led recovery . . . we knew it had to be one full generation ahead [of competitive products]. We worry about everybody out there, but this is leagues better. We make the best truck. That is why it is so important for us to get this right."

Getting it right meant more than designing a good product. Ford Motor Company struggled with launching products during the Nasser era, and externally there were doubts as to whether the automaker could put an all-new vehicle into production without a series of profit-draining glitches. Scoring big with the new truck—the first of 65 new products planned over the next five years—meant more than designing a head turner. Ford had to build it and ship it on time and without flaws.

Internal confidence was high, based on preproduction reviews. Lyons boldly predicted that the company would set a sales record for full-size pickups in 2004. That meant selling more than 912,000 trucks to break the mark established by the F-Series in 2001. With the new Dearborn Truck Plant at the Rouge coming on line in the summer of 2004, joining Ford's plants in Norfolk, Virginia, and Kansas City, Missouri, full production would be in place for an entire year beginning in 2005.

"[Lyons] signed up for it," Ford said, "so we are going to hold him to it."

A celebration for "Job One" for the new F-150 was held at the Norfolk truck plant in summer 2003 when the truck was ready for mass production. Bill Ford was there, along with Governor Mark Warner and UAW vice president Gerald Bantom. Norfolk shift workers lined the walls behind media and special guests, cheering when Ford came rolling into the plant on a ramp, driving a brand-new, sporty red SuperCab Lariat F-150 while Toby Keith's "Ford Truck Man" blared on loudspeakers. Bill Ford emerged, blushing at the rock star entrance, but showed pleasure at being upstaged.

"That," Ford said, "is one great truck."

At the moment, it was also a more expensive truck for the company to build. Ford had pushed engineers and designers to deliver a can't-miss, bar-raising product. They did, but all those extras cost more when the truck went into production. Estimates were that the product symbolizing Ford Motor Company's bet that it could rely on new products to restore automotive profitability cost $1,200 more per unit to make. This gave some analysts who covered the company pause, particularly in light of pricing pressures due to America's car wars. Ford's plan, however, was to give the customers a superior product and launch it properly, earning trust and respect and, ultimately, higher profits. Engineers would work with suppliers and remove over-engineered components after the launch to "get the costs out."

"There's no question," Ford said, "that we have to cut cost on the truck. But it's more important we get this launch right."

Moving to center stage at Norfolk Assembly, Ford was broadly smiling. Before him were the elements of success that matter most to Ford Motor Company at the moment: the new F-150 truck and the people charged with building it. Hanging behind him were the emblems representative of everything at stake—Ford's blue oval and the UAW logo.

"This," he said, pointing to the F-150, "is the most important model to our turnaround."

Japanese automakers may just be getting around to building full-size pickup trucks, but they invented flexible manufacturing—the process that allows for multiple products to be built on a single assembly line. Toyota, Honda, and Nissan have been building vehicles on interchangeable lines for years, allowing the companies to adapt rapidly to volume and product mix demands. Ford management had considered adopting the process off and on for years, but ultimately opted against it because cost and changeover constraints outweighed the advantages. A Mustang plant built Mustangs, and an F-150 plant built F-150s.

But the challenge of producing 65 new or all-new models in five years, combined with Ford Motor Company's increasing need to maximize productivity, led to a dramatic move in the way the company builds cars and trucks. The company that invented the moving assembly line reinvented itself again during its 100th year, installing next-generation flexible manufacturing at plants building the new F-150.

Ford Motor Company took advantage of its controlling stake of Japanese automaker Mazda to study the specifics of flexible manufacturing and find new-generation solutions that could be employed in the United States to help the automaker become more efficient at the beginning of its second century of business. Ford's Norfolk Assembly converted to flexible systems first during the F-150 launch. The new flexible manufacturing allows the automaker to build up to eight different models off two vehicle platforms (the backbone of a car or truck). The process works by employing standardized cells, or modules, that can be interchanged on the line to launch new products. The result is optimized capacity and quicker response time during changing market demands. For example, Ford Motor's body shops employing flexible manufacturing are no longer held captive by a single product. The company now has the capability to mix product, more quickly meeting customer demand.

The man charged with leading Ford Motor Company's manufacturing changes at the start of the company's second century of business was Roman Krygier, group vice president of Ford Global Manufacturing and Quality. A company veteran since beginning in 1964 as a trainee foreman in the Chicago Stamping Plant, Krygier is a Purdue University and Massachusetts Institute of Technology–educated engineer who fellow executives say has never lost sight of Ford Motor Company's commitment to its employees and to quality.

Krygier, 60, previously only knew Bill Ford at "arm's distance," but got the chairman's attention during the first quarter of 2001 when he stepped into a vital leadership role at a company plant in Cleveland, Ohio, involved in crisis. Tensions were running high at Ford Motor Company's Cleveland Casting Plant in March 2001—a time the automaker was in deep turmoil—when two workers died from Legionnaires' disease. Ford briefly closed the plant and Krygier went onsite, taking the company lead in remedying a dire situation.

More than 2,500 people worked at the plant, which manufactured iron engine blocks, heads, crankshafts, and bearing caps for a variety of Ford engines used in a wider variety of cars, trucks, and SUVs. The company could not afford to put employees in danger—nor could it afford to let such an important plant close.

"If we had lost that site," Krygier says, "we would have lost North America."

Krygier led the company's efforts to close and disinfect the plant, while working with federal, state, and local officials to ensure employee safety. The Cleveland plant reopened in April 2001. Krygier earned the praise of Ford's chairman, who sent a handwritten note in appreciation. Krygier keeps it prominently displayed in his office today.

"Thank you," Bill Ford wrote, "for your response on behalf of the employees and families . . . thank you for living the values that all the others only talk about."

When Bill Ford became CEO later the same year and needed someone to lead the way to improved quality and manufacturing efficiency, he turned to Krygier. By 2002 Krygier was a part of Ford's small group of executives included in Monday operational committee meetings and was drafting plans to change the way Ford Motor Company builds cars and trucks.

At the office, Krygier says Ford is a "genuine" leader who gives top executives freedom to do a job with the caveat of "high accountability." Outside of the office, Krygier says Ford is personable and typically uninterested in talking business. Krygier's oldest son played professional hockey and coaches Krygier's grandson in youth leagues in the Detroit area. Bill Ford's son plays games at the same arena, and Krygier has been known to run into his boss on weekends at the rink.

"I hear someone calling my name," Krygier says, "and it's Bill Ford."

Ford asks Krygier how his grandson is doing, avoiding the obvious. But Monday morning at the office, it is all business with high accountability to deliver for the company.

"That's just the way he is," Krygier says. "It's a breath of fresh air. In a time of crunch, people will deliver for him."

The plant investments, coming at a time when the company was financially strained, were approved as a necessity for Ford Motor Company's future. Plans easily could have been delayed, helping in the short term.

"Bill knows the business," says Krygier. "He knows we have to invest in product and we have to take the money we have available and apply it where it can be leveraged effectively."

In the summer of 2003, Ford Motor Company's manufacturing revolution was under way. The Norfolk plant came on line with flexible manufacturing first because the goal at the company was to tier in the process during major product changes. Other Ford plants building the F-150—Kansas City and the new Dearborn Truck Plant—would be outfitted with the new flexible system and would ramp up sequentially as production of the truck hit full stride. After Norfolk came on line, employees and managers from the Kansas City and Dearborn facilities studied the process.

"We used to ask questions," Krygier says, "about implementing flexible manufacturing years ago, but the market was not as fragmented [with product] at the time. I don't know how we would have gotten it in anyway, because you have to put flexibility in with product change. Now, with so many new products coming, the timing was right."

The delay allowed Ford Motor Company to benefit from improved and more cost-efficient systems, implementing flexible systems as new product comes to market. Standardized manufacturing calls for standardized design and engineering, resulting ultimately in more communization across the board for a global automaker that needs all the simplification it can get. Krygier expects half of the company's facilities to be converted by mid-decade and three-fourths to be converted by the end of the decade—delivering savings to the automaker of $2 billion. The ultimate benefit, though, is that Ford Motor Company modernized its manufacturing at precisely the moment many in the automotive world were suggesting Detroit's demise due to an unwillingness to change.

"Necessity and need came in," Krygier said. "Now, more competitors are coming in with differentiated products. If we don't differentiate, we will lose ground."

The challenge, of course, was to implement the new manufacturing systems at Ford Motor Company's most crucial moment—the launch of its new F-150. The entire company was focusing its energy on delivering its best launch ever. Flaws in the new flexible scheme causing delays or quality glitches could do irreparable damage. But Norfolk delivered, and the new truck was well on its way.

"The product," Krygier said, "is excellent."

Problems were also few. The new F-150 rolled off the assembly lines and to dealers across the country in time for a national release date in September, coinciding with the start of the National Football League season kickoff. Prelaunch hype was the best Ford Motor Company had ever experienced for a product, creating backorder demand of almost 50,000 trucks. The company had entertained hundreds of automotive journalists in San Antonio, Texas, in the summer over eight waves of a two-day launch program, letting them drive the truck through winding prairie back roads, down rocky creek beds, and up and down dirt hills. Reviews were overwhelmingly positive. The *Detroit Free Press* said the new F-150 was "the best pickup truck ever," while a writer with the *Detroit News* proclaimed after driving the new truck: "They got it right. Now they've just got to sell a ton."

The new truck was priced to move, with base models starting at $19,125—the same as the 2003 model. The manufacturer's suggested retail price (MSRP) for the entire 2004 F-150 lineup ranged from $19,125 to $35,570. Thanks to low interest rates, customers buying a 2004 model on a 60-month plan would pay roughly the same per month as they would have three years before. With only the Norfolk plant building the new trucks in the beginning, supply was behind demand, but Ford executives wanted all dealers to have a truck on their lot by the September 4 kickoff, and they made it happen, shipping 20,000 F-150s across the country and getting at least one to each of Ford's 3,800 dealers. In Hastel, Texas, the sight of the new trucks being delivered to an area dealership got one traveler so excited he stopped and checked into a motel just so he could buy one of the first trucks when they went on sale the next day. In Detroit, area Ford dealers broke tradition and opened their doors on a Saturday to show off their new prized product.

Since Ford was still selling 60,000 F-150s in a slower month, the company could not afford to phase out its previous model. So, while the new truck was launched, the renamed Heritage edition of the F-150 remained in production, giving the company a double-edged approach. The new 2004 F-150 cost more for Ford to build in the beginning and it was priced competitively with the Heritage model. But, while the Heritage model had a package of incentives to keep it competitive with the $3,000 to $4,000 Chevrolet had on the hood of its Silverado, the new 2004 F-150 sold with virtually no incentives.

"Every nickel," Jim Padilla said, "that we spent on the F-150 was worth it because it puts that truck in a new dimension with the competition."

Executives hoped superior product design and engineering would yield higher profits in the form of reduced incentives. The idea was that when competitor General Motors responded to the F-150 launch by offering even deeper discounts on its Chevrolet trucks than already in place, Ford would counter by offering deep discounts on its Heritage model, fighting to protect profits on the new truck.

"People will pay more for a product because it is better, especially if it is clearly superior," said Ford Division president Steve Lyons.

At the news conference where he announced the pricing for the new F-150, Lyons boldly predicted that despite the modest price increases and the inherently higher costs in the new truck, the 2004 F-150 would deliver at least as much variable profit as the outgoing model. In addition to carrying much lower incentives, the new truck would sell in a more profitable mix than the outgoing truck, with a higher take rate for the upscale FX4 and Lariat models, more Super Crew models, and a higher rate for options such as a floor shifter and four-wheel drive. Lyons suggested the new truck was so much better than the Silverado, it would push the Chevy truck off many buyers' consideration lists.

"It's simple," Lyons said. "Best truck wins."

To support its massive investment in the new F-150, on kickoff weekend Ford Motor Company launched its biggest-ever advertising campaign. Led by advertising manager Rich Stoddart and Truck Group marketing manager Doug Scott, and in conjunction with ad agency J. Walter Thompson, the three-month ad blitz sought not only to restore the F-150's loyalty rate above 50 percent and move trucks from dealer lots in record numbers, but also to draw traffic to Ford dealerships that would help vehicle sales across the board—showing the world Ford Motor Company was back, stronger than ever before.

"We were launching," Scott says, "from a position of strength. We can say, 'Ford Tough' and consumers know what that means."

But to meet Lyons' goal of selling a record number of F-Series pickups, the product had to be launched into the hearts and minds of American consumers, while the quality had to be confirmed by the automotive critics. The approach was not to simply play the same old game of advertising trucks—of one-upmanship of power and torque—but to create an overnight awareness that the new F-150 will forever change American customers' expectations for full-size pickup trucks with more power, more quietness, and more comfort than ever before available.

"This," said Scott, "is not about the past 26 years. It is about the future. This truck is the gold standard of how we build our products."

Toby Keith's new "Ford Truck Man" song launched the truck advertising campaign, and the singer/songwriter agreed to let Ford Motor Company actively participate in his 2003 "Shock'n Y'all" tour by using a Ford "transformer" truck on the stage during his 60-show national tour. A one-of-a-kind 2004 F-150 actually transformed onstage at the beginning of Toby's performance, providing a unique platform from which to entertain more than 1.5 million fans. Keith, also, got his own new F-150 and parked it beside his F-250 and F-350.

"When it was delivered," he said, "I knew they had gotten it right."

The new F-150 truck and its accompanying promotional efforts signaled an aggressive shift for the company in recognizing and taking advantage of its leadership position. Instead of worrying about competitive maneuvers, Ford had made a charge away from the pack. Nissan's Titan was on the way, along with Toyota's bigger Tundra. General Motors was pouring incentives on its Silverado, but Ford Motor Company kept driving its message through television and print ads and even a vibrating MSN home page: "Only one truck deserves to be the next F-150."

"It is no secret," said Marty Collins, marketing manager for the Ford Division, "that GM is trying to screw up our big launch, but we are not going to let them. This new truck is way ahead of the [competitive] curve. With many products, like our midsize cars, we've been behind in past years and trying to play catch up. We are not going to do that anymore."

The combination of new F-150s, discounted Heritage models, and national advertising helped Ford Motor Company set an all-time record for September 2003. The company sold 81,872 F-Series trucks in the month, easily beating the previous September record.

"Dealers," Bill Ford said, "love it and the quality of the launch was excellent. That was not a slam dunk. It is almost impossible to overstate the importance of getting this launch right. But we did it. We got the product right, and the quality of the product is very good."

The mix of trucks sold was even richer than Ford Division had expected—more than 67 percent were Lariats and FX4s, with more Super Crews, more 5.4-liter V-8s, more floor shifters, and a greater percentage of four-wheel drives than had been programmed in the division's aggressive planning. This rich mix boded well for the company's ability to achieve its 2003 profit targets.

The truck also provided to the automaker the industry's highly sought halo effect, sending buyers into showrooms and increasing sales on multiple models, including the Ford Escape (up 29 percent), Ford Expedition (up 52 percent), and Lincoln Aviator.

"The new F-150," Jim O'Connor said, "is doing exactly what we expected our clean-up hitter to do—drive in truck buyers to Ford dealer showrooms."

Bargaining
for a Future

Ford Motor Company was making undeniable progress
in revitalization efforts as its 100th anniversary successfully passed and the early reviews of its new pickup
truck exceeded most internal and external expectations. But
as the automaker began its 101st year in business, all eyes
were focused on the most important event in Ford's fledgling
second century—impending contract talks with the United
Auto Workers.

Few industry watchers expected labor negotiations to result
in a crippling strike, since Ford and U.S. competitors General
Motors and Chrysler were dealing with declining U.S. market
share and unprecedented pricing pressures. Union officials
and employees were well aware of the difficult environment,
in stark contrast to the most recent negotiations, in 1999,
when domestic automakers dominated in share and profits.
There was considerable concern, however, that Ford's revitalization plan would suffer a big blow if the company did not
earn union concessions in regard to health care costs and
overcapacity. Ford Motor Company needed to close plants
and it needed to find solutions in paying for escalating health
care benefits. Ford provided eligible employees, retirees, and

surviving spouses with comprehensive health care coverage, and the total expense for covered hourly employees was $2.5 billion in 2002, with average annual increases of more than 10 percent.

"We're not going to go backward in health care," UAW president Ron Gettelfinger proclaimed.

Gettelfinger kicked off national UAW negotiations with a photo opportunity—a ceremonial handshake with Dieter Zetsche, chief executive of the Chrysler unit of Daimler-Chrysler—but speculation was rampant over which company the union would lead negotiations with. Historically, when it formally begins negotiations every four years, the UAW has selected a lead automaker for bargaining, basing contracts with the other two on its successful first. A former Ford employee who rose through the union ranks from his job at the company's Louisville, Kentucky, truck plant, Gettelfinger had participated in the 1999 talks, but these would be his first in the role of leader of the entire UAW membership. His challenge was daunting: having to make costly demands from American automakers while simultaneously allowing them enough strength to battle foreign automakers who were increasingly creating nonunion transplant jobs in the United States.

Ford Motor Company's Joe Laymon had been named vice president of corporate human resources by Bill Ford in late 2001, becoming one of the highest ranking African Americans in the auto industry. The job put Laymon in the leadership position for Ford's 340,000 employees worldwide. It did not, however, give him the responsibility of UAW negotiations and relations. That job fell under Ford's North American division and was not a corporate responsibility. Charged with leading the labor talks was Shamel Rushwin, a 1999 Nasser recruit who specialized in vehicle operations—not human resources. As Ford's vice president of North American business operations, Rushwin had previously worked in manufacturing at General Motors, Volkswagen of North America, and DaimlerChrysler before coming to Ford, but had little experience as a personnel specialist.

As negotiations for the UAW 2003 contract neared, Laymon grew increasingly concerned that Ford Motor Company was not putting its most effective foot forward with the union. Labor, he believed, should be a function of human resources. Labor talks, he believed, should be led by executives with the most experience in domestic negotiations. In recent years, the UAW had dealt with Ford's internationally flavored leadership, including Alex Trotman and Jac Nasser, and Laymon was not sure Rushwin was the right choice. Ford needed to stay on track for its five-year revitalization plan by closing five North American parts and assembly plants, including four in the United States, and containing soaring health care benefits. There was little room for error during the all-important centennial year labor negations. While Laymon respected Rushwin as a seasoned automotive manufacturing and operations executive, he had concerns over his lack of negotiation skill and experience.

Also on Ford Motor Company payroll was 30-year company veteran Dennis Cirbes, who had assisted in the 1999 talks. As the date for 2003 formal negotiations neared, Cirbes sat on the sidelines as a second team player while Rushwin, with little bargaining experience, remained in place to lead the Ford team. Concerned, Laymon stepped in and talked with Rushwin about the crucial negotiation process, suggesting he take special classes on the subject of negotiation. Rushwin agreed. But by early 2003, with formal UAW talks set to begin in the summer, Laymon determined something more drastic had to be done. Reluctantly, he went to Bill Ford, telling him point-blank that "the company should not put before the UAW a person who has never before negotiated a contract."

"It would have been an insult," Laymon says.

Bill Ford listened closely as Laymon outlined his strategy for how he believed Ford's labor negations should be run and who should be involved. Laymon wanted Dennis Cirbes, who had six years of Ford factory management experience and previous bargaining experience, to serve as the company's negotiation point man, reporting to Laymon as vice president of labor affairs. The move would put negotiations back into the corporate structure with the rest of employee relations and take responsibility out of operations at Ford's North American division.

The importance of having the right team in place during UAW talks was not lost on Bill Ford, who had the benefit of knowledge from generations of family involvement with labor. Henry Ford had hired Harry Bennett as an enforcer when the union tried to organize more than 60 years before, resulting in a bloody battle at the Rouge in 1937, but by June 1941, Ford and Bennett had successfully negotiated with the union, and the Ford family had recognized its importance ever since. Henry Ford II, in fact, was noted for his sensitivity toward labor, and delivered a rousing speech in 1946 on "human engineering" that urged the auto industry to stop its efforts to "break the unions." Bill Ford's father also conveyed the importance of the company's relationship with the organization that represented its hourly workers at an early age and got his son on Ford's 1982 labor team. As chairman in 1999, Ford showed a compassionate side himself. He did not like the sometimes prevailing "us versus them" approach and wore the UAW's "Bargaining for Families" button while negotiations progressed.

When Laymon sat before him suggesting that Ford Motor Company was not putting its best foot forward in labor relations, Ford listened. He recognized that Laymon, with previous negotiations experience at Xerox and Kodak, had a valid point, and urged him to meet with key UAW figures to determine the pulse for a possible team change. The first person Laymon went to see was Gettelfinger, who had been elected to the organization's top post in 2000.

"He listened," Laymon says. "He had plenty of opportunity to voice objection but did not. I knew it was time to make a change."

Time was pressing and Laymon did not want Ford Motor Company to be at a bargaining disadvantage due to the late lineup switch. He quickly assembled a new team, charging them with labor policy and negotiations covering Ford's 90,000 hourly employees. The move was made public on February 13, 2003. Ford's new chief of labor relations was 57-year-old Dennis Cirbes, who promised to focus on a better understanding of the problems before going to the solution. Cirbes, who had played college football at Purdue and served a year in Vietnam, was joined on the team by vice president of manufacturing Roman Krygier, with final input from Bill Ford.

"It was the first time in my career," Laymon says, "that I asked for a neighbor's property. It was something I felt I had to do. Bill Ford was courageous enough to say, 'I agree with you.'"

With less than five months remaining before formal talks would begin, speculation increased about which automaker Gettelfinger and the UAW would choose to lead negotiations with. Still plagued by problems during a restructuring effort, Ford Motor Company was seen as an unlikely choice. Gettelfinger also was not likely to choose his former employer during his first negotiations as UAW president. Chrysler was in a weakened state as well, and negotiating with that company would mean navigating through its German Daimler-Chrysler leadership. All that remained was General Motors. Seen as the strongest of the three at the time financially, GM was fighting to keep U.S. operations running at near capacity by leading a national charge in the incentives war.

Recognizing that tradition was not nearly as important as protecting members and UAW jobs, Gettelfinger crafted a groundbreaking strategy: to negotiate simultaneously with all three automakers. The plan was to talk with all three at the same time, keeping each informed of progress and problems along the way. Gettelfinger hoped the UAW would find strength in numbers rather than weakness in isolation with a less-than-strong lead company. The move was also, in many ways, a show of unity by the union with American automakers during increasing presence in the United States by foreign automakers building nonunion plants. All three companies were on equal footing, including Ford.

"It was clearly," says Cirbes, "a breakthrough strategy for the UAW, and for us it was not a bad strategy."

The UAW strategy demonstrated that its leadership believed their competition was the "transplants"—the Asian and European auto companies that were building cars and trucks in nonunion American facilities.

"That's fine with us," Cirbes says, "because that is our competition too. I think their process of stating who the competition is was important, because it was not a case of the UAW playing GM off against Ford, or Ford off against DaimlerChrysler."

By working with all three automakers at once, UAW team members obtained input from Ford labor leaders who otherwise likely would have been shut out of the process under the old lead company scenario.

"To Ron's credit," Laymon says, "he chose a model that allowed us input and almost put us at a competitive advantage because we had a team in place that was trusted and respected by the union."

———

Ford executives take great pride in their key UAW relationships, focusing on the positive elements that since the early 1980s have been more mutually beneficial. "It is not exactly a friendship," Dennis Cirbes says, "and it is not a true partnership. It starts with having mutual respect of each other and each other's needs. We can't have success without each other.

"When times are tough," he adds, "the union is willing to step up and do what they can to help, and in return they hope their members will get the benefits of the ultimate success of the company."

The media was thrown off by the unusual UAW approach of working with all three U.S. automakers at once since no announcements of the change had been made. Experienced labor writers in Detroit are accustomed to focusing on the talks at one company at a time. In past bargaining years, the media literally camped out at one company's headquarters, working their sources and awaiting news of a settlement or a breakdown in talks. Once a settlement was announced, they pulled up stakes and followed the UAW to the next company. Not so in 2003. With no named lead, media had nowhere to go, literally.

As a result, speculations continued into early September as to which company would be chosen as the lead, while Gettelfinger and associates worked behind the scenes with all three companies at once. The process was difficult at first, Cirbes says, and many were skeptical it would work, until the pieces began effectively coming together. On Ford's side of the negotiations, Cirbes and Krygier worked closely with Laymon, while the three of them kept Bill Ford informed along the way. Ultimately, they received much-needed attention from the UAW because of their desires to more effectively align Ford Motor Company's manufacturing capacity with customer demand; to realign employee guidelines at Visteon (its biggest parts supplier, made up of former Ford component plants employing workers grandfathered with Ford benefits); and to control health care cost increases.

"It was a different role for Bill," Cirbes says, "than he had in the 1999 negotiations because [as CEO] he was in a different job. But it was a tremendous benefit having him because the union membership is very pleased to see a Ford family member running the company."

By the end of September, final touches were made to agreements between Ford Motor Company and the UAW that were viewed in many circles as positive to both. The new deal gave Ford and its domestic rivals relief in the battle against foreign automakers by allowing the closing of plants and enough job cuts to close a gap in productivity.

Highlights of the 2003 UAW-Ford contract include the following provisions:

- Closing Cleveland (Ohio) Aluminum Casting, Vulcan Forge (Dearborn), and Edison (N.J.) Assembly by the end of the year, while merging Lorain (Ohio) Assembly with Ohio Assembly Plant within four years and reducing St. Louis Assembly to one shift of production in 2004.

- A $3,000 cash payment in 2003 and a cash payment in 2004 equivalent to 3 percent of an employee's wages.

- A 2 percent general wage increase in 2005 and a 3 percent general wage increase in 2006.

- A change in the cost of living allowance formula to exclude the cost of medical inflation from consumer price index calculations.

- Two $1,000 vouchers for retirees—one during the first year and one during the third year of the four-year contract—to be used toward the purchase of a new Ford, Lincoln, or Mercury vehicle, and annual cash payments of $800 for current retirees.

- The 20,000 UAW-represented Ford employees working in U.S. Visteon plants will have the opportunity to transfer to Ford plants as openings arise.

- Visteon has the ability to negotiate in the near term competitive wages and benefits for new hires.

"We were in a difficult environment," Bill Ford said. "Ron Gettelfinger was trying to manage all three companies at once during concurrent negotiations, and so there were a lot of things that went into this that made all of us wonder if we could pull this off. We wondered if it could be the kind of contract that was truly good for both sides, and I think the answer to that is yes.

"They know where we've screwed up the company, and they know where they can help."

The agreement gave Ford Motor Company the ability to reduce manufacturing capacity by one million units and more freely transfer workers among plants with close proximity to each other. And while Gettelfinger and the UAW allowed Ford to close plants and move workers in the interest of leveling the playing field with transplant companies, cash payments and benefits for members were secured in return.

"It will enable Ford to restructure," Padilla said of the agreement. "It was a balanced settlement with enough positives for everybody. Ron and Gerald Bantom showed a lot of leadership."

Bill Ford might be a millionaire by birth, but he is frugal by nature, particularly when it comes to the line items on Ford Motor Company's budget.

"He hates waste," Laymon says.

As the automaker progressed in the early months of its second century of business, Ford continued to look deeper into the company for areas to cut costs without jeopardizing product development or quality. He considered the amount of money Ford was spending on internal fleet cars—vehicles driven for free by employees, suppliers, even journalists—and ordered reductions. Ford even looked at the amount of money spent by employees and divisional departments on magazine and newspaper subscriptions. He pays for his own subscriptions and suggested that too many others inside the company were duplicated.

"You can't," he says, "cost cut your way to prosperity forever. But a company of this size will always have some inefficiency by definition, so we have to work hard every day to get those out."

With his high-profile cycle of the company's centennial over and the end of television commercials featuring him, Bill Ford stepped out of the limelight for a time and worked to keep executives and employees focusing on back-to-basics efforts, including the cost cutting and product development.

"This company," he says, "has a history of not doing well when it loses focus."

The company's increasing stability, however, allowed Bill Ford to step up his efforts behind the scenes in determining how Ford Motor Company could lead the world into its second century in the transportation revolution. He had a vision when he took over as chairman in 1999 that the automaker would make a difference in the world as the leading provider of 21st century transportation solutions. But in his first 18 months on the job as CEO, he had to spend most of his time undoing the damage of failed big plans. Ford says his ultimate mission, though, never changed. He wanted Ford Motor Company to consistently deliver the basics of good business so that when the automaker evolved in its new century of business with innovation, the ride would be smooth and less frenetic and disrupting than previous attempts at change.

"Great products," he says, "are just a start. They get you into the game. But they are not good enough to keep you there. It takes some corporate responsibility, building a better world."

The new Rouge, with its living roof and environment friendly design, was less than a year away from opening, and the Escape Hybrid, the world's first mass-produced hybrid-electric SUV, was on the way—tangible signs that Ford Motor Company was making progress toward fulfilling the vision of its chairman and CEO. But Bill Ford's grand vision still called for so much more—specifically, how Ford Motor Company could set the pace for transportation leadership in its second century of business just as it had during its first. The idea was not to look for ways to recklessly spend stockpiled

cash—which totaled more than $30 billion in late 2003—
like Nasser did in 1999, but to look to areas that aligned with
his mission of building great, groundbreaking products that
contribute ultimately to a better world.

Ford considered buying Segway, the maker of the electric
personal transport scooters, but decided against it because "it
was not right for us." He continued to keep his eyes open for
glimpses of transportation future, studying all forms, including rail and air. But he was not looking to make acquisitions
for the simple benefit of short-term value on Wall Street.

"He will never," Laymon says, "piss that money away because of what [he and the company] went through before."

To help facilitate this long-term vision, Ford appointed
then-CFO Allan Gilmour to head a group of Ford Motor
Company's brightest strategists. He charged the committee
with working behind the scenes of daily operations to review
all company global activities, seeking information useful in
forming long-term vision to guide the company beyond the
end of its revitalization plan, scheduled to conclude in 2007.

Said Ford: "It's taking a critical look at us today and then
anticipating where the world's going to be in 10 or 20 years,
and asking, 'Are we aligned to get there?'"

Beyond the committee led by Gilmour, Ford continued to
spend quiet time outside the office contemplating the future
of the company and the future of transportation, reminiscent
of others in his genealogical and corporate history—Henry
Ford and Henry Ford II.

————————

For Bill Ford, the office is a place for work, but never-ending
details and demands make it a difficult place for individual vi-
sioning. So he tries to find time in an office at home, or while
working out or going for a run in the Ann Arbor suburbs, to
think about the future of Ford Motor Company and the future
of global transportation. In return, he brings elements of

home to the office to balance his busy life and keep his wife and children within constant reach.

On one particular day, a familiar visitor stops by Ford's office five minutes early for a scheduled Thursday afternoon appointment and finds the CEO on the telephone in the office of his executive assistant, Ann. He is talking with his wife, Lisa, about a busy slate of upcoming family events. Ford hangs up the phone and welcomes his guest into his 12th floor corner office at Ford Motor Company's World Headquarters. Ann, he says, keeps all of his children's events on a master calendar, including teacher conferences and sporting events. Ford talks about his oldest daughter, in her senior year at private school in Ann Arbor. She's a three-sport athlete, looking at colleges. She is considering Princeton, his alma mater, and wants to play a sport there. He cannot hide his excitement at the prospect.

The standard public relations line at Ford Motor Company to interviewing journalists is that the boss protects his family and will not talk specifically about them. Yet with this interviewer, Ford always speaks eagerly about them like any proud father. When someone mentions a Michigan scholar-athlete award won by his daughter, Ford looks around for a newspaper clipping.

The upcoming weekend will be busy, he says, with multiple children's sporting events and accompanying parental duties. Ford family activities will start at 4 A.M. on Saturday when he rises early to help set up chairs for his younger daughter's cross-country event. Later that morning, one of his sons has a hockey game. Later in the day, he will head to the soccer fields to watch his daughter play. Topping the weekend off, the Lions play at home on Sunday and Bill Ford, of course, will be there, too—family in tow.

"I took my son to the [Detroit Red Wings] hockey game last night," he says. "It was fun, but it was hard to watch the game. There are so many people connected to Ford that sit by me, I spend most of the time talking."

As Ford talks, the large glass windows behind him reveal a

sweeping view of the land developed by his great-grandfather. Rising in the distance most prominently above the flat river low country is the 600-acre, recently modernized Rouge complex. Anchoring Ford's office is a massive, burled maple desk once owned and used by his grandfather, Edsel Ford. There is an acoustic guitar in the corner—Ford plays folk music—and tropical fish swim in a tank above rows of family pictures. The office furniture is made of wood from sustainable forests and upholstered in biodegradable material, and plants are everywhere, including potted flowers in bloom. Wall coverings are made of hemp. Perched on a counter along a wall is an espresso machine, which Ford uses himself, making and drinking one to two each morning.

"I don't usually drink one in the afternoon," he says, "unless it's been a really long day."

On a shelf in Ford's office is a picture of the day he got his black belt in Tae Kwon Do, chopping six wooden blocks in half with a bare hand. The picture was taken by Dan Murray, the company photographer and his former instructor. Another picture is a framed newspaper clipping of a story that ran the day after he took the job as Ford Motor Company's CEO. It shows a smiling, young-faced man. Two years later, at 45, Ford still looks youthful, but a quick glimpse reveals changes that have occurred since he took charge of the company. Ford's cheeks and brow are more emphatically lined, evidence of battle. No more frequent fly-fishing expeditions to exotic parts of the world, and no more scurrying around Richmond, Virginia, searching for still-standing treasures and landmarks of the Civil War. For the moment, his life comes down to his family's happiness and the success of Ford Motor Company.

"That does not leave room for much else," he says.

Outside of his immediate family, Ford stays in close contact with his parents, siblings, and cousins, as well. His father and Edsel Ford are actively involved in Ford Motor Company affairs as two of the automaker's most influential directors. They both maintain offices at the company and are known to work together when sharing concerns within the company as board members. It is not unusual, in fact, to see them walking the halls together on the 12th floor of Ford's World Headquarters.

"I hope," says Joe Laymon, "we don't ever walk away from being a family company. Instead, we say we are [a family company] and are damn proud of it. The legacy of this family and this company is too rich. This is something we can build on."

When it comes to running the company, Bill Ford Sr. gives his son full-fledged support, offering advice only when solicited. As for his mother, she is the only person known to still call him by his childhood name, Billy, on a regular basis. Like any good mother, she worries about the pressures her son faces in a demanding job, having witnessed firsthand (with the Firestones and the Fords) the toll such responsibility can take on a person.

As fall 2003 eased across Lower Michigan and hundreds of acres of sunflowers around World Headquarters beamed in full maturity, Ford Motor Company appeared to be largely through its most significant problems and well prepared for the onset of the frigid season, so harsh the year before. The closely watched UAW contract had been wrapped up effectively, and the F-150 continued selling at a record pace, following the best product launch in the automaker's history. But when a company the size of Ford has problems like it did from 1999 to 2001, the time it takes for others to recognize the swing of the pendulum and improving indicators can take what seems like forever.

"There is a lag factor out there," Ford says, "between how you are doing and what the perception of you out there is."

Such was the case in October 2003 when most internal signals were moving in a positive direction at Ford Motor Company. Dealers were coming back on board, enthused by the promise of oncoming product. Consumer purchase considerations numbers were improving as Ford Motor Company's cor-

porate image shot up the charts following its centennial celebration. Most employees were behind the company again,
finding strength in stability and in a singular focus on building and selling cars and trucks; and profitability was slowly
but surely returning.

Some external opinions, however, were drastically different. A book written by *New York Times* journalist Micheline
Maynard was published, suggesting a rather bleak future for
the American auto industry. Her book, *The End of Detroit*,
stated essentially that Ford Motor Company and its Detroit
counterparts lacked humility and were unable to react fast
enough to global market changes to fend off foreign automakers, including Toyota and Nissan. Stacks of the black-covered
books sat in large piles in Dearborn bookstores, effectively
pronouncing the death of America's last industrial strong-
hold, auto manufacturing. Never mind that Ford Motor Company owned a controlling share of Japanese up-and-comer
Mazda and played a vital, direct role in that company's new de-
ployment of product, including the Mazda 6 and the Mazda 3.
And never mind that Japanese companies had full access to
sell cars in the United States while American companies still
faced significant barriers in selling cars in Japan, thus tilting
the scales. The book still hit right at the heart of Dearborn.

"When I read about books coming out talking about the
death of Detroit and the end of the domestic auto industry,"
Bill Ford says, "part of it makes me madder than hell and part
of it makes me smile.

"I remember when David Halberstam wrote that book
called *The Reckoning* [chronicling the demise of Ford and the
simultaneous rise of Nissan], and it was back right at the time
we had begun a spectacular turnaround [while Nissan had begun to stumble] and his timing could not have been worse. So,
right about the time people start writing these stories is about
the time that we start to show them that they are wrong.

"We are better than we are being given credit for right
now," Ford says. "But then, I force myself to step back and say,

you know, back when we were getting into trouble, the world did not realize it either."

At almost the same time, credit watch agency Standard and Poor's announced that it was considering a downgrade of Ford Motor Company's credit rating. Weeks later it delivered the widely anticipated downgrade to "BBB" level—just above junk-bond status. S&P cited poor cash flow and profitability, and expectations of only limited improvement over the next few years, as its reasons for hammering Ford's credit rating. Even though S&P also issued a stable outlook on Ford, calming concerns of many investors, the news was generally not good.

"This company," said Carl Reichardt, "has a large, unfunded pension plan, which is a heck of a big problem. But to go back to 1981, our cash position was not good. Cash is king and this time sales have remained strong. But rating agencies aside, a lot of folks look at us and take solace from our cash position."

Led by Bill Ford, company executives strongly opposed the S&P move, citing an improved 2003 earnings outlook, reduced costs, plans to introduce 40 new products in the next year, and "exceptionally strong liquidity." Still, the continuing weak prognosis for the North American auto market, as price wars and the slumbering economy ebb on, caused S&P enough concern to deliver Ford Motor Company another frustrating blow.

"Not only do I not understand it," Ford said, "I don't think it is right. If you look at our liquidity today, it is almost staggering. Between the credit, the parent company, and our credit lines, we have almost $80 billion in liquidity, so our ability to pay our bills is unlike any corporation in America. Given the fact that we are on a roll . . . I don't get it."

A Town
Hall Meeting

W hen Bill Ford has a message to deliver to the people of Ford Motor Company, he does not hesitate
to stand before them. In the tradition of Henry
Ford and Henry Ford II, he is not a renowned orator when it
comes to the word-for-word, meticulously crafted and prepared speech. But when it comes to talking casually and hon-
estly in front of employees, Ford has an ability to connect
with the audience and effectively communicate the matters
at hand, and he is not afraid to play to this strength. He
prowls the stage, blending passionate pleas with an Ivy
League intellect and neighborly smile. He gets that twinkle
in his eye, suggesting, "We're in this together." People sit up
and listen.

When Ford conducts a town hall–style meeting with employees, he uses a prepared outline as a guide, but he speaks
freely about issues facing the company, even accepting unfil-
tered questions from the audience. In late October 2003, from
the same stage in the auditorium at World Headquarters
where exactly two years before he announced he was taking
over as CEO from the departing Jac Nasser, Bill Ford took almost an hour to talk with employees about his first two years

on the job, while also seeking to reassure them that despite some negative media reports, Ford Motor Company was not broke, near its death, or in demise.

A capacity crowd filled the auditorium while he walked and talked, flanked by a preproduction model of the 2005 Mustang and the company's new Freestar minivan. Times were still tough, he said. Frankly, he was not sure when they would ever cease being tough in the hypercompetitive 21st century global auto industry. But Ford Motor Company had made meaningful progress in two short years and was now on much firmer footing, contrary to the opinions of some outsiders.

"When I took over," Ford said, "I felt like I was holding up a collapsing building with an umbrella. Everywhere I looked there was trouble. Nothing seemed firm, nothing seemed set. It became clear to me that we had to fix our base business, refocus this company on the car and truck business, and get out of the stuff that was distracting us and was not adding much to the bottom line."

In two years, he said, Ford Motor Company had stabilized financially, restored its financing division, invigorated its product lineup, and was once again looking for growth opportunities. He hailed the conclusion of the new, four-year UAW contract, which gave the company needed leeway to better align manufacturing capacity with demand, and talked about the importance of the successful F-150 launch, as well as a recent trip to Asia, where he worked to position Ford Motor Company for growth in key emerging auto markets.

"I met President [Gloria Macapagal] Arroyo of the Philippines and Prime Minister Thaksin [Shinawatra] in Thailand," Ford said. "It is clear that both of them value the Ford presence incredibly.

"In China, it is impossible to describe how fast that country is modernizing. We got a late start but are catching up well. We are taking production from about 20,000 vehicles up to

150,000 vehicles and will probably have to go beyond that relatively soon."

Specifically, Ford was referring to the company's plans to invest more than $1 billion in building a new plant in China, the world's fastest growing auto market. Ford Motor Company was behind some competitors like General Motors and Volkswagen in establishing a strong manufacturing network in the rapidly developing country. Its only plant was in the remote city of Chongqing, and general industry speculation was that Ford would fuel its China expansion from there. But, by working closely with the government, the company was now building a second, more modern car plant in eastern China, near Shanghai, to serve the booming area around the country's vital commercial hub. As a result, the automaker may have ultimately positioned itself better than others.

"We were late," Ford said, "but sometimes you do luck into things."

Located in Nanjing and in partnership with Changan Automobile Company, the new plant would be in an area that more easily accesses the country's bustling eastern provinces, resulting in a better employee pool and more efficient delivery to masses of more affluent buyers.

"Going back to my great-grandfather," Ford said, "we've always believed that we need to build cars and trucks where we sell them. It is growth for Asia, not taking away from this market or Europe."

Closer to home, Ford praised the efforts of fellow executives and employees for delivering seven consecutive quarters of financial performances that beat Wall Street estimates, helping Ford Motor Company turn the corner in two years "the old-fashioned way, through hard work and determination."

"We keep knocking our naysayers down for a loop," he said. "Credibility was one thing we sorely lacked when we came in, and there is nothing that will build credibility like beating what you say you are going to do."

_____

The company, Ford told employees, had proven it could success-fully launch new products in North America, beginning with the new 2003 model Ford Expedition and Lincoln Navigator re-leases in 2002 and continuing through the F-150 in 2003.

"We were told," Ford said, "by the outsiders—in fact, it was largely true—that we did not know how to launch product anymore. When we launched the Expedition-Navigator, it was really the first big product launch that this management team had had. We were all crossing our fingers and toes and everything else we could cross, hoping it would go well, and it did. Then the subsequent launches went well, and that was a huge stake in the ground for the credibility of this company and our collective confidence as a management team that we could pull this off, and we did it."

Ford said external statistics gauging quality for Ford North America were on the rise, increasing by more than 16 percent in two years, while capacity was being reduced through plant closing. Additionally, he said, $2 billion in nonproduction costs had been eliminated in 2002 and $3 billion in automo-tive costs were eliminated in 2003.

"The biggest travesty that happened," Ford said, "was that we went from the eighties and nineties being a quality leader and a company that was really driving hard on quality, to a company that had lost the plot rather quickly in quality. It is easy to lose and tough to get back, but get it back we have."

Globally, Ford said the company had divested many non-core operations, including most of its ownership from 1999 and 2000 acquisitions such as Kwik-Fit and Greanleaf, adding $1 billion in cash to coffers, but, more important, getting rid of daily distractions. "Our ability to manage them was ques-tionable at best, and they were not adding really anything to our bottom line, and they were a huge distraction," Ford said.

Most important, profits were returning. The company that had lost $2 billion in 2001 (not counting significant one-time charges and write-offs) was projecting a profit of $3 billion in 2003 behind the strength of drastically improved Ford Credit operations. Ford Motor Company also had improved its cash position by more than $9 billion (totaling more than $26 billion) over two years, Ford said.

"I don't want it to be a cushion," he said, "or an excuse for anyone to spend more money needlessly or take their eye off the cost issue, but it is a good thing to have because it gives us the financial flexibility to chart our own future. We have the cash to do anything and everything we have to do to make us successful. Unlike the early 1980s, when we were struggling as a company and facing a number of issues, at that time we were also out of money. It is very different this time around, because we have the cash."

Problems, however, continued after two years, Ford said. European operations were still struggling, domestic market share pressure kept increasing, incentives continued at historic levels, and the competition was only getting stronger.

"There are no safe havens anymore for our products," he said. "We can't just retreat to the SUV and truck market and call it a day. We've got to be profitable in every single segment we play in, and we have to have a growth plan in every single segment we play in, and we are up against some tough players. But guess what? We are just as good as they are and in many cases we are better. We've just got to get our act together and go after them.

"Where does all of this put us now?" Ford asked. "I'd say we went from about bottom of the barrel to about middle of the pack. But is that good enough? No. I did not join this company to be average. We aspire to be great, because that is our heritage. It is going to be a tough road. I think next year is going to be another tough one. And frankly, I don't know when it ever ceases to be tough. But I like our chances, because we have always proved we can do it.

"'Built Ford Tough,'" he says, "isn't just a slogan. We're at our best as a company when our back is to the wall. We're at our best when we have to be scrappy innovators and be fighters, and that is the environment we are in. We've come a long way in two years and have some breathing room and a little bit of confidence, but the times when we sort of let go of that equation are when we are fat, dumb, and happy. Our company is at its best when we've got to show the world we really are a great company."

———————

At the end of his talk, Ford answered questions from the floor about such concerns as what Ford Motor Company planned to do about its lack of an entry-level product below the Focus in North America, and its ongoing struggle to find more commonality and reuse among vehicle programs worldwide.

He walked to the floor to shake hands, answer more questions, and mingle with employees. A crowd of dozens of employees quickly circled around him. A woman extended her hand. Ford accepted it, smiling.

"I'm a Lions season ticket holder," she said.

"Great!"

"Is [Lions coach Steve] Mariucci pleased with [quarterback] Joey Harrington?"

"No," Ford said, "and yes. I mean, he is not pleased with all of the results, but he's pleased with the progress he is making. With a young, talented quarterback, he knows there is a learning process."

———————

The Lions, like Ford Motor Company, were in a rebuilding mode, with a new coach, a new downtown stadium, a new quarterback, and a renewed commitment by the team's ownership to deliver a winner for the Motor City. Football fans throughout southeast Michigan, including many Ford employees, were starving for a winner and looking for Bill Ford to deliver one.

The Lions went to the NFL playoffs six times in the 1990s, including a trip to the NFC championship game in 1991, but had been among the NFL's worst teams since 2001. It was apparent three-fourths of the way through Mariucci's first season as Lions head coach that the team wouldn't be making the playoffs, but the roster of young, developing stars was showing promise. There were back-to-back home wins and a 22–14 stunner over Green Bay in the annual Thanksgiving Day game, the tradition preserved for Detroit at Ford's behest. So excited was Ford after the holiday win that days later, when meeting for a roundtable discussion with a dozen or so of the top automotive journalists in the world, he could not resist bringing it up first.

"I suppose," he said, smiling as he walked into the room, "you all want me to talk about the Lions game."

Ford works to separate his interest in the Lions from his duties as chairman and CEO of Ford Motor Company, but privately talks almost daily to team general manager Matt Millen and has a youthful enjoyment of the team. But he plays to win in everything he does—whether on the ice playing hockey as a teenager, sparring in martial arts matches as an adult, at work in the auto business, or in football. Out of the public eye and away from the extended hand of a fan, he can be demanding.

"Bill Ford," says Joe Laymon, "is a very, very smart and intelligent man. But there is a part of this man that, unless you get close to him, you don't see that fierce competitiveness, because of his humility.

"He wants to win, period."

————————

As winter set in, the acres of sunflowers surrounding Ford's World Headquarters in Dearborn had long been drained of color from the season's first heavy frost in Lower Michigan, but there was a different feeling inside the building than there had been the previous two years, when dreary days magnified a bleak picture. Two years before, North American auto operations were "hemorrhaging red ink." Just one year before, Ford Motor Company lost $130 million in the fourth quarter alone.

On the second day of December 2003, the temperature was in the low 30s and the wind was whipping at more than 20 miles per hour, but the sunshine was almost abnormally bright and had been for almost a week. It glistened off the first few floors of the Glass House with a vengeance, reflecting the mood inside. The uncontrolled losses of the prior two years had stopped, and profits were foreseeable in the short-term future due to a product pipeline that was beginning to flow with the F-150 and the new Ford Freestar and Mercury Monterey minivans.

At the annual Ford Motor Company media Christmas party, held this time at the Ford Community and Performing Arts Center, which sits less than a quarter mile down Michigan Avenue from Ford Motor Company World Headquarters, executives were upbeat, relieved to finally be talking about plans for the future instead of solutions for the past.

"I think we are all feeling pretty good," Nick Scheele said.

Bill Ford attended, but did not give remarks like he did in his first year as chairman and CEO. This was his third Christmas on the job and he was learning what works best. He likes to move and be social, not standing still as a target for a mob of media to circle around, whipping out notebooks and pigeonholing him for quotes. Lee Iacocca liked a crowd. Jac Nasser loved a crowd. GM's Bob Lutz loves a crowd. Bill Ford prefers one-on-one interchanges repeated a hundred times as opposed to once, one-hundred on one.

"He likes this to be a time to visit with [media] in a friendly environment," a Ford manager said. "He's not comfortable drawing all the attention at a party away from everyone else."

One moment he was talking in a corner about fly-fishing, telling about how his wife unknowingly let the line and fly float between her legs while wading in the water the first time he took her along, but still managed to catch a fish. The next, he was breaking toward a familiar face. Mark Truby was running late for the party, having been stuck at the office, meeting a deadline. The former Ford beat reporter for the *Detroit News* who had covered the company during its fall from grace and return from near disaster, Truby had been promoted to business editor of the newspaper, leaving what was the juiciest gig in town for breaking stories just as the company began to settle down and drop from the negative headlines. In journalism circles, it's called graduating with your source. Ford saw Truby and immediately gravitated toward him, slapping him across the arm and delivering a broad smile.

"Hey, man," he said. "I hear you've become a businessman now. That's great."

Two days later Jim O'Connor, the tireless leader of Ford's North American sales and marketing division, was in the office early, despite returning late the night before from Texas, where the new F-150 had won Truck of the Year honors from the Texas Auto Writers Association. He had attended a dinner to accept the award. It ran late and there were organizational issues, but he humbly stayed until the end, pleased that journalists in the most important state to America's best-selling vehicle recognized a good thing. It's the way O'Connor approaches the job every day. In 2002 alone, the 40-year company veteran went to 178 dinners across North America and was well on his way to eclipsing that in 2003. When traveling, O'Connor frequently stops unexpectedly in local dealerships as a show of support, dispelling the widespread notion that all Detroit auto executives suffer from debilitating ego.

"We've made progress, but are not yet where we want to be," says O'Connor. "It takes time to rebuild. You just have to start bringing them back in and hugging them again."

The efforts were paying off. Internal surveys ranking dealer satisfaction had climbed steadily over two years, and retailers were beginning to enjoy the benefits of new product as the

F-150 sold at a record pace. Dialogue was back in play and opinions from the field were given renewed voice.

Just like Ford Motor Company's improvement in an array of other internal problems that had magnified during the tumultuous years of 1999–2000, dealer relations on the mend showed the automaker was on steadying ground. Problems at a company the size of Ford will never entirely go away, of course. There will always be issues, but the problems facing the company after two years of leadership from Bill Ford and his management team had changed in scope. Now, instead of mostly having to put out fires at World Headquarters and elsewhere within the organization, Bill Ford was focusing on such external forces harming the company as the national health care crisis. With Ford Motor Company's total obligations for health care and life insurance for employees and retirees exceeding $30 billion and steadily on the rise, he determined the company could not afford to wait for solutions too slow in coming.

"We need a new model," Ford said. "The system does not seem to be working very well."

He asked confidant and Ford vice chairman Allan Gilmour to write a proposal for fixing America's health care problems. Ford said America's unsolved health care issue was "driving investment decisions away from the United States, and that's wrong." For every vehicle it built, Ford Motor Company spent $1,200 on employee and retiree health costs, while manufacturing companies in countries that have government-funded medical care spent almost none, making it much more attractive to expand operations outside of the United States.

"I just think that as a country," he said, "if we have a model that isn't working and a model that is driving jobs overseas, then we'd better take another look at it."

In the time between Gilmour's retirement from Ford Motor Company in 1996 and his return in 2002 at Bill Ford's request, he served as chairman of the Henry Ford Health System's board of directors, leading cost-cutting reform. Ford believed Gilmour would be the right person to draft an initiative that could lead to change if it gained grassroots support from other corporations, perhaps even automakers, before going to Washington to seek formalization.

"I've asked Allan to involve others in the [auto] industry when the time is right," Ford said. "He's uniquely positioned to do that because he knows the issue very well. He's seen it from both sides. Plus, he's got great external credibility so when it's time for him to interact with Washington, Allan will do so with authority."

The broader issues like the national health care crisis plaguing Ford Motor Company are larger and arguably much more difficult than the dozens of nagging internal nuances inherited by Bill Ford when he took over as CEO. But they are more in line with what he set out to accomplish when he first took over as chairman of the company in 1999: using big business as a driving force for leading visionary change in the United States and, ultimately, throughout the world. While they may be more imposing, such issues make his motor run, and as his third year as chairman and CEO began to hit full stride, the new lines carved on his face during two years of sometimes agonizing stress were increasingly loosening into smiles and optimism. Wheels were turning again as Bill Ford the CEO moved from constantly putting out the fires of the moment toward seeking future solutions, backed by knowledge gained from the most painful battles held on hallowed grounds.

"It is better," says Laymon, "that he experienced these things early in his leadership of the company than 8 to 10 years down the road."

The Year of the Car

Anyone thinking Bill Ford lives the good life as heir, CEO, and part-owner of a pro football team to tinker with in his spare time, need only meet J Mays, Ford Motor Company's group vice president for design. A native of Maysville, Oklahoma, Mays has emerged as a celebrity in this dawning age of design, where the automobile is the center-piece of increasing consumer taste for fashion reflecting passion. One minute he's driving around the Napa Valley with Apple and Pixar founder Steve Jobs, listening to music and sipping fine wine with the top down; the next, he's addressing the art world on car design at the Smithsonian Institution in Washington.

So respected is Mays in art circles that he is the first American car designer to have a museum exhibition devoted exclusively to his work—at the Museum of Contemporary Art in Los Angeles, no less. "Retrofuturism: The Car Design of J Mays" was the show organized by museum curator of architecture and design Brooke Hodge. It ran from November 2002 to March 2003, featuring designs Mays led at Audi-Volkswagen, BMW, and Ford Motor Company, drawing inspiration from fashion, architecture, and industrial design.

"It's a pretty bloody exciting business," Mays says.

The 49-year-old design executive enrolled in a drafting program in high school because he wanted to become an architect. But after graduating from Maysville High School in 1972, Mays studied art, then journalism at the University of Oklahoma, before announcing to his parents that he really wanted to be a car designer. He then enrolled at the Art Center College of Design in Pasadena, California, one of the nation's top auto design colleges. He graduated in 1980 and went to work for Volkswagen and Audi in Munich, Germany, easily adapting to and even thriving in the European environment. Mays remained abroad for nine years, ultimately working for BMW on such projects as exterior design proposals for the popular BMW 5 and 8 series. By the time he returned to the United States in 1989 as chief designer of Volkswagen of America's Design Center in Simi Valley, California, the man from Oklahoma was viewed by colleagues as more European than American.

At Volkswagen he was responsible for design and branding of the Volkswagen Concept 1, which ultimately became the popular New Beetle. Mays not only led development of the car, but also pushed the German company to gamble on the remake of its iconic original Beetle. It paid off, reviving Volkswagen's sagging U.S. presence and launching Mays as a star on the rise in an industry hungry for American identity.

When he joined Ford in 1997 after being recruited by Nasser, Mays went to work on the remake of the Thunderbird, which drew industry raves at the 1999 Detroit auto show, and also developed such radical concepts as the Ma, a kit-of-parts car that is 96 percent recyclable.

"I've had the fascination," Mays says, "for 10 years in trying to tell stories with sheet metal. For three days Steve [Jobs] and I drove around . . . talking about the similarities between movies and autos. If there is no story, there is not a movie. The same is true in my work. If there is no story, there is no automobile. We do this by bending sheet metal to tell a story that consumers can relate to."

After Bill Ford took over as CEO and charged the company with a product-led revival, Mays' responsibility and importance at the company increased significantly. He was promoted to group vice president, overseeing design at Ford and Lincoln-Mercury as well as Aston Martin, Jaguar, Land Rover, and Volvo, and maintains such a high profile at the company that he often appears at media functions as the front man.

"J is a pretty important guy around here these days," says one Ford manager.

Although tooling around in sports cars on the weekend or speaking at the Smithsonian may be perks of his past success, Mays has the weight of one of the world's largest companies on his shoulders: The future of Ford Motor Company depends on having dozens of completely new or radically changed products in the pipeline. The automaker can only rely on cost savings and better incentive management for so long. Bill Ford pushed the company to heavily invest in product development at the same time it was cutting other costs, committing to longer-term rebuilding through car and truck revival. As the company continued to make remarkable progress in its revitalization efforts in the early stages of his third year on the job, it was becoming increasingly clear that for sales to grow, thus increasing revenues, more head turners like the all-new F-150 are needed.

"Everybody here," Mays says, "feels a bit of pressure to push forward. It was nice having that misty feeling [during the centennial], but we are about to push the accelerator down."

While it used to be that the main requirements for car hits in America were reliability, horsepower, and handling, this decade quickly began to be defined as the age of design, where power and handling remain critical but the importance of superior styling is rapidly on the rise. While Bill Ford professes he is "not able to draw a straight line" and says little about time he spent in design as a modeler, he should know. His grandfather, Edsel Ford, was revered for his eye for design, as was his father. Bill Ford Sr. still maintains an office in the company's Dearborn Product Development Center, just two doors down from the office of J Mays.

Shortly after taking the job at Ford, Nasser suggested to Mays that he stop in to meet Bill Ford Sr. "I was supposed to say hello for five minutes," Mays says. "I came back 30 minutes later with season tickets to the Lions."

When Bill Ford took over as CEO, staking the company's revival on the shoulders of product, Mays asked to take Ford and his father on a joint tour of the design studio to view cars and trucks in development. The tour lasted almost three hours. Bill Ford Sr. offered few opinions at first, Mays says, but when prodded, started talking about such details as execution of lines.

"He gave incredible critique," Mays says. "I was amazed. This guy has been around this industry a long time."

For Ford Motor Company, the concept of design as a driving force is not so foreign. The automaker that introduced the affordable sports car with the Mustang later revived the U.S. car industry with the Taurus, and it was now in the midst of setting a new standard in pickup trucks by combining luxury design and power so effectively in its new F-150.

"The design studio is the most exciting part of this business," Bill Ford says. "Product design is also becoming the differentiator."

But when you are in the business of delivering home runs, the perfect execution of design becomes a very fine line, creating the ultimate challenge. Reeling off edgy concept cars is not so hard for Mays and other talented designers. Finding the balance between breathtaking style and vehicles that will sell in mass quantity is the secret, and the pressure point, for Mays and company. He drives a Jag and a Land Rover but understands that many Americans want and need midsize sedans and family minivans.

"When I was at Audi," Mays says, "it was an elitist brand. Now I'm at a populist brand. The difference is like the difference in Fellini and Spielberg. We do blockbusters here."

That's exactly what Ford Motor Company delivered on its new F-150, and the effort was paying off nicely at the end of 2003. The automaker was selling record numbers of the truck and its popularity among customers and journalists was exceeding all expectations. But while the product's success allowed for many internal sighs of relief as the year came to an end, Ford had always been good at building and selling trucks. In recent years, as Japanese companies took aim at the American car market while domestic automakers focused on trucks and SUVs, the focus on the car had been lost to a degree in the United States, and Ford Motor Company was no exception. The Ford Taurus (ranked 8th, with 300,496 units sold) and the Ford Focus (14th, 229,353 units sold) were among the 15 top-selling vehicles in America in 2003, but the Taurus was showing its age as sales declined, and the company needed new hits, reminiscent of the 1980s when the sedan successfully fought off foreign imports.

Bill Ford, J Mays, and others inside the company knew that Ford Motor Company could not afford to sit back and concede the car market, particularly when foreign automakers were targeting profitable truck segments. The first goal at Ford was proving the company was still the leader in its hallowed ground, trucks. But as the F-150 successfully moved from launch, sights were set on reminding the world that the company that had grandfathered mass transportation by car could still generate hits 100 years later.

As 2003 came to a close, Ford Motor Company was in the final stages of planning its "Year of the Car" campaign to focus on a wave of new products launched as the backbone of the product-led revitalization. To make these Ford Division 2005 model year cars winners, Mays and Ford Motor Company were counting on the beginnings of an emerging theme based on what the automaker has always done best: combining rural toughness and functionality in product with urban desirability.

"We're in an interesting, transitional period right now," Mays says. "If you go back to Henry Ford and the Model T . . .

that was one tough vehicle. There was a direct correlation between that and the F-150 and our SUVs."

The dilemma, says Mays, was how to move this generally rural and suburban brand and theme closer to today's youth movement, which is urban in nature. The idea was to take the "Ford Tough" core philosophy in trucks and expand it into a theme that runs through cars as well, giving Ford autos in the future "a distinct point of view that is very Ford and very Detroit as well." A classic example is the original Mustang and other sporty cars of the 1960s.

"You'll end up with an urban toughness with cars," Mays says.

———

Ford Motor Company's "Year of the Car" campaign was based on five new car and crossover models scheduled to enter showrooms in 2004 (as 2005 models), as Ford dealers replaced more than 60 percent of their total volume with all-new models by the end of the year. By including all-new cars this early in its promise of delivering 65 all-new products in five years across its North American product lineup, Ford's leadership aimed to send a counterattack to its foreign competitors that had taken a big piece of this market away.

New vehicles to be launched as part of Ford's "Year of the Car" included these:

- A freshened Ford Focus. Launched first in Europe in 1998 and later in the United States in 2000, the Focus has been selected as one of *Car and Driver* magazine's 10 best cars for four consecutive years. (The 2005 model was slated to debut in April 2004.)

- Ford GT supercar, 550-horsepower, supercharged V-8 engine, with limited production and a $139,995 base price, designed for true performance car enthusiasts who relish a thoroughly modern, street-legal remake of the classic Ford GT40 race car. (July 2004)

- Ford Freestyle, an all-wheel-drive crossover vehicle that combines attributes of the SUV, sedan, and minivan. (July 2004 production)

- Ford Five Hundred, the company's new flagship sedan with SUV-type room and seating. With the largest trunk in the industry, the Five Hundred can stow a stunning eight golf bags. (July 2004)

- Mustang, a beautiful and more modern, livable, and safer version that has not lost its street swagger. The Mustang GT packs 300 horses under its hood. (September 2004)

- The 2006 Fusion, an all-new midsize sedan to be positioned between the Focus and the Five Hundred, taking inspiration and design cues from the Ford 427 concept car. (Arrival date sometime in 2005 as 2006 model)

The leader of this pack may be the remake of its all-time best-selling sports car, the Mustang, simply because of its 40-year history and vital role in American pop culture. In fact, the car is so popular in the United States that more than 250 Mustang clubs exist and annual gatherings of enthusiasts are held in 16 countries on five continents. Scheduled to launch in the fall of 2004, the all-new Mustang is the first radical redo of the product in 10 years and the best Mustang by all accounts to launch since the original hit American roads in 1964.

"This car," Mays says, "has transcended being an automobile. It is part of the good life this country is associated with. When Europeans think about what they like best about America, they think about the '64 Mustang. It's the quintessential American car. It cuts across all cultures, from blue collar to Wall Street . . . it knows no ethnicity."

Just as with his leading role in the remake of the VW Beetle and Ford's Thunderbird, Mays hoped the redesigned pony car would strike a cord with American consumers hungry for the most appealing elements of the past, updated with today's engineering and design. The product creation team used an all-new platform and "clean-sheet design approach" to the new Mustang, despite its retro appearance, which plays off the signature long hood and short rear deck and includes a sharklike nose, "imparting an attitude not seen since the 1967 model." But making the car more comfortable than its popular predecessor is a larger wheelbase (a six-inch improvement), increased interior space, and small touches like added rear windows for backseat passengers. The energized Mustang, along with the new Ford GT supercar, is intended to "create an emotional magnet that will draw people back" to the Ford brand.

"[The Mustang] has got everybody's temperature up around here," says Mays.

With full responsibility for Ford's North American operations, Jim Padilla speaks more bluntly about how the company's new pony car must deliver.

"The Mustang," he says, "is a got-to-have vehicle."

While the Mustang is based on a futuristic update of an icon, Ford's approach to its other new products was to search for the attributes that made trucks, SUVs, and crossovers so popular, integrating these qualities in an attempt to redefine the North American sedan, resulting in a purpose-built, functional car with an urban toughness. The flagship of Ford Motor Company's new car lineup and the vehicle that best displays this character is the new Ford Five Hundred, which will replace the Taurus as the retail leader among Ford's cars (the Taurus will continue as a value proposition primarily for fleet sales). It is important to Ford because, even though SUVs and trucks reign, midsize cars still account for nearly 20 percent of total industry volume (3 million vehicles), comprising the single largest segment. But while buyers migrate to sedans, many want some of the same strengths and attributes of SUVs, like more cargo space and command of the road. So Ford's production creation team wanted to put more utility into its new cars.

"We took a look at the attributes that make crossovers popular," said Phil Martens, president of product creation for Ford North America, "like high-package 'command' seating, and sought to deliver some of those qualities in a sedan. While the industry tries to create new car-based crossovers, the Ford Five Hundred stands alone as the first crossover-based car."

With all-wheel drive, the Five Hundred is based on a new, purpose-built crossover platform, resulting in its atypical dimensions for a passenger car. The sedan has the largest trunk available anywhere (as mentioned, it can hold eight full-size golf bags) to go with its big-car interior in a midsize body, and the driver and passengers sit four inches higher than in the average midsize car. Just as the Ford Explorer in 1990 and later the Expedition found success as designers placed passengers higher on the road, the goal is the same with the Five Hundred, using a sedan.

"This," Steve Lyons says, "is not another Taurus."

In line with Ford's strategy involving Lincoln-Mercury to update its product lineup with "Fords plus a lot more," the company planned to release an upmarket version of the Five Hundred as the Mercury Montego.

The Freestyle is another example of Ford Motor Company's commitment to build many of its new products from the ground up. They did not use an existing minivan or SUV platform as the basis for the Freestyle, Martens says, because to be successful as a new type of crossover, it required a unique footprint. So Ford went after developing a new type of cross between a car and an SUV, different from its major competitor, the Chrysler Pacifica, which is based on a cross between a car and a minivan.

"I think," says Mays, "the market will bear out the differences. The Freestyle is tough, but luxurious on the inside, but very SUV and rugged on the outside."

The all-wheel-drive crossover vehicle is targeted for active families, offering multiple seating configurations and safety features developed in conjunction with Volvo, a division of Ford Motor Company's Premier Auto Group. In fact, the Five Hundred and Freestyle are built off a Volvo architecture.

"Of all the previous acquisitions," one Ford executive says, "I think Volvo will prove to be the wisest. There is a lot of synergy there."

Ford is finding domestic synergy from its other global 1990s acquisitions as well. Another car planned in the company's future to shore up sedan sales is the Fusion, a version of the popular Mazda 6 sedan, scheduled to arrive in Ford's North American dealer showrooms (with derivative versions for the Mercury and Lincoln showrooms) in 2005. Because Ford needs good new cars fast, it cannot afford the time and money it takes to develop an entirely new architecture, so it borrowed from Mazda "and probably saved 16 months" in the process. The Fusion also includes a version of Mazda engines, taking the best elements from the popular car developed in Japan when Ford's Phil Martens ran retention and development operations at the company during a critical juncture. When Martens arrived at Mazda, the company was in the midst of a product drought and, under his leadership, "bet the farm," putting four entirely new architectures and frames in place. The result was critical hits with the Mazda 6, the RX-8, and the Mazda 3.

"That company is entirely different now," he says.

The goal is for Ford's car lineup to make the same transformation with new, can't-miss products in North America based on a mix of new designs and elements of strength from global positioning. "We can't afford," Jim Padilla says, "the complexity we have today, but it is going to take us a while to get there."

It is a challenge Martens is aggressively taking, but he is well aware of the impediments he faces, from Ford's previous difficulty launching good products to its inability to lead through fast product action. "When Nick Scheele and Jim Padilla came asking me to come back and rewire what was being done here," Martens says, "my first intuition was, I did not know if we could get it done. I was experienced enough to know how difficult the situation was.

"In my room at the [Dearborn] Ritz-Carlton, I wrote down what needed to be done. I knew we had to get people in the right jobs and we had to grow back engineering competency. You *can't* subcontract that."

Within his first year on the job and with Padilla's leadership and support, Martens eliminated more than 1,200 external contract workers in product development, built an entirely new leadership team, put in a structured meeting cadence of weekly planning and review, and announced North American platform reduction. He also looked in multiple corners of Ford Motor Company's global presence for pieces that would work with his new puzzles.

"You want to win regionally," Martens says. "But to succeed, you have to work globally. We should take advantage of our global network, and that's what we are doing."

So influential is Martens in his role of leading Ford's North American product development that Padilla, speaking to a room full of hundreds of company employees, said Martens is the "single leader" in making final decisions in product development.

It's a strategy similar to the one Ford is using in its global luxury division, where 43-year-old Mark Fields is leading a highly profitable resurgence of the company's prestigious brands packaged in the Premier Auto Group (PAG). The division lost almost $900 million in 2002, but in the final days of 2003, it became obvious in Dearborn that the PAG was turning the corner and would actually post an operating profit based on a double-digit global sales increase, making Ford

Motor Company the largest seller of luxury cars in the United States. The products driving the success included Jaguar's XJ sedans and Volvo's crossover XC90. Fields' strategy was to protect the integrity of Ford's prestigious luxury brands, which include Aston Martin and Land Rover, by actually reducing platform sharing outside of those brands, while increasing sharing inside of each brand, ultimately protecting the perceived value of the exclusive brands.

In other words, it was okay to share a Mazda platform with a Ford, because those brand products fall in the same general price category. It may not be as acceptable to customers for a Jaguar to be built on a Ford or Mazda frame. So, instead of profiting through short-sighted vision by mass production of prostitution, Fields has led the PAG to focus on luxury, quality, and individuality within each brand. By the end of the year, it was becoming apparent that the company was learning how to better utilize its size and diversity by better understanding the dos and don'ts of commonization and standardization.

"Allan Gilmour says to me we are the biggest little company he has ever seen," says Bill Ford. "We have to break through that, and I think we are."

The automaker was making undeniable progress as 2003 came to a close. Many external and internal indicators were pointing in a positive direction, and there was a noticeable mood shift throughout executive and management offices as well as among the critics who, within the same year, had predicted such dire results as a deepening slide. A primary reason for this change was the success of the F-150. Employees had been challenged, from product design and marketing in Dearborn to factories in Norfolk and Kansas City, to deliver to America the best truck ever built. With the majority of its new products more than a year away from showrooms, there was no room for failure or even moderate success. At the end of the year, it was obvious to everyone remotely familiar with the industry that Ford Motor Company had gotten it right with the new F-150. Sales were moving at a record pace and headway was being made behind the scenes on getting cost out of the product, setting the stage for greater profitability in the near future.

Even with a higher manufacturing cost base than was desired in the beginning, the company was seeing customers paying more on average for each new F-150 truck than expected, as more than 50 percent of the buyers were opting for the two highest trim levels offered in an F-150, the FX4 and the Lariat. The truck had come in at launch with about $1,200 in additional costs, causing concern among some Wall Street analysts, but executives had made the decision to push ahead with product release, hoping to deliver a superior product that would turn heads and deliver superior results. And now the plan was working. Three months of sales results showed that nearly three-fourths of all buyers were choosing the 5.4-liter engine in the new F-150, when the company had predicted roughly 60 percent would do so; and 47 percent of all buyers were leaving lots with four-door Super Crew cabs, while the company had predicted that 39 percent would do so. All this translated into higher than expected profits for Ford. Meanwhile, Ford chief financial officer Don Leclair said the company was also in the process of whittling down its costs in the F-150 and would eliminate almost $1,000 by the end of 2004 through engineering changes and reduced supply costs, yet create "no real changes in the content that the customer will be able to discern."

The wave of good news continued in late December 2003, when Ford Motor Company announced a new agreement with chief supplier Visteon that addressed pricing costs as well as costs related to the approximately 20,000 UAW-represented Ford employees working at Visteon after its June 2000 spin-off from Ford. On the same day, the automaker announced it was raising guidance for the 2003 fiscal year and profits were expected in the range of $1.05 to $1.10 per share, as opposed to the $.95 to $1.05 it had previously stated. The increase in earnings, said Leclair, reflected continued cost savings, strength of the F-150, and the ongoing strength of Ford Motor Credit, which was expected to deliver $3 billion in profits.

At the end of the December 22 trading day on the New York Stock Exchange, Ford Motor Company's stock was the most actively traded issue, jumping more than 10 percent to a 52-week high of $16.79, a price-to-earnings multiple of 21. On the same day, Coca-Cola's stock closed at $52 per share, with a price-to-earnings ratio of 18.

CHAPTER

14

From Escape
to Reality

The 2004 Detroit auto show began on a cold, cloudy day in early January with imminent snow in the forecast for the metro area. But inside the downtown Cobo Center, palms were sweaty among Ford executives and managers who had gathered to see if the new F-150 would garner the award viewed in North America as the most important in the auto industry.

The auto show kicks off each year with the announcement of the North American Car and Truck of the Year awards, and Ford executives and employees believed they had a justifiable winner with the F-150. The public was already suggesting as much with its record support, and awards for the truck had already been gathered from the likes of *Motor Trend* magazine and Texas auto writers. But this annual designation by an independent panel of top automotive journalists is among the most coveted in the auto industry and, while a loss would not have been devastating, a win would be the crowning moment to four years of hard work throughout all levels of Ford Motor Company design.

Among the finalists for truck of the year were the F-150 and Nissan's new Titan. Nobody from Dearborn wanted the

American icon to lose the award to a foreign upstart. The Japanese may have made two decades of inroads in cars in the United States, but the pickup is a uniquely American thing, and Ford has long been the leader in pickup trucks. This valuable turf is one the company wanted to protect. Jim Padilla, Steve Lyons, and Phil Martens joined a handful of Ford Motor Company employees among a standing-room-only crowd of industry insiders and journalists from around the world as the announcement was made:

"The 2004 North American Truck of the Year is America's best-selling pickup of all time, the Ford F-150."

"This," said one Ford employee, "is one we just had to have."

Three hours later, several thousand journalists and industry onlookers filled most of the available seats inside the Cobo Arena as Ford Motor Company unveiled to the public its "Year of the Car," led by the all-new Mustang coupe. Just as Ford had fought to defend its truck turf, foreign automakers were keenly aware of the company's impending resurgence in the American car market. Detroit automakers allowed rivals to steal domestic car business in the 1990s while focusing on more profitable SUVs and luxury cars, but the awakening in Dearborn was turning heads, because even though the U.S. car market was shrinking, it still accounted for 47 percent of all vehicle sales, and foreign-based automakers controlled more than half of that.

A widely held industry assumption was that of all the domestics, Ford Motor Company had the best chance of taking back control over the domestic car market because it could leverage strengths of its global ownership in strong car companies like Mazda and Volvo and also had a history of delivering hits like the Taurus when they were desperately needed. One notable sign of the renewed interest in Ford's new car lineup was that just 12 months earlier, when the company unveiled its new F-150 for the first time in the same basketball arena, the seats were full, but the crowd included not only journalists but hundreds of Ford Motor Company employees bused in from a nearby manufacturing plant for the unveiling. In 2004, it was all pure interest and easily the biggest crowd of journalists ever attracted to the show.

"Just look around," said Ford's Jim O'Connor. "You can see and feel the difference."

During a sit-down dinner event later that evening for a few dozen top journalists who regularly cover Ford or the auto industry as a whole, the company unveiled its leading 2004 concept car, a remake of the once wildly popular Shelby Cobra, designed with the help of 80-year-old Carroll Shelby. Like the GT, the Ford Shelby Cobra supercar signifies a time when fast, sexy, Ford sports cars ruled the international roads. Shelby had run the Ford race team that won at Le Mans in the 1960s and had created the original Cobra, but he had bitterly parted ways with the company 35 years ago, even going so far as to sue Ford. In 2001, it was Edsel Ford II who asked Shelby to come back into the fold, and designer J Mays jumped at the chance to work with the legend in bringing back a 600-horsepower concept version of the Cobra.

As Shelby stood onstage with the Cobra concept, cameras flashing, it was obvious this was as much about Ford Motor Company rekindling its old relationships as it was about the car. In the audience, journalists attending the event were scattered among tables to dine with different Ford executives, as is tradition in the industry. Seated at Bill Ford's table, with his agreement, was Keith Naughton, the *Newsweek* journalist who wrote the story six months before that had so bothered the CEO.

The biggest story involving Ford at the 2004 Detroit auto show, however, was outside of Cobo Center, away from the splashy, rock star treatment given to hot new products. If you've seen one grand entrance of a car or truck, you've seen them all. Turning heads were the dozens of Ford Escapes continually dropping off guests in the circular drive at the front entrance of Cobo. The vehicles were preproduction models of the company's forthcoming 2005 Escape Hybrid, to be the world's first mass-produced hybrid electric SUV.

Using top products to ferry journalists and guests to Cobo is a tradition among automakers, who recognize the opportunity to show off products at the most visible entrance to the world's most important automotive showcase. On this day, General Motors used its Suburban SUV to taxi guests, while Ford, in marked contrast, chauffeured journalists in its 2005 model year Escape Hybrid, destined to become the world's cleanest and most fuel-efficient SUV. Scheduled for late summer 2004 delivery, the vehicle offers the same cargo capacity and capability of Ford's traditional Escape, while providing 36 miles per gallon fuel efficiency in city driving, compared with 19 miles per gallon for the regular V6-powered Escape.

"When I came back here," Phil Martens said, "it was clear to me that the Hybrid Escape was one of the five most important programs in development."

Visually differentiated from typical gas-powered versions of the small SUV only by a small "hybrid" emblem on the rear, the Escape Hybrid lowers emissions and saves fuel with a system that automatically stops the engine while it is idling, and then, operating on clean electric power, restarts instantly when it is time to pull away from the traffic light. The hybrid system also provides electric assist at speeds below 40 miles per hour, further reducing emissions and improving gas mileage. The battery is constantly charged by a generator that transforms braking energy into electricity.

The Escape Hybrid was not Ford Motor Company's first significant entry into environmentally friendly vehicles. The automaker had been selling the partial zero-emission (PZEV) Focus nationwide since October 2003, as one of just two global automakers making superclean models available in dealerships all over the country. The PZEV (pronounced

PEE-zev) Focus looks and drives the same as the traditional Ford Focus, but has the addition of a steel tank that prevents fuel vapors from leaking, a superefficient catalytic converter, and an engine specially designed for clean combustion. The result is a car that reduces emitted smog-forming pollutants by more than 80 percent from the already clean standard of an ultra low emissions vehicle (ULEV). The PZEV technology costs roughly $500 more per vehicle to make, but Ford Motor Company was absorbing most of that cost in hopes of getting more of these clean machines on the road.

"[PZEV] has taught us how to deliver [effectively] zero emissions," Martens said.

Another product coloring Ford's environmentally friendly product future is the Model U, unveiled at the 2003 Detroit auto show as a concept car. Featuring a reconfigurable interior and exterior and an environmentally friendly hydrogen internal combustion engine mated to an electric transmission, the Model U concept resulted in a hybrid that meets PZEV emissions standards with virtually no pollutants. Company insiders believe that one day the concept could morph into a production vehicle that will be as important to the company and American transportation as the Model T was almost 100 years ago.

The Escape Hybrid, however, was the most significant environmentally friendly vehicle of the moment for Ford Motor Company. It was also the first hybrid of any type offered by an American automaker. Japan's largest automaker, Toyota, became the first company in the world to mass-produce and sell hybrid cars when the Prius was released in 1997. But, long the leader in trucks and SUVs, Ford Motor Company was beating competitors to market with a hybrid vehicle that could meet the demands of today's environmentally conscious American driver who may not want to cram into a small car.

As the global auto industry moves over the next two decades toward what many experts believe will be a complete shift away from gas-powered vehicles to hydrogen-powered fuel cells that emit nothing but water vapor, gas-electric hybrid engines are a transitional technology providing immediate benefits to consumers seeking environmentally friendly alternatives. Ford's hybrid system was built as a "true global program," combining parts and technology from around the world as engineers searched for the best pieces available to provide the best result. The company licensed some technology (20 patents) from Toyota to incorporate into its system and used parts from European suppliers to build a uniquely American hybrid engine. In turn, Toyota licensed a number of patents from Ford, covering catalyst technology and diesel power controls, and Ford expects to ultimately license as many as 100 patents on its unique hybrid system.

Bill Ford, who predicted drastic changes to traditional gas combustion engines long before others in the auto industry publicly considered such a notion, made the commitment to offer hybrid vehicles as environmental solutions shortly after becoming Ford Motor Company's chairman in 1999. While Ford Motor Company's first major hybrid project was overdue and over budget because of the company's detailed study of evolving technologies, he wanted to make sure that when they did it, they did it right. Customers will expect performance and quality, not experimentation, particularly in an SUV.

"Many people," he said, "are becoming impatient, but I believe our industry is poised to take real leadership in this area."

Ford Motor Company, which also plans to produce hybrid versions of its Fusion sedan and Mercury Mariner SUV, deliberately scheduled an extended and more methodical launch phase for the Escape Hybrid in an effort to establish the product as one driven as much by the automaker's commitment to quality as its desire to provide alternatives. Even though the company plans to sell only 20,000 Escape Hybrids in its first year, and indications are that it will not be a profitable program until volumes increase, it is the pacesetter for hybrids from the American industry.

"We are going to be slow to ramp up to ensure quality standards," said Mary Ann Wright, chief engineer of the Escape

Hybrid program. "But we believe we have got it right because it is an appealing product. It is attractive to environmentally conscious consumers and it also functions like a base Escape. It's truly a no-compromises solution."

When final sales and balance sheets for 2003 were posted early in 2004, the news for Ford Motor Company was good. For the first time since 2000, the automaker reported a net profit for a full fiscal year. Earnings also topped Wall Street estimates, as Ford posted a $495 million gain behind the strength of radically improved credit operations and improved automotive operations due to cost cutting and better incentive management.

"I'd rather be one of those guys," Bill Ford says, "who underpromises and overdelivers."

But on the heels of the earnings announcement came concern from outsiders that Ford Motor Company was being passed in total global sales by Japanese automaker Toyota, losing its long-held position as the world's second largest automaker. Preliminary sales reports from the year had Toyota selling 6.78 million vehicles worldwide, compared to Ford Motor Company's 6.72 million vehicles. Many in the media made a big deal of the news, while Toyota executives tried to downplay it, no doubt recognizing that moving from underdog to giant tends to make people look at you differently. Few in Dearborn were losing sleep over the figures, though, because Ford managers were focusing on the challenge in front of them, namely profitability, and not worrying about global sales tallies. Still, the inequity of the situation—the openness of the U.S. market to all comers, compared with the insularity of the Japanese market—occasionally got under the skin of domestic auto executives.

"I would wish we had the same opportunity in their home

market that they have in ours," said Ford COO Nick Scheele. "We were the market leader in Japan until we were kicked out in the early thirties. . . .

"Let's be honest about it. We can't sell vehicles in any numbers in the Japanese market. They sell 2 million units in the Japanese market. Let's take that out and then see where we are."

Additionally, Ford Motor Company executives had made a conscious decision in 2002 to focus on profitability and not chase market share at a loss. Ford Division reduced by 50,000 units the number of Tauruses being sold to rental fleets, and greatly restricted the rental sales of popular new vehicles like the 2005 Escape. Cranking large numbers of vehicles through rental fleets results in a flood of almost-new used cars just a few months later, hurting the resale value of the vehicles. While Ford lost some market share because of these moves, it strengthened its financial results. The new Escape model, for example, now carries a very high residual value of 50 percent of its original price after 36 months. Strong residual values are a competitive advantage because they make a vehicle more affordable for a customer to buy or lease. Ford could have pushed more cars into Hertz, its rental unit, to pick up market share to protect its overall share, but instead allowed rival GM to flood more discounted fleet in its own backyard.

"I think we've seen that biggest does not mean being the best," Bill Ford said. "We can't manage for volume growth. We have to get the basics of our business right and then the growth will take care of itself."

He noted also that Ford did not count sales of Japanese automaker Mazda in its annual figures, despite owning a controlling interest with one-third of that company, which sold roughly 1 million units globally in 2003. Still, he agreed that there are always lessons to learn from competitors.

"I think that Toyota has just been consistent," Ford said. "We have changed our strategy, it seems, almost every year for the last 10 years. If I can do anything for this company, it is to see that we stay the course. We'll fine-tune as the world changes and new opportunities arise, but the best thing for Ford Motor Company is that we are in the car and truck and financing business. . . . That is what we are going to focus on year after year. When we look back in 20 years, we'll be very pleased with what we've done."

As the company continues to move through its 101st year in business, more progress is being made in cost cutting and reform in line with Ford's five-year plan to restore profitability through automotive operations. By using efficient Mazda as a template for cost-effective product development, and by searching for an additional $500 million in costs to cut (on top of the $3 billion cut in 2003), primarily through price reductions from its largest suppliers, Ford Motor Company continues its ongoing march to financial and operational reform.

"The pressures of continual cost discussion are just a way of life," said Phil Martens. "They will go on forever."

Progress through reduction can be painful, however, as was the case when Ford Motor Company's Edison Assembly Plant in Edison, New Jersey, closed in late February 2004. Nearly 7 million cars and trucks were built at the Edison plant during its 56-year operation, and the facility had a rich history with the company. The plant opened in 1948 during the company's post–World War II expansion and was the first place outside of Detroit that a Lincoln was ever built. Among the vehicles built through the years in Edison were Falcons, Comets, Mustangs, Pintos, Bobcats, Escorts, Lynxes, and, finally, Ford Ranger and Mazda B-Series pickups.

But while most of the 900 workers remaining on payroll when the plant closed were understandably sad, most also claimed to understand the need for Ford and other U.S. automakers to reduce capacity and were appreciative of joint efforts by Ford and the UAW to deliver lucrative retirement or layoff packages and offer them transfer opportunities to other Ford plants. So engaged was the company in encouraging employees to transfer that the human resources department, under the direction of Laymon, arranged presentations telling them about quality of life, community, and work amenities available elsewhere at Ford plants in the country.

The last two vehicles rolled off the Edison line on February 26, 2004. The Ford Ranger pickups were raffled off to employees, who hung around at the end for cake and soft drinks and to reflect on years of hard work producing American automobiles. In the end, about 350 employees retired, accepting from the company a lump sum payment of $35,000 on top of their normal retirement, while others planned to transfer to other Ford plants, moving with full salary, relocation expenses, and, in most cases, a less expensive cost of living than they had experienced in New Jersey. The rest of the Edison workers were laid off with a significant portion of salary and benefits through 2007, a result of the agreement between Ford and the UAW.

"We must move on," said employee Gregory Neal, 40, on the day the plant closed. "Ford is a family. They're going to take care of their people until the end."

For many Ford Motor Company employees, the benefits of hard work and commitment to the five-year revitalization plan were finally paying off. In early March 2004, the company announced to employees that it would pay bonuses to middle and senior managers once again and also reinstate a partial match of salaried worker contributions to 401(k) retirement funds, sending an important signal that company finances were continuing to recover, based on the strength of a couple of new products, improved vehicle quality, and cost cutting. For Bill Ford, the return of bonuses after a two-year absence translated into his first payout as CEO. He accepted the money—roughly

$1.5 million—but donated the entire amount toward a college tuition fund for children of Ford employees.

Ford Motor Company also stated in regulatory filings in March that it was on track to reach its mid-decade earnings goal of $7 billion in pretax profits, and expected 2004 profits of $3.5 billion to $3.8 billion ($1.20 to $1.30 per share). This was a major reversal from just two years before, when the automaker lost just shy of $1 billion in 2002, Bill Ford's first full year on the job as CEO.

"To have that kind of turnaround in the kind of markets we are facing," Ford said, "is tremendous, I think. It shows the hard work and dedication of people who love this company."

The best news in Dearborn was that even with the dramatic improvement, most inside the company believed it was only the beginning. The progress had been made with generally flat sales as the company awaited the arrival of most of its new products, including the Five Hundred, Freestyle, and Fusion. But even as Ford waited, some of its current strengths were getting stronger. The Ford Focus was the only domestic car named among *Consumer Reports* top picks for 2004, and it garnered two awards. The magazine said that with improved reliability, the Focus rated as the best small sedan and the most fun car to drive in America. Sales of the company's flagship F-150 were also getting stronger, on its way during Ford's "Year of the Car" to setting an all-time record for truck sales. The only thing standing in the way of Steve Lyons' goal of setting a record for F-Series units sold in one year was limited production capacity. They were selling them as fast as they could build them in 2004.

There was also pride in the opening of the Ford Rouge Center, where visitors from around the world can see and experience American automobile manufacturing like never before. The facility that was once the site of Bill Ford's worst day ever is now the culmination of his determination: an American manufacturing facility that protects the environment and workers, while allowing visitors an unprecedented educational and touring opportunity. Rouge tours that originally began in 1924, drawing as many as 250,000 annual visitors, ceased in 1980 when the age of the dated complex became an issue. Now F-150 trucks are being made with Ford's new-generation flexible manufacturing system, under the world's largest living roof, before the eyes of many visitors who have never seen the pumping heart of the American industrial revolution in action.

Beginning in May 2004, the Epcot-like Ford Rouge factory tour gives the 17 million visitors to the Detroit area each year the option of taking a crash course in auto manufacturing and entering into the unusual sights and sounds of actual assembly. But where Epcot relies on the illusion of reality, the Rouge tour is based on bottom-line American reality. The Rouge is history, the dreams of Henry Ford, merging with modern innovations, the dreams of his great-grandson.

"Henry Ford would be stunned," Bill Ford says. "He would like this plant because Henry Ford was always pushing the envelope and he had this ethic of reusing and recycling. This could have been easily cancelled along the way, but . . .

"This plant represents the future of Ford Motor Company."

CHAPTER 15

Great Products, Strong Business, Better World

Marking the definitive end to a contemporary story involving Ford family leadership and Ford Motor Company proves difficult since the saga is a continuation of one that began more than 100 years ago and one that shows all the signs of continuing well into the future. At 46, the great-grandson of Henry Ford is just getting started. And, in its 101st year of business, with more than $160 billion in annual sales, 327,000 employees, and dozens of new products on the way, Ford Motor Company is far from finished.

But, like any true tale of tragedy and triumph and much in between, this one does have its conclusion, based on the very fact that as Ford's first year of its second century in business comes to a close, the pieces are in place for the company to make a major impact on the world for another 100 years, just like it did in its first. That concept would not have seemed reasonable three years before, as the company teetered on the edge of disaster and Henry Ford's great-grandson prepared to step into its leadership role.

When Bill Ford went to work in early 1999 as chairman of the board of the company bearing his name, many people outside of Ford Motor Company were not sure what he brought to the table other than heritage. The company appeared to be in such global control that it needed little more than for him to stay out of the way, keeping his wild-eyed beliefs to himself—like the one about the impending end of the internal combustion auto engine in our lifetime, or the one about building a new truck plant with a living, sedum-based roof. Ford spoke out anyway, disregarding what others thought, and aimed to use strong business as a means of contributing to a better world, while letting Jac Nasser do his job of running the company day to day.

But America's corporate environment was entering turbulence, and the explosion at the Rouge shortly after they took office was a foretelling event for Jac Nasser and Bill Ford as well as for Ford Motor Company. Nothing was as solid as it seemed, and no matter how hard anyone worked or what they tried, the company's future was not in a web site, dozens of acquisitions, or an entirely new culture. Instead, the future of Ford Motor Company was scattered among the many parts of its prominent past, from employees and dealers to products like the Mustang and icons like the rusty old Rouge. These pieces needed cohesion, modernization, vision, and, most important, an understanding, guiding hand. Bill Ford apparently recognized this, and when it appeared the company had little to no chance of succeeding under Jac Nasser or his approach of remaking the automaker, he single-handedly stepped up from his easy life as chairman and made a drastic change, taking over operations and internal obstructions that had gotten so bad that short-term success was not even a thought—only survival.

To steady the listing ship, Ford surrounded himself with seasoned automotive professionals who, like their leader, quickly earned the trust of most of Ford Motor Company's people. The new management team stopped all the foolishness that was ripping the soul from the company and talked only about such mundane disciplines as manufacturing fundamentals, belt-tightening, and execution. Ford pulled back from his vocal position of creating more corporate environmental leadership and attacked bleeding holes with pressure. Perhaps he had made a mistake as chairman, jumping the gun by espousing so much change at the same time Ford Motor Company was moving in many directions.

He was quick to learn, though, and publicly focused mostly on core business when it became apparent that too much was happening too fast. Externally, he took a beating from environmentalist accusers, who said he was abandoning morals and commitments and who complained loudly if promising projects met unfortunate delay. Internally, however, Bill Ford kept pushing, refusing to give up on hybrids, sustainable manufacturing, or corporate citizenship honesty, even though some around him often pleaded for just that.

From the start, the people of Ford Motor Company rallied around their fourth generation family leader, who professed to bleed the same blood as they—blue. Employees, both A players and B, tightened belts and burned lights late into the night, desperate to show the world that the automaker was alive and well and still an industrial giant to be reckoned with. Some problems continued, as did mistakes. But slowly, month by month and quarter by quarter, the company that for a spell was blowing in a swirling wind began showing it was grounded in repetition, concentrating on the most important elements of automotive industry success, including product design, quality, and value, and all at a faster pace than ever before.

As one of America's oldest companies matured, so did its leader, learning some aspects of the job on the fly and adjusting to a new life of nonstop responsibility and celebrity. Ford's style emerged as one blended with charm, conservative tradition, and new age industrial imagination. He picked apart budgets dollar by dollar, the company's richest employee serving as its symbol of frugality. He put all his eggs in one big basket—new product—and concentrated on the ones who could make it happen, the people throughout his company. When the company successfully rallied around one team-effort grand slam, the F-150, employees were convinced they would deliver more.

The push to survive created the need for Ford's many global divisions to reach across diversified lines for product and operational solutions, resulting in the first true glimpses of globalization at Ford Motor Company. Lessons were learned from Volvo and Mazda and others in between. Closer to home, the traction in Dearborn led to an attitude change reminiscent of Ford Motor Company's glory days when the blue oval was an American rallying symbol, winning at Le Mans, serving up the Mustang, and reintroducing a quality-made, European-looking Detroit sedan. The marketing theme "Look Again" was history, on its way to being replaced by something with a swagger more worthy of an industry leader.

And in April 2004, the financial world and shareholders took notice that Ford Motor Company was in fact achieving what many less than one year before said would be impossible. Ford announced that its profit for the 2004 first quarter was nearly $2 billion, double the consensus estimates of Wall Street analysts as the company took advantage of rising sales and continued cost cutting. Perhaps more importantly, Ford showed it was still gaining advantage in North America against domestic competitors, increasing pricing and profits through revenue management. The results, the ninth consecutive quarter Ford Motor Company beat estimates, were breathtaking comparatively. A little more than two years before, Ford Motor Company was cutting 35,000 jobs and announcing a $5.45 billion loss. Less than 12 months before, persistent bankruptcy rumors still plagued the company. Ford's nearly $2 billion in quarterly earnings was more than a surprise in the business world; it was vindication for more than 300,000 company employees.

The day after the earnings announcement, Bill Ford made official management changes reflective of the company's post-centennial strength. David Thursfield would retire immediately as chief of international operations. Nick Scheele, who previously delayed retirement plans to help Ford recover, remained as president, but turned over his duties as Ford's chief operating officer to "back to basics" guru Jim Padilla, credited with leading the company's surge in North America.

Some big headaches were still around, namely the never-ending battle to maintain quality; the ever-increasing challenge of designing vehicles that keep up with a fast-moving, hypercompetitive global auto industry; and the difficulty in making money in an incentive-driven market. Health care expenses were likely to increase by double digits again, and the company's pension liability was growing bigger by the minute. But on the other side of the most important year in Ford Motor Company's modern history, one thing was abundantly clear: Bill Ford stepped in when he had to and led Ford back from near disaster. Then he successfully guided the company through a crucial, and exceedingly difficult, passage in time. Ford Motor Company emerged profitable, with a promising future colored by new product, renewed focus, and the world-changing ideals of its leader.

ACKNOWLEDGMENTS

Writing a book is never easy, particularly when tackling a subject as complex and rich in detail as Ford Motor Company. But I have learned that the hardest tasks in life are made easier by relying on the help of good people. I was never shy in soliciting help for this project and was fortunate that many went out of their way to provide assistance.

Nobody played a bigger role than Jon Harmon of Ford Motor Company. He first met with me in Dearborn upon my initial request for complete access to the company and its top executives, including Bill Ford. Harmon was no doubt too busy from his never-ending duties as director of public affairs for the Ford Division to deal with my repeated requests for help and information, but he stuck with me for almost two years anyway. I'm sure he grew weary of my quick-trigger e-mails, but he never showed it, treating my every whim and request like it was the most important issue of the moment.

Special thanks also go to Jon Pepper, who leads Ford's integrated communications division and is a former newshound and business columnist who never lost focus on the value of truth or a good story.

Another person in public affairs I relied heavily on and came to know and respect is Miles Johnson, assistant manager for car public affairs in the Ford Division. On many occasions, Johnson called me with answers before I even asked questions. He took me into the bowels of the company and into executive offices (and to a few too many fast-food joints), and made my job of research and writing much easier.

Dozens of others at Ford Motor Company took the time to work with me and answer many questions in my effort to get this story right, and never asked for anything in return but accuracy. At times, situations inside the company were tough while I was around, but doors were always open, and that made all the difference.

———————

Dearborn, Michigan, is an unusual place. Originally empty river lowland on the outskirts of Detroit, Dearborn was transformed in the early 1900s by Henry Ford into a centerpiece of world manufacturing, driving a community that continues to reflect his impact today. There is the Rouge manufacturing complex; the Henry Ford Centennial Library; The Henry Ford museum; Henry Ford Medical Center; Henry Ford Elementary School; the Ford Community and Performing Arts Center; the Ford Product Development Center; and dozens of others.

But underneath the two-dimensional nameplates is a diverse group of middle-class Americans who settled in Dearborn because of the opportunity offered by Ford Motor Company, and who share a love of country, politics, competition, and, most important, the automobile. This strong-willed, multicultural citizenry, which includes America's largest Arab population per capita, has led to the city being called by national pundits a political mecca for its ability to draw stops from the country's top politicians. More than anything, Dearborn is diversified, industrial, and passionate.

I know this firsthand, having spent what my wife would call too much time there for a year and a half, working on this project. I got to know the people—meeting them on public golf courses, in restaurants, at the library, in stores, or in a taxi. Whether I was pulled up for wine and dinner at Kiernan's Steakhouse, Ciao, or Big Fish, many locals remembered my name from trip to trip and always welcomed me back, making Dearborn, Michigan, a very Southern kind of northern place that I will always appreciate.

This book may never have come to fruition without the immediate and never-ending support of Matthew Holt, executive editor at John Wiley and Sons. We jibed the first time we ever talked, and our professional relationship has gone only uphill since. He knew from the first moment he heard about this contemporary story about America's most storied manufacturer that it was one he wanted to publish. He never took his eye off the ball, gaining the crucial support all along the way from Professional/Trade Group vice president and publisher Larry Alexander, who knows a little about Ford Motor Company himself.

A special thanks to the talented marketing team at Wiley, including Michelle Patterson and Laurie Frank Harting, who made this book a top priority and gave it all available resources and energy. Thanks to Wiley senior publicist Michael Onorato, particularly skilled at identifying news worthy of promotion. Also at Wiley, senior editorial assistant Tamara Hummel played a very helpful role.

Special thanks to my agent for this project, Elizabeth Frost-Knappman of New England Publishing Associates, whom I consider a friend and one of the best in the sometimes difficult business of publishing. Her laugh is contagious and her advice always valuable. Others at NEPA who deserve thanks are Kristine Schiavi and Ed Knappman.

The list of those deserving special mention includes Lyman Magee, for solid copyediting; Richard Howorth, for being a good mayor, friend, and bookseller; John Grisham, for showing the way; John Porretto, for maintaining a coon-ass mentality while becoming one of America's top auto industry reporters; and Ward Nelson, for watching me sweat over golf balls on the side of a mountain between interviews in Michigan and writing pages at home.

Finally, nobody deserves recognition more than my wife, Kent, who has a boy's name but a striking woman's beauty and a knack for always doing and saying the right thing.

NOTES

The most useful and informative business books are built from the inside out, whenever possible, and every effort has been made to achieve that here. Days and weeks in Dearborn over a year and a half yielded valuable insight from Ford Motor Company employees and executives and key automotive industry observers, allowing me to rely almost solely on information obtained firsthand.

However, many good and valuable outside sources were viewed and used as backup and supporting material, and I would be remiss not to give credit where credit is due. In the book sector, the sweeping works of Robert Lacey, *Ford: The Men and the Machine* (Boston: Little, Brown, 1986), and Douglas Brinkley, *Wheels for the World* (New York: Viking, 2003), provided comprehensive understanding of Ford family and Ford Motor Company history, while respected and well-written auto books like *Comeback* (New York: Simon and Schuster, 1994), by Joseph B. White and Paul Ingrassia, and *The Reckoning* (New York: William Morrow, 1986), by David Halberstam, helped me better understand the cyclical nature of America's largest industry. Another book, *Dot.con* (New York: HarperBusiness, 2002), by John Cassidy, provided insight into the technology bubble of the 1990s. I also read portions of *Tragic Indifference* (New York: HarperBusiness, 2003) by Adam L. Penenberg, for an understanding of the Ford/Firestone crisis.

In the magazine and print sector, special mention must be given to *BusinessWeek*, for steadfast and reliable reporting on the auto industry week after week and year after year, and to the *Detroit News*, the *Detroit Free Press*, and the *Wall Street Journal*, for covering the U.S. industry on a daily basis better than any other news organizations in the world. A special mention must be made also of Crain's *Automotive News*, and *Ward's Auto World*, some of the best trade publications around.

CHAPTER 1   *The Rouge*

Page 4   "I think they wanted me to have . . ." *Detroit Free Press*, Tuesday, June 10, 2003

Page 12   "This game does not belong to you . . ." *Time*, December 8, 1997

Page 12   "I grew up in a wealthy neighborhood," *Time*, May 14, 2001

Page 14   "Jac's been the catalyst," *BusinessWeek*, September 28, 1998

CHAPTER 2   *Lessons in Leadership*

Pages 25–26   "a leading consumer company for automotive products and services," *BusinessWeek*, October 11, 1999

Page 29   "Anyone . . . who is going to hide behind legal fences . . ." *Ward's Dealer Business*, January 1, 2001

Page 32   "We're forming Internet joint ventures left and right . . ." Douglas Brinkley, *Wheels for the World: Henry Ford, His Company, and a Century of Progress* (New York: Viking, 2003)

Page 33   Often, Nasser acted more in haste . . . *Ward's Auto World*, January 1, 2000

Page 36   "This leadership effort is about as scaled up . . ." *FastCompany*, April 2000

Page 37   "the hair stand up on the back of your neck
                 . . ." *BusinessWeek*, September 28, 1998

CHAPTER 3   *Ground Zero*

Page 43   "There were a lot of people . . ." *Time*, May 14,
                 2001
Page 44   "I define . . ." *BusinessWeek*, September 28,
                 1998
Page 44   "So I got an X-Acto knife . . ." *Detroit Free
                 Press*, June 10, 2003
Page 49   "environmentally safe manufacturing processes
                 and materials," *Wired*, February 2002
Page 49   "I went up to his office and he said . . ." ibid.
Page 51   "I remember thinking . . ." *Time*, May 14,
                 2001
Page 55   "This company . . . has always . . ." ibid.
Page 56   "I couldn't believe it . . ." *Detroit News*, May
                 24, 2000

CHAPTER 4   *Dark Days in Dearborn*

Page 58   "They are among the most popular . . ." Adam
                 Penenberg, *Tragic Indifference* (New York:
                 HarperBusiness, 2003)
Page 60   By August 2000, the NHTSA had more than
                 doubled . . . ibid.
Page 66   "We all know sadly enough . . ." *Detroit News*,
                 June 21, 2001
Page 70   "It says a lot . . ." *Ward's Dealer Business*, Au-
                 gust 1, 2001
Page 71   "Single-handedly . . ." CarConnection.com,
                 September 16, 2002

CHAPTER 5   *Taking Charge*

Page 75   . . . a civil rights activist and occasional Southern bootlegger . . . *Detroit Free Press*, August 21, 2002

Page 84   "It was a very normal conversation . . ." *Newsweek*, November 5, 2001

CHAPTER 6   *The New Face of Ford*

Page 103   "They realize . . ." *Ward's Dealer Business*, March 1, 2002

Page 105   "We needed to take back the voice of Ford . . ." *USA Today*, July 28, 2002

CHAPTER 8   *Surviving the Cold of Winter*

Page 134   "The reality . . ." *New York Times*, March 14, 2003

Page 141   "Ford . . . is holding the line on vehicle prices . . ." Reuters, April 16, 2003

Page 144   "Frankly . . . it's back where God intended it to be." *Detroit News*, June 5, 2003

CHAPTER 9   *Momentum*

Page 148   "I was only reluctant . . ." *Automotive News*, November 11, 2002

Page 148   "It is hard . . . for me . . ." ibid.

Page 159   "Red Poling, when he was . . ." *Detroit News*, July 17, 2003

CHAPTER 10 *America's Best-Selling Truck Is New Again*

Page 164   "The F-150 is certainly the make-it or break-it vehicle . . ." *Detroit Free Press*, January 6, 2003

Page 176   "The new F-150 . . ." Associated Press, October 1, 2003

CHAPTER 11 *Bargaining for a Future*

Page 178   "We're not going to go backward in health care . . ." Reuters, July 16, 2003

Page 187   "It's taking a critical look at us today . . ." *Forbes*, June 23, 2003

CHAPTER 13 *The Year of the Car*

Page 206   But after graduating from Maysville High School . . . *USA Today*, June 16, 2003

CHAPTER 14 *From Escape to Reality*

Page 225   "I would wish we had the same opportunity . . ." Reuters, January 25, 2004

Page 227   "The pressures of continual cost discussion . . ." Dow Jones Newswires, February 18, 2004

Page 228   "We must move on . . ." *New York Times*, February 27, 2004

INDEX